Acknowledgen

When he was in his mid-sixties, my father Stan asked me to write this story as a record for my family. Over the years I had kept my sisters up to date with my adventures through occasional postcards, phone calls and letters. But there was still so much more to tell.

My father regretted not sharing his personal history, realising how important it was for following generations, and he didn't want me to make the same mistake.

I'm sure my father would be pleased with Don't Postpone Joy. I dedicate this book to him.

There are a number of important people who encouraged and trained me, and at times participated in my adventures, and they too deserve recognition.

To departed friends:

My father Stan Taylor

My stepmother Rosemary Taylor

Philip Warburton, Karen Walter, Geoffrey Bugg, Donjalle Gina Burns, Douglas George, Lockie Richards, Beth Fife, Ross Wallace, Stephen Tattersall, Mathew Martin and Carl Johnson.

My family and close friends in New Zealand, Australia, Canada, England and Switzerland. They know who they are.

My riding teachers and those who helped my dreams come true: Selma Brandl, Julie Peterson, Denis Pigott, Julie Pigott, Ted Harrison, Nick Holmes-Smith and Lorrayne La Framboise. Judith Peters from Centennial Park Trust, Gillian Brennan, my assistant, friend and eyes, and Lorayne Tennet, who transcribed my work.

The team of health professionals headed by Associate Professor Dr Mark Thomas in New Zealand, and Professor Dr Andrew Lloyd in Australia, their registrars, Dr Cassy Workman, Rick Osborne who was my main nurse in Sydney, and Colleen from Ward 68; and Grafton Pharmacy, Auckland.

A special thank you to the Royal New Zealand Foundation of the Blind, especially the tutor who taught me to touch-type, the vocation support officer who helped me learn about anatomy and physiology for massage, and the deaf division for funding my hearing aids.

Thanks also to the National Audiology Centre for changing my world from a silent place to a sound-filled one.

I am also grateful to Debbie Tawes and Celebrity Speakers, and my publisher Random House.

Ownership of this work was returned to the author in 2011.

This book was first published by Random House in February 2005.

This edit now complete in June 2012 is published under the authors name.

Prologue

I am sitting in an old vinyl armchair in a warm maternity hospital room, cradling my two-day-old great-nephew Taylor and wondering how someone so new can have such a huge amount of hair on his tiny head.

As I gently cuddle him with one arm, I stroke the fine, downy topknot with my other hand and listen to his soft breathing. He's waking up, ready for his lunch, and I feel him unfurl like a little ponga frond, his arms and legs stretching out from under the shawl he's wrapped in. In that moment, emotion floods through me, bringing tears to my eyes. Not just the 'Oh how nice, what a cute new baby' feeling that everyone gets when they hold a newborn. For me, this goes deeper, much deeper. It's a feeling of unadulterated hope.

Just the day before, I was in another hospital room on the other side of Auckland City, with drips feeding into my veins, machines going 'bleep' all around me, and nurses popping in to poke me with various instruments. 'Why on earth am I doing this? I am so utterly sick of it all! I've had enough!' I had screamed inside, while I gritted my teeth for yet another medical test.

For eight years I have gone through this routine of hospital treatment, just to stay alive for another eight weeks. That's how often Auckland Hospital gives me chemotherapy, a cocktail of nausea-inducing drugs pumped into my flagging body to keep my life-threatening illness under control. However horrible this treatment is, I have to give it credit for working because I really should be dead. Three times doctors have given me a deadline, in the true sense of the word. The last one was just four days, but that was three years ago and I'm still here. How's that for beating the odds?

But sometimes, when my body is puffy with fluid retention, when it aches and I feel as if I can barely bend down to pat my dog Barney or make myself something to drink because I'm too weak to close my hand around a cup, I wonder if it's worth it. Then I have moments like this one with Taylor. As I carefully hand him to his mum Anna for a feed — staying close enough for him to curl his small toes around my finger and for me to hear his snuffles of contentment — I know I've done the right thing by refusing to give up. My sister Yvonne, a proud grandmother for the first time, leans close to me and describes every detail of Taylor's appearance — his button nose, his big, dark, almond-shaped eyes like Anna's, and the way he crinkles his face up when he's about to cry. I don't want to miss a single thing and I listen intently, building a picture of Taylor in my mind.

As she speaks, I have one of those moments when I wish that my sight was better, even for a fleeting second, so I could see Taylor's face in all its precious detail. The extra time my treatment has given me has come at a cost. A drug administered to me for my illness over a three-year period caused my body to be poisoned with heavy-metal toxins and strangled my optic nerves, leaving me virtually blind. One of the side effects of choosing life, I'm afraid. When Taylor finishes his feed I lean close, straining to catch a glimpse of him, and through the murkiness I can make out those almond eyes. Oh, he is so beautiful. At 51, I'm on my way out after a wonderful life and here is this perfect little human being, who carries my family name, Taylor, all ready to take on the world. My greatest wish is that he will have a life that has been as full as mine.

A childhood filled with heartache taught me to survive. Those lessons, on how to get through when everything looks hopeless, went with me as I travelled the world. I had adventures and met amazing — and some terrible — people. I loved with all my heart, I lost, and twice, I almost got married. I worked hard, I lived hard and I made things happen.

My dreams, however remote they seemed to others, became reality — even when it meant personal sacrifices that some would find shocking and hard to understand. When the future looked utterly bleak and projects doomed to failure, there was always a way for me to come out, not just standing upright, but dancing.

However you view my life by the end of this book, you are certainly not likely to use the word 'mediocre'. I stomp on mediocrity with a tall pair of riding boots caked in horse sweat, and I plan to go out that way too.

With my time limited now, I find it frustrating that so many people don't feel they can pull on those boots too and do a bit of stomping. Why are there still so many who are prepared to accept second-best and plod on without ambition? Even though my body is falling to bits faster than a secondhand Russian car, my mind is still searching for new challenges at the pace of a brand-new Ferrari. That's why I am now a motivational speaker, telling people how to break out of their comfort zones, grab opportunities and make the most of everything that comes their way. It's how I believe in living.

It's why I refused to give up my dream of going to the Olympics. And it's why, after I had finally achieved that goal, I refused to give up life when a tiny insect, a sandfly smaller even than Taylor's pinky toenail, bit me and gave me a rare and devastating illness. I am the only person in the Southern Hemisphere with Leishmaniasis donovani (also called kala-azar) thanks to that sand fly. It transmitted a microscopic parasite, picked up from a dog that it had bitten, into my bloodstream. The parasite is in my bone marrow and destroys it. Only regular doses of chemotherapy keep the parasites at bay long enough for my body to recover and carry on. I am also the only person in the world to have HIV at the same time and survive. Most people who have both illnesses die within 20 months. I've never liked to stick to the textbooks.

As Taylor falls asleep in Anna's arms and his toes uncurl from around my finger, I realise that I'm actually very lucky. Not just to be here still, but also to have such an amazing tale to tell, a real modern-day Boy's Own adventure of passion, sacrifice, daring, endurance, heartache and joy. Maybe I'm not dead yet because it would take so long for my life to pass in front of my eyes or maybe a greater power has decided to let me continue because I still have so much to do. It's certainly baffling the medical experts — and my loved ones, who have had to say goodbye to me on three heart-breaking occasions.

It dawns on me, as I get up to leave Taylor and Anna at the maternity hospital and return to my own hospital room for yet more treatment that I don't know if I will be here to tell Taylor my story in person. 'Well, he'll just have to read it instead,' I think to myself, and leave him to his nap. And for some reason, as I walk from the hospital and out into the watery sunshine of a glorious winter's day, I'm smiling.

Chapter 1

It was a simple poached egg, sitting on a lightly toasted piece of bread, accompanied by a china cup of freshly brewed tea. The napkin was folded neatly; the knife and fork were shiny from polishing. I had

set it all out on a breakfast tray and laid the tray carefully across my mother Joan's lap as she sat up in bed. And yet, Joan was staring at the breakfast with a grumpy expression on her face. Standing beside the bed in my school uniform, I shuffled nervously from one foot to the other, my hands clenched into tight fists behind my back. I wanted to blurt out a whole list of excuses in one breath.

'The toaster took too long, Kay needed a drink of milk, I lost my reading book, Dad wanted a cup of tea, I forgot the time, the alarm clock was broken, the bread needed to be sliced ...'

Of course, I said nothing. Not a single word.

The problem was not so much the food. It was the fact that I was five minutes late with her breakfast.

'Oh Peter, you know I need my breakfast brought to me at 7.30,' said Joan, leaning back in her single bed with a huge sigh, her hand fluttering at her throat. It was a Victorian fit of the vapors being played out in a 1960s household.

I bit my bottom lip and looked at the floor.

'Well, what do you have to say to me?' she said with a sigh.

'Sorry,' I mumbled. I always felt so terrible when I let her down.

Outside the bedroom door, I could hear my sisters Yvonne and Kay getting their shoes from the cupboard and putting them on.

'I can't do my laces, I need Peter to do my laces,' wailed Kay, with all the impatience of her five years.

'Shhh, he'll be out in a moment,' said Yvonne, worried that her mother would hear. It was a well-founded fear. Joan seemed to bristle when she heard Yvonne's voice. It had always been that way. I was adored but tortured, Kay was tolerated, but Yvonne, then aged six, seemed to clash with our mother more often than we did.

I went to take away the breakfast I had worked so hard to make, mouthing more apologies, but Joan put out a hand to stop me. 'Oh, it's fine. Just leave it, Peter. I'll eat it,' she said. 'Otherwise you might have it, and you do seem to be putting on weight.'

She was right. I was starting to put on weight, but not from eating her leftovers. Sneaking biscuits and other sweet treats gave me temporary relief from my painful situation. I was only eight years old and I ran the entire household.

Everything depended on me. I was in charge of the house. I made packed lunches, I cooked the meals, I did the laundry, and I cleaned the house to the point that when my mother inspected, running a finger along ledges and shelves, it was as spotless as a hospital operating theatre. In the mornings I helped the girls get dressed, brushed and braided their hair, and made sure they had no toast crumbs on their little noses. Short for my age, I bustled around my father like a little housekeeper, getting his breakfast and helping him get ready to go to the cattle auction house where he ran the sales. A short, stocky, dapper Englishman with sparkling blue eyes and a cheeky smile, he was the perfect auctioneer.

Some mornings Joan would remain in her bed and we wouldn't see her until we got home. On others she would appear before we left the house, just to give poor Stan a final browbeating. She would come through in her dressing gown, smoking a cigarette and launching a tirade at my father. Stan just took it and would leave with his head bowed. We would follow in his footsteps like ducklings, happy to escape for a day away from the house. This was my life in 1961.

Joan no longer slept with Stan, preferring her small, neat, single room with its basic utility furniture. The only splash of bright colour among the brown wood was her jewellery box, a fabric-covered container for all her fake diamonds.

We lived in a beautiful home in the comfortable upper-working-class neighbourhood of Kamo, in Whangarei. For years my parents had dreamed of getting a property with a new, purpose-built family home just for them. They finally achieved it, and now had an impressive four-bedroom house with open-plan living areas — from the modern kitchen to the large lounge — and beautifully tended gardens. It was exactly what Joan had always wanted, and the envy of our neighbours.

My sisters, Yvonne and Kay, had one room, my parents another, and I had a bedroom all to myself. In the early days of moving to the house, Joan and Stan still slept together. And then there was the spare room, which was filled by Nana soon after we moved in. Nana was Stan's mother, a short, round, bespectacled, fiery creature from England. She had done the rounds of her children and relatives on the other side of the world and the news of our large house meant it was our turn to host her. I can imagine her children in England cried tears of relief as they waved her goodbye at the docks. Nana arrived in Auckland and we drove down there, crossing from the North Shore by ferry, to pick her up from the ship. Six months later we would repeat this exercise with relish as we finally packed her off.

Nana and Joan did not like each other at all.

'Common Australian, swanning around like Lady Muck,' Nana would hiss to a weary Stan, as he sat at the dining table working through big bundles of cattle sales figures. 'You know, Stan, you could have done so much better.'

'How long is she staying for? Can't you hurry it up and send her home?' Joan would complain as Stan put down the telephone after spending the evening negotiating sales of pigs.

All I knew was that Nana wouldn't let us have fruit but hoarded a stash of her own in the spare room where she slept. That was enough to make me wonder about how good her heart might be. I later found out that she had had a tough life, married to a master baker who was never home, and bringing up her family with the help of her sisters. Stan had had little male influence on his life, which was why he was such a wonder with the ladies. And even with Joan for a while.

During Nana's stay Joan went back to midwifery, doing night shifts and sleeping while we were at school. Her starched headdress and her hair in a neat French roll at the back of her neck made her seem highly organized amid the chaos of a family breakfast. Nana looked after us for six months, until even Stan was unable to cope with her any more. We waved her goodbye and imagined the English relatives groaning as they read the letter announcing her return home.

But Nana's departure didn't make things better, strangely enough. In fact, that was when the decline set in. Back at work Joan had retasted life outside the family, and she now seemed unhappy than ever. What started as mild niggles at Stan, as he worked endlessly to keep her in the style she desperately wanted, became full-blown explosions of anger and despair. She was miserable and frustrated by her situation. Some nights Stan would come home early to drink with Joan. If he went out with friends she would wait for him, ready to berate him about leaving her alone. When they drank in the lounge I stayed awake, listening to the rising voices. Eventually I began hiding behind the bathroom door that led to the lounge area. I knew that if things got too heated I could pop out and save them from each other. Of course, that meant I didn't get to sleep until the early hours, and my schoolwork began to suffer.

'Peter's reading and spelling is well behind his age,' was a frequent comment on my report card. This despite the fact that I actually spent more time at school than most of my peers, because I felt like I was walking on eggshells at home.

'It's really late, Peter. Shouldn't you be going home now?' my teacher would say gently.

'Can I just wash these paint pots? Or put the chairs away neatly?' I came up with endless excuses to remain at school, but inevitably I would have to make the walk back home.

'Tubby, hey Tubby Taylor,' the other kids shouted as I trudged back along the road with my buddy Alan. Often we would go to the creek, to hunt for freshwater crayfish and hide out in our secret safe place, a tiny clearing in the trees. It was edged with a broken old stone wall that was covered in clematis and honeysuckle. We would sit there, eating fresh walnuts and Totara berries, two friends sharing silence. But beneath the quiet I harboured a secret. To me, Alan was more than a friend. I liked him in a different way, a way that I couldn't understand at the time, and would certainly never have confided to him. It was something that would become clearer as I grew older and experienced more of life, but this wasn't the time for that kind of thing. So we threw stones in the creek and wondered how big an eel could grow. Boy things like that. I guess I already had a fickle heart though. As much as I liked Alan, there was one person I liked even more. The girl with the pony.

Carol was a neighbor, and together we used to make toffee apples and fudge to sell at the gate for pocket money. It wasn't my sweet tooth that kept me doing this. Carol had something I wanted: her old grey pony, Tammy.

'When can I ride Tammy?' I asked her, for possibly the 700th time that year.

'When there is enough blue in the sky to make a pair of sailor's pants,' she replied. 'Now help me wrap up this toffee apple. It's sticking to everything.'

I must have been feeling foolhardy one day because I refused to go quietly after the usual sailor's pants put-off. I looked at the sky and realised there was more than enough blue to make not just the pants, but an entire seafaring wardrobe for the anonymous sailor.

'Look,' I said, pointing up at the huge azure expanse. 'There's heaps of blue. Come on Carol, let me ride Tammy.'

Carol stared at me. 'No,' she said firmly.

But I wasn't having it. I had waited weeks, months, and I was more than fed up.

'Do it! Now! I want to ride Tammy,' I said. Carol laughed and did what girls of that age always like to do — she ran so I would chase her.

'Right, that's it,' I panted, racing up towards her house. She darted inside the glass back door and slammed it in my face. I put out my right hand to stop myself, and crash, my hand went through the pane. I withdrew my hand immediately, not feeling much pain but seeing ribbons of blood suddenly pouring down my pale arm.

Holding my hand closed I ran to our house and stood at the door, waiting. Joan was on the telephone. I knew it was rude to interrupt so I stayed quiet, holding my hand together. I didn't want to go in because the floor had been washed and I would drip blood on it. So I waited patiently for Joan to finish her call. As soon as she put down the receiver I croaked out, 'Mum.'

'What is it, Peter?' She turned toward me and I opened my hand, holding it out. Her face turned pale as she saw the blood trickling out from my palm, and she clasped it closed again.

'Don't open it,' she said, switching to nurse mode. Carefully, my hand was wrapped in a towel, and I was driven to the doctor. The sickly sweetness of the ether as the mask was held over my face in the operating theatre stays with me still. I sank into blackness.

When I woke up they had stitched my sliced palm together, although the glass had cut the tendons to the second finger and to

this day it still sticks out. Later I waved my bandaged hand at
Carol but she still didn't give me a ride on Tammy.

Joan worked on and off after Nana left, then she hurt her back. She
had damaged two vertebrae at work, as sometimes happens to
nurses, and the pain was excruciating. As she lay in her little room,
moaning in agony, pethidine helped to take the edge off the pain
And send her into a woozy half-world. She became addicted to the
painkiller, so that eventually, after her back problem was cured,
she
had to be weaned from the drug. When I was 10, I sat beside her
during the nights when the pain was too much for her to cope with
alone, holding her hand and listening as she rambled about her own
childhood.

'It was terrible, Peter,' she would say, her short nurse's nails
digging into my hand. She always kept her nails short, but liked to
paint them with shiny polish. I thought they were beautiful.

'I hated what my mother did to me,' she would ramble. 'She was
horrible. Do you know, she gave me away when I was only eight
months old? She didn't want me.'

I did know. I had heard the story many times before. But each time
I heard it I could relate to the little girl who was dumped at an
aunt's house in the lonely Australian outback, along with her two-
year-old sister Betty. Even at my young age I knew that this
trauma had shaped Joan and stayed with her as she tried to parent
her own children.

When Joan was 16 her mother, Myrtle, went to live in Rawene, on
the Hokianga in northern New Zealand, and Joan tracked her
down. Myrtle, a woman who enjoyed faking spectacular heart
attacks at convenient times, had another husband then, a gentle
bloke called Alec. Vain and insecure, she couldn't handle the
petite, dark-haired daughter with the piercing blue eyes, who had
appeared from nowhere.

'She thought I was having an affair with Alec, and she kicked me
out,' Joan sobbed, her voice slurred with pain. I nodded and
murmured soft words to her. 'After I left, a terrible thing happened
to poor Alec.'

Yes, poor Alec. A bulldozer driver, he was clearing trees one night
in a remote spot and a tree fell, crushing his legs. He was pinned to
the ground for a whole night, and when he was found the next

morning, the shock had turned his hair pure white. One leg had to be amputated. If that wasn't hard enough for the man, Myrtle decided she didn't want a disabled husband and left him. She would have another two husbands in her life.

'She abandoned me, you know,' Joan gulped, tears pouring down her cheeks as she fought another wave of pain. 'I was just thrown away, like a piece of rubbish. It was so unfair, Peter, so unfair.'

I nodded gently. The pain of rejection was fresh for her, and my heart ached every time she expressed it.

And then Joan would slur her way to the story of meeting Stan. He was newly demobbed from the British Army after serving in India and Malaya, and working as a bus mechanic. She was a beautiful young nurse from Australia, who fell for his charms and expected a better life than he could ever give her. After they were married she happily worked with him as a share milker on four farms, even living in a tin army hut just after I was born. All because she dreamed he would give her more.

I remember those sharemilking days as happy, hopeful times. At night I would cuddle in with Joan and Stan at the age of three because I was scared of the moreporks in the bush.

'its okay, Peter,' Joan would soothe me gently as I buried my face in her nightdress, feeling safer beside her. 'It's just Mrs. Morepork calling her husband home for his dinner.'

We had pet lambs, went on feeling trips, and ate eggs from our own chickens. Joan was proud of me, the gorgeous blue-eyed boy who captured everyone's hearts with his sunny smile and good looks. As toddlers, Yvonne and I would sit with baby Kay in a spare milking pen early in the morning while Joan and Stan milked the herd. We had a mattress to sit on, and snuggled up with blankets and quilts. When we were a little older Stan installed a wind-up phone between the house and the cowshed, just a few metres away, so we didn't feel alone. At nights he would rub his stubble on our faces to make us laugh, and Joan would smile as she watched us. One year she even made me a beautiful birthday cake in the shape of a carousel, with animal crackers as the horses. Eventually Stan got the job at the auction house and sold pigs too, so there was no need to milk. The perfect home, the house that Joan had always wanted and waited for, was built. But that just tipped her into wanting more. It seemed that whatever Stan did, Joan was not satisfied.

'He let me down,' Joan sighed as she lay in her drugged and pain-addled state. 'He always lets me down. All I want is to have a good life, a better life.'

'Why did you marry him, Mum?' I asked, holding her hand a little tighter.

I almost didn't want her to speak, and she didn't. Joan just looked at me and drew her hand away from mine. She tucked the thumb of her right hand into the fist of her left hand, as she did when she was angry, and stared. In that moment, in that dark little room, I knew.

She had been pregnant with me. I was the reason she had married Stan. I thought it was my fault that she was so unhappy, and later — aged 16 — I vowed never to have children myself. Instead, my horses became my children. But like children they brought me joy and heartache, as well as taking me to the biggest sporting events in the world.

It wasn't until I was in my thirties that I discovered just how traumatic Joan's early life had been and the secret anguish she had hidden from us all. Only then did I finally understand this complex, troubled, amazing woman.

Chapter 2

Stan put down the spanner, wiped his oily hands on the front of his overalls and called me over. He was in the garage, working on his car.

'Hey, boy, who are they for?' he asked cheerily as I walked up, a bunch of wild flowers in my hand.

'Mum.'

Stan frowned, and then forced a smile.

'Do you want to see me do a valve-grind on the car and learn a bit from your old man, eh? Come on, give it a go. You might even like it.'

I didn't know what to do. I didn't even know what a valve was, let alone why it should be so exciting and educational to grind it.

'Okay, Dad,' I said, feeling apprehensive but putting the flowers carefully to one side, away from the tools. Usually I said no when he asked me to do something like this, and would see him become dismayed and annoyed.

I tried to grind the valve in the paste, pushing it around half-heartedly. In the end even Stan could see that I was just going through the motions. In fact, I was counting down the grindings until I could wash the muck off my hands.

'Ah, you're too tied to your mother's apron strings,' Stan muttered, jerking his thumb to indicate that my trial by valve was over. Then he ducked his head back under the bonnet of the car and carried on clanging away at the complicated metal guts of it.

Stan was a good honest type, a real bloke, all mouth and trousers, and he couldn't hide his disappointment in me. I was a softie, a quiet, gentle boy with no interest in cars, bikes or any rough and tumble. I think Stan was secretly quite pleased when I was caught letting off crackers in the letterbox of the old couple who lived at number 18. The rougher boys who lived in our street had egged me on, telling me I had to prove I was a man. Still, I felt terrible and I took my punishment happily because I knew old Mr and Mrs. Smith would nearly have had heart attacks when those crackers went off.

I was a loner mainly, and if I was in a group I would be the sensible one. Horses and ponies were the big passion in my life, even at this early age. I was 11 and it was 1964.

To me, horses were uncomplicated but challenging, and I couldn't hide my fascination with them. Day after day I followed friends who had horses, just hoping they would let me have a ride. I walked for miles and miles with them. The day Stan asked me to get blokey and tinker with the car I had already trailed for hours after a friend's horse, picking flowers for Joan as I went. Stan finally found out what I did on those long afternoons out of the house when he drove past and saw me walking behind a horse and rider.

'You walked how far? What on earth for?' He was utterly amazed.

'I wish I had a pony,' I said, shrugging my shoulders. It had never occurred to me just to ask.

'Right, well, you'll have to go to pony club for a season and learn how to ride properly. Once you know how to look after a pony, we'll see what we can do,' Stan replied, ruffling my hair.

I raced into the house to tell Yvonne. She was just as pony-mad as I was.

'Dad says we can go to pony club and maybe get a pony!' I yelled. We danced like mad pixies around the house, until Joan said we had to stop because she had a headache and needed me to get her some cigarettes. My feet flew to the shops that day.

Yvonne and I began going to pony club, sharing an old part-Clydesdale with six other kids, and that's where my love of horses became the passion that would take me to the Olympics. Horses were also the way to find common ground with my father, something valve-grinding could never do. After I'd spent almost a year patiently traipsing behind that old horse with a clutch of other pony-mad kids, waiting for my turn, Stan was willing to take the next step.

'Right,' he said one Saturday morning, picking up his car keys as I finished my chores. 'We're off to look at a pony.'

I could hardly believe what I had heard. But Stan wasn't messing about.

'Come on: drop that duster and hop in the car. Do you want this pony or not?'

As soon as I saw Prince, a charming little bay pony with a cropped mane, my heart was a bubble of sheer happiness. He was perfect — a sweet-natured 12-year-old, the same age as me, and a gentleman in every way. I let him sniff at my pockets and rubbed my hand through his stubby mane as Stan negotiated a price with his owner, whose son had grown out of him.

'Hello Prince,' I whispered into his velvety ear, as his sweet breath puffed against my jumper. Stan walked over, grinning broadly. 'He's yours,' he said.

Prince moved into a paddock beside my primary school, and my schoolwork became even worse as I spent my days staring at him lovingly from the classroom window. I would race through my chores so I could spend every moment at his side. I loved caring for Prince, from picking up his piles of manure to grooming his coat and picking out his feet. When I rode him, I felt as if I had been sitting on a horse all my life. It felt incredibly natural, and the right place for me to be. Once I had mounted Prince and we set off together for a lazy hack along the riverbank I forgot about Joan, my bad grades and the fact that my parents' marriage was in crisis.

Six months after Prince came into my life, Stan bought Yvonne a pony too. Amigo was a patient mare with the longest back I have ever seen on a pony. She was the equine equivalent of a dachshund. At pony club, she could fit seven children along her back and won prizes for 'Pony with Most Kids On Board' at our little shows.

The horses also gave Stan a reason to spend more time with us. Always a country man at heart, he learned to shoe using Amigo. It was a clumsy business initially, with hot horseshoes dropping onto the grass and nails going in crooked, but Amigo put up with it. If it got too much for her the only sign of annoyance she gave was a well-timed blast of hot air from her nether regions. Stan would laugh and wave away the smell. 'I get the message, girl,' he would say, as Yvonne and I collapsed in laughter.

Stan particularly enjoyed the gymkhanas and shows, buying a 1953 Bedford truck, which he nicknamed Magabelle, to take us there. As Yvonne and I took part in potato races, where you had to drop spuds into buckets from horseback, or mini-showjumping contests, he would lean on the fence with his friends, talking about cows and how well the ponies were doing. He had a look of contentment that

I had never seen before: it was all because he was spending more time away from Joan and seeing the kids happy as a family.

Prince also brought me a good dose of much-needed self-esteem, plus a new circle of horse-crazy friends. Now that I owned a pony I went from being the fat school outcast to being someone with a bit of credibility. A group of eight of us would trek around Kamo, stopping to buy ice cream, swimming in the waterhole and looking down, literally, on the kids who only had bikes. We rode bareback and thought we were tough, a gang of pony-riding renegades.

In the long summer evenings I would head out with Kennedy, my latest best friend, on his mare Black Bess, to steal fruit from the neighbours' gardens. It was a bit like a tricky circus act, balancing on Bess's wide hindquarters while reaching for peaches and plums. I was at intermediate school by this time and Kennedy and I were inseparable. It wasn't only horses that brought us together. His parents had just divorced because his father was an alcoholic who disappeared for months on end. When I talked about my parents fighting, he understood and would nod his gingery head. He knew exactly what it was like.

Joan's mood improved a bit after she went into hospital and had the vertebrae in her back fused, which helped ease her pain. We visited her regularly, and I was always fascinated by the array of stiletto heels that were left at the door to the ward. These were the days of glamour, from high-heeled shoes to huge beehive hairstyles.

Even when Stan and Joan began to dislike each other, they still loved to socialise with their friends. Sitting with Joan while she got ready for a night of glamorous partying was my favorite time with my mother.

'What do you think? The pink one or the blue one?' Joan would hold out her gloved arms, a different diamante bracelet on each wrist.

'Definitely the blue, because it matches your eyes, and you need to wear the brooch too, with the little chiffon scarf,' I would say excitedly, jumping up to fetch items from drawers and wardrobes.

'What about shoes? Plain black or something fancier?'

'Black. You need to keep it plain because the jewels are so colourful.'

It was the same every time she went out. A hand would beckon me into her room, and I would help choose everything from the right shade of stockings to the appropriate earrings. As she expertly applied thick black eyeliner, her lipsticked mouth open in concentration, I would sit on the bed, my face unconsciously mimicking everything she did. Once Joan was perfect I could relax and wave her out the door, knowing she looked utterly beautiful. I loved those nights with her.

Every so often Stan and Joan had a party at home. Maybe it was a hint of things to come, but I was always the barman and waiter, serving up the cocktail onions and stuffed olives. I loved being the organizer and coming up with inventive new delights for the guests. Our parties were considered very flash in the neighborhood, not least because of delicacies like stuffed olives. I folded napkins, mixed cocktails and cleared glasses. It was good training for the adventures in food and drink that lay ahead. I learned a lot, in those early days, about what made people tick during a night out.

With all that cocktail-mixing and being a mini-host I was often too tired to do my homework, but I wouldn't have missed those nights for anything — though even when the last guests had left, I was on duty in a different sense. Stan and Joan were now drunk and alone, and that's when the darkest side of our family came out. I shivered behind that toilet door more times than I can remember, wincing at each cruel curse they hurled at each other, feeling sick to the pit of my stomach yet feeling a need to listen in.

Joan's back operation curbed her social life quite a bit, which meant less arguing, as this was something she and Stan only did after parties and drinking. For three months she wore a plaster cast from neck to groin, and she was pretty limited in what she could do. To fill in time she helped out at the school as a teacher aide. She always wore one of two caftan creations, the only things that would fit over the cast. The other children would tease me: 'Your mum's only got two ugly dresses.'

When Joan came home from hospital after getting the cast removed the first thing she did was ask me to run a deep, hot bath. 'And bring me that half-bottle of sherry from the cabinet, Peter,' she called, disappearing into the bathroom.

I stared when I saw her lying there, the layers of grey dead skin sloughing off her body under the water. It wasn't her naked body that shocked me. I was used to seeing it, all of it. Joan seemed to take pleasure in showing off her figure and had no modesty, even with her growing son. As she lay in the bath I was horrified by what was happening to her skin. It was coming off in big pieces, rippling in the bathwater like sinister, slimy seaweed.

'Oh, stop staring and pass the bottle,' Joan sighed. She didn't come out for hours.

Freed from her cast, Joan got back into the swing of life in a big way. For her, that meant going out — her way of escaping her unhappy situation. Instead of being on the sofa when I got home from school, she wouldn't be there at all, and her little car would be gone from the driveway. At first it was only occasionally, and then it became more frequent. Eventually Stan noticed.

'Right, Peter, get in the car,' he would sigh, when he arrived home to find the couch empty of Joan.

With a leaden heart I would climb into his green Wolseley and he would drive to the Kamo pub. Through the darkness we would see the lights of the bar flickering and hear music. Stan would pull up in the driveway and look at the cars in the carpark. There was Joan's little vehicle. Stan would purse his lips, back out and drive home. As long as he knew where she was, he put up with it. She was safe in the pub.

On the last night of their marriage, in 1966, I was 13 years old. Stan sat up drinking quietly in the house, waiting for Joan's key in the lock. I lay in my bed, blankets pulled up to my chin, sick with worry. As soon as the front door opened I crept along the corridor and into my usual place behind the door. This had been an almost nightly routine for close to five years.

The argument started in low, angry mutters, and then it grew. This time they raged at each other like never before and I suddenly snapped. I couldn't take it any more. This wasn't how a family was supposed to be. I raced out into the lounge and threw myself between them. When they saw me, a pale-faced child in pyjamas, they were shocked into silence.

'No!' I screamed at them, my voice hoarse with despair. 'No more. That's it. I can't stand it; none of us can stand it anymore. You have to get a divorce.'

Chapter 3

Kay burst into tears as she stood in the mud, her well-polished shoes sinking into the goo. 'It's horrible,' she wailed, and Yvonne put an arm around her, trying not to look at Stan.

I said nothing. The miserable-looking three-bedroom house, surrounded by farm buildings and scrubby paddocks, was a far cry from our smart Kamo home. But it was a better place in my opinion, for one simple reason: Joan wasn't here.

Less than a month after I had stood in the lounge telling my parents that they should split up once and for all, Stan, my sisters and I were making a fresh start. At first Stan had dug his heels in about a divorce, even though marriage to Joan was clearly tearing him apart too.

'Not until the girls have left school,' he said, when I gave them my ultimatum that night. 'It's not fair to split up a family when the children are still young.'

'That's years away. There's no way we can go on for that long,' I said fiercely, holding my hands together to stop them shaking.

'Right, there's nothing else for it then. Let's ask the girls.'

I went to get them from their bedroom. Yvonne and Kay followed me back to the lounge, rubbing sleepy eyes and looking confused.

'Girls — do you want to go on with two parents who will fight and argue until you leave school, or do you want to live with one happy parent?' I said bravely.

Joan glared at the girls, her face stony and cold. Stan looked flushed and upset, his eyes darting from Yvonne to Kay and back again. I waited.

'A happy one,' mumbled Yvonne. 'No more fighting.' Kay nodded, her eyes huge and scared. 'Happy,' she whispered, reaching for my hand and cuddling into my side. Stan shook his head and sighed, rubbing his big hands through his dark hair.

'Well, that's it then,' he said. 'Joan?'

My mother said nothing.

Within days Stan had packed in his job at the auction house and taken a sharemilking position at Puwera, just south of Whangarei. Some people thought he was crazy to give up a good job for such a lowly one. But at heart Stan was a simple, hard-working man, and after years of working long hours to satisfy an unhappy wife, this was his chance to show his real devotion to his family. He knew we deserved a life very different to the one we had led in our Kamo show home.

And it was exceedingly different.

Sparsely furnished, little more than a big wooden box divided by walls, the house was basic but clean. The farm was 200 acres of hard, exposed land, tough going when there were 90 dairy cows trying to survive on its sparse grass. The steps from this house led straight into a cowpat-splattered milking yard instead of the roses and lush plants of the Kamo garden.

Yvonne and I knew we would be able to keep our horses here and spend all our free time with them. We didn't mind about the harder living conditions. That wasn't the case for little Kay, though. She was afraid of horses and liked her creature comforts. She couldn't remember our early years, when Joan and Stan had sharemilked together. Her memories were of plush carpets, cabinets full of precious china, a warm log-burner, and beautifully manicured lawns to turn somersaults on during sunny school holidays. To her, this was damp, grim and grey.

'I don't like it. I want to go home,' she said, tears dripping off her quivering chin.

'Hey, hey, love, it'll be okay,' Stan told her, hugging her against him. 'Honestly, poppet, this is a better place for us. We've all got each other. It'll be fine.'

Yvonne and I exchanged looks. For a second it had sounded as if Stan was trying to convince himself as much as he was trying to convince Kay.

Within a year, Kay went to Auckland to live with Joan. Her dislike of farm life never abated, and even a little pony of her own didn't convert her. The pony scared her, she refused to ride him, and eventually he had to be sold because he got so fat from lack of exercise. It was tough for Stan to accept that he couldn't make all his children happy. After Kay left he was quiet for a few days, probably wondering if there was anything he could have done to keep her there. In truth, Kay was happier with Joan's urban lifestyle than with Joan herself. In the end the situation would turn sour for her, but initially she found it a better option than the muddy farm.

I moved to Whangarei Boys' High School, which was on a convenient bus route. After a long and happy friendship, Prince and I had finally parted. Just before the separation I'd been bought a new pony, Pasadena. A glitzy, ritzy chestnut with a fiery temper, he was a far cry from placid Prince.

Both Yvonne and I found farm life perfect. We didn't have much money or a life of luxury, but for the first time in many years we were happy. Stan worked like a man half his age, milking the 90 cows single-handedly in the draughty walk-through shed. The hours were hard but he was always nearby if we needed him. On Friday nights Stan would pile us into Magabelle, the truck, and off we would go to Whangarei to buy food. We all sat in the front, although the one in the middle had to sit on an upside-down nail box with a lumpy old cushion on the top. Yvonne and I would bicker about who had to perch on it, but neither of us really minded. On the way back we would have treats. Stan got a packet of marshmallows, I had a
chocolate block, and Yvonne got a tin of condensed milk.

Life was fun. We hired a television set and would sit together on the sofa, giggling at The Flintstones, Stan more than us. Yvonne and I would tease the half-hibernating frogs in the trough, poking their sleepy, slimy bodies to wake them up. Mushrooms were picked fresh from the cow dung pile, and occasionally we got fresh duck or pheasant. Yvonne and I would gallop on our ponies from one end of the farm to the other. Last one in had to complete the outside chores, while the winner got to cook dinner. I began to experiment with otherwise dull recipes, learning about the tastes of different spices, when we could get them. It was the start of a passion for flavor that continues today. As I got further into my teens I began to get crushes, but not on girls. The object of my affections was the handsome farmer who had the next smallholding along the road. Of course, I never admitted it to him, or to anyone. It never occurred to me that I might be gay. I just thought it was part of my life that I had to keep quiet, and that's exactly what I did.

One evening during our first year on the farm, as I sat on Pasadena watching a Northland sunset and listening to the birds in the bush surrounding the pasture, I came to a realisation: I was happy. Of course, I hadn't reckoned on Joan. As if she could sense happiness and had a mission to turn it to misery, she suddenly appeared in my life again.

'Hello, Stan.' Joan looked totally out of place amid the trucks and the green paddocks of the A and P show. She was perfectly made up, her dark hair sprayed into a shiny bouffant style, wearing a tight skirt and high heels that sank into the soft ground. Stan turned around, his face pale at the sound of that pinched Australian twang. 'Aren't you going to say hello?' Joan said. Stan frowned and moved away from the two men he had been chatting to about some new piggery being set up in the area.

'Joan,' he sighed, standing a short distance away so that if she took a swing with her handbag it would miss him. 'What do you want?'

'Oh, that's right. No "Hello", no "How are you?". Typical.'

'Don't bloody start, Joan.'

From this unpromising start, the conversation escalated into a full row. It ended in Joan stomping off, her heels wobbling, and the farmers' wives glancing with a hint of jealousy at this city woman who had no idea of dressing for rural comfort. Tiredly, Stan rubbed his face with his hands, shook his head, accepted a couple of pats on the shoulder from friends, and went to judge one of the Jersey classes. Yvonne and I watched from a safe distance, grooming our ponies in readiness for the next class.

Stan quickly regained his composure after the very public spat and we could see him standing in one of the smaller show rings, pulling on a white judge's coat and picking up a clipboard. The circling cows, groomed to perfection, had already put thoughts of Joan to the back of his mind. Judging cattle was a serious business, after all.

I was coming back to the horses, sipping a bottle of lemonade, when I saw her. She had Pasadena by his head collar and was leading him away from the pony area where he had been tethered. I dropped the bottle and ran, my boots sliding on the mushy ground. 'Mum! Mum! What are you doing?' I skidded to a halt and tried to grab the halter. She held it out of my reach.

'Now, Peter, you know he's not yours. I'm simply taking back something that I own. That's all.'

She began to walk off again. Pasadena jerked his head, as if sensing that something wrong was happening.

'No, you can't,' I gasped, holding the other side of his halter and digging my heels in. 'What do you mean? He's mine. You can't take him.'

She unfurled my fingers from the halter and pushed me away roughly.

'Wrong, I'm afraid. I bought him, so he actually belongs to me. And I'm taking him back.'

'What? No, that's not true. Dad bought him. He bought him for me.'

'He might have appeared to have bought this horse, but he used my money. My money, meaning this is my horse. And I know someone who wants to buy him, so I can get my money back. Believe me, Peter, I intend to do just that. Now, go back to your father.'

Utterly devastated, I sank to the ground and watched as she took Pasadena from me. Yvonne came running towards me.

'Are you okay? Where's Pasadena?'

'She took him,' I moaned. 'She took him.'

When Stan realized what had happened he was furious. He immediately went to find Joan and another huge row started. Yvonne and I watched from the safety of the truck, Magabelle.

'It's going to be all right, Dad will sort it out,' Yvonne said. From the look of Stan's slumped shoulders and head-shaking it seemed like he was losing the battle, but I wasn't going to let Joan win the war.

'That does it. I'm not sitting here, letting her get away with this.'

I shifted from Maggabelle's passenger seat to the driver's seat. Although I had driven the tractor a few times on the farm I was far from being a confident motorist. In fact, I had never been behind the wheel of any other vehicle. And this steering wheel was huge. I tried to remember what Stan did when he drove Magabelle. The key was in the ignition. I turned it and felt her shudder into life. The gears crunched and squealed as I tried to find the right one.

'But you can't drive,' Yvonne wailed. 'You'll get into trouble. Dad will be furious.'

'I can't think about that just now. Keep an eye out,' I said, gritting my teeth.

Magabelle kangarooed out of her parking space and toward an area where a number of horse trucks had been parked up. I had a feeling that Joan would have put Pasadena there, ready to go into his new owner's truck. Yvonne watched out of the side window to make sure Stan and Joan were still fighting.

'Be quick, it looks like she's about to storm off again,' she said suddenly. 'Look out for that car. Oh, sweet Lord. You almost clipped it there. Oh no, be careful. Too fast.'

Then her tone changed, from panic to excitement.

'I can see Pasadena, Pete. He's tied up outside that red truck.'

I kept Magabelle running and dashed towards Pasadena. Joan wouldn't be far away if her row with Stan was over, and she'd be wilder than ever, especially if she saw me getting my horse back. Yvonne opened the back doors of our truck and I walked Pasadena in.

'Come on, boy, easy now,' I said, trying to look relaxed so anyone passing by wouldn't be suspicious. Thankfully it was quiet because some dog display was going on in the ring: crowds can never resist a performing pooch or two.

As soon as Pasadena was safely tied up inside Magabelle, Yvonne and I climbed back in. 'Get out of here, Pete.' Yvonne was terrified. To the crimes of truck theft and illegal driving I had now added horse rustling, and I would be in deep trouble with not one but both parents.

I drove as carefully but as quickly as I could, and eventually found a quiet lane not too far away from the show grounds. Yvonne and I sat there, talking through the possible scenarios, until Stan tracked us down. As I watched him striding toward the truck, I swallowed hard. Yvonne held my hand. We knew I was in for a huge row, the biggest of my life.

Stan swung the door open. I waited. What would it be? Cold silence, outraged yelling, a disappointed lecture? It was none of these. Stan was quiet and exhausted.

'It's okay. She's gone. Let's get your pony, Yvonne. Time to go home. Oh, and I'm driving.'

The smiles were hesitant, but full of relief. It was all going to work out in the end.

Later that week Joan reappeared. 'I'm here to get some of my china,' she said.

Stan went out without a word, leaving her to go through the cupboards, taking what she could find. She put it all into a cardboard box. I waited outside for her to leave, feeling nothing but cold loathing. I was also ready to leap into action and ride Pasadena away from her if I had to.

Finally Joan emerged from the house, stopping on the steps and wrinkling her nose at the mucky farmyard. I glared at her from a nearby wall. She teetered down the flattened pathway and through the puddles, then stopped beside me.

'If you want that pony, you'll have to buy it from me,' she said acidly.

'I can't afford him,' I said, wondering how cruel she could be to suggest I had that kind of cash at my young age.

'Ten cents.'

I could hardly believe what I had heard. I stared at her.

'What?'

'I said ten cents. Get it now and the horse is yours. If you don't have it by the time I get to my car, I'll take it you don't want the horse.'

I was off that wall and into the house before she could change her mind.

'Quick, Yvonne, find me ten cents. I have to find ten cents!' I raked frantically through drawers and pockets, even down the back of the sofa. Yvonne ran into Stan's room and came out holding a shiny ten-cent piece in her fingers.

'You beauty,' I said, wishing I had time to kiss her. Joan was almost at her car, the crockery clinking in the box as she reached for the handle.

'I've got it,' I puffed. I pressed the coin into her outstretched hand and tried to catch my breath.

She inspected the coin, eyebrows raised, then popped it into the pocket of her jacket and got into the car, closing the door.

'Wait! Wait!' I hammered on the glass with the heel of my hand. 'Does that mean he's mine? Is he mine?'

Joan sighed, slowly lit a cigarette, then wound the window down.

'Look what you're doing to my nice clean window with your sweaty hand. You really do need to lose weight, Peter. Honestly, you're geting fatter and fatter.'

I didn't care what she thought of my size. I just wanted to know about Pasadena.

'Is he mine?' I was almost crying. 'Have I bought him?'

She began to wind up the window, enjoying the chance to prolong my torture. When the glass was an inch from the top she puffed cigarette smoke through the gap and said the words.

'Yes. The horse belongs to you now.'

Then she drove off, smiling.

I didn't feel grateful to her. And for the next two years, I didn't speak to her.

Chapter 4

Rosemary was her real name, but we called her Bud. She was a riding-school teacher, from an upper-class English family, quietly spoken and polite.

'Stan, I wonder, would you mind training my dog for me?' she asked one day after I had been for my riding lesson on Pasadena. Stan shrugged and smiled. 'Sure. He needs a bit, doesn't he? Runs you ragged.'

He laughed and Bud blushed, her English-rose cheeks pinking up beautifully. I watched from my perch on the fence, where I was pretending to pet Pasadena while really keeping an eye on the two of them. Even if they were oblivious, it was already obvious to me, at the age of 13, that love was in the air.

Bud and Stan made a deal over the dog: Stan would train the wayward Border collie and Bud would give me free riding lessons. I was thrilled, until their blossoming relationship got in the way. Soon, Bud's visits didn't need the excuse of dog training and she openly spent her time with my father. The riding lessons also foundered as they spent more and more time together. The dog would end up sitting outside the house with me and Pasadena, waiting for Bud to reappear. I don't know which of us looked more fed up. It's a pity the training stopped, because he ended up tearing into a cow and had to be shot.

Bud and Stan were the perfect match. They both knew what it was like to have the spouse from hell. Bud had been married for years, 21 to be exact, until she found out her husband was having an affair with his secretary. Her three children had grown up and left home by that time. She was educated, attractive and lonely. Stan had put Joan behind him as best he could; he liked working the dairy farm and was just as handsome as ever. He had started to get a bit lonely too, and before long Bud was living with us.

I loved the idea of my father having a riding instructor as a girlfriend. Bud was also kind, tolerant and made Stan smile. Yvonne, however, had a different view.

'Who does she think she is?' she huffed, after Bud had asked her to put her school shoes away. 'It's not like she's our mum or anything. We were fine before she came.'

'Oh, she's not so bad really, when you get to know her,' I said, ever the peacemaker.

'No way,' was Yvonne's firm response.

But within a short time Bud had worked her magic. Slowly we began to love this gentle, kind woman who could be strict but was always fair. Even so, I could understand Yvonne's reluctance to allow another mother figure into our lives. We had been through a lot with Stan.

Not long after the incident with Joan and Pasadena at the show, Stan had developed a nasty rash on his hands.

'The doctor has no idea what it is,' Stan sighed, looking at his blistered and swollen hands. 'He gave me another cream. I doubt this one will work either. It's a bloody pain.'

The rash got so bad that Stan couldn't milk the herd. So, Yvonne and I stepped in. We would work alternate milking shifts, while Stan ran the separator room and loaded the cows into the milking pens. It meant waking at 4am to milk before school, or finishing at 6pm while the other cooked the evening meal and fed the calves. This took up fourteen months of those two Joan-free years, when I refused to have anything to do with my controlling, manipulative mother.

I got my driver's licence at the age of 15 and was able to take the horse trucks to shows when Stan couldn't grip the steering wheel. Every day before we left for school we would leave out his lunch and a thermos of tea. His hands were covered in huge, oozing cracks that needed dressing twice a day. He wore long white wedding gloves — turned inside out so the seams didn't rub on the wounds — to work with the stock during the day. After endless tests the cause was finally found: he was allergic to the hormone oestrogen, which was secreted from the cows' udders.

'So does that mean we have to leave the farm?' I asked, filled with horror.

Stan shook his head and chuckled. 'Don't worry, Peter. We're staying put. I just have to wear long rubber gloves when I milk, that's all.'

After Bud arrived, he had an extra pair of hands to help him. They went on to milk together for another decade and his hands never broke out in that awful rash again.

Once Bud had been accepted by Yvonne, life was good. Stan had found someone who loved him unconditionally, and Bud had learned to trust again. The only downside was school. I hated it. I often hitchhiked home at lunchtime rather than stick out a full day in that place.

'What are you doing home?' Stan asked crossly one day when he caught me hanging out in the house, listening to the radio. I remember 'Hey Jude' was playing as he shook his head and gave me an ultimatum.

'Right, if you don't want to go to school, you can quit and work on the farm,' he said. 'I need some help and you're as good As anyone.' Then he turned and went back out into the chilly rain. I listened to his gumboots sloshing through the puddles and swallowed hard. Mud, manure, rain, grumpy cows and icy winds. The thought of working on the farm in the middle of winter was far from appealing.

I agreed to stay on at school and not sneak off early, although my grades didn't improve. I did have ambitions: I wanted to be a chef. But when I opened my School Cert results, my heart sank.

'What did you get? Surely it can't be that bad?' Yvonne asked as we leaned against the cream stand at the road side. With results like these my chances of getting into catering college looked grim.

'I got 48 percent in geography,' I sighed. 'That's my best result. The worst one is French.'

'How bad?' she whispered.

'Unlucky for me 13 percent.'

'You can appeal the geography one, surely?' Yvonne suggested, trying to be cheerful but not quite getting there.

'What's the point?' I had sunk into misery and was wondering what on earth I would do. 'I know one thing, though. I'm not working on the farm. I need a job.'

A week after school finished, I started at the McKenzies department store in Whangarei.

'We insist on punctuality and a smart code of dress at all times. There are lots of prospects at this store.' The assistant manager droned on, but I wasn't listening. I was eyeing the confectionery department, the big clear bins filled with lollies.

'Can I work there?' I asked.

'Confectionery? Well, yes, if you like. There's also the china department, menswear, kitchenware, gifts …'

I always found a way to get back to the confectionery department, even though I did a certain amount of time in the other parts of the store. Soon I was in charge of 'pick and mix', filling my days with lollies of all descriptions. My devotion to the job was spotted by the manager, and one day he called me to his office.

'Now, Peter, I just wanted to let you know that we are very pleased with your progress. Very pleased indeed.'

He was large, red-faced, shiny and pompous. I wondered what magical goo he used to slather his hair across the top of his bald patch. In fact, I was trying so hard to work out what the product was —

wallpaper paste, egg white or glue — that it took me a few moments to realise he had offered me a promotion.

'So, what do you say, Peter?'

'Pardon? I didn't quite catch that, I'm afraid,' I said politely.

'I said, would you like to be an assistant manager. You have all the makings of a decent assistant manager and it's quite an honor, you know, to be . . . why are you laughing? What's so funny?'

His smile had disappeared and he was glaring at me. I couldn't stop giggling.

'Whatever is the matter with you, boy?' the manager demanded.

'I . . . I . . . just can't believe you offered me that job,' I managed to splutter between gasps of laughter.

He relaxed a little and leaned back in his chair.

'Well, of course, as I said, it's a real honor to be offered such a prestigious position.'

'No, no, you've got it wrong,' I wheezed, trying not to double over with mirth. 'I don't want to be an assistant manager. In fact, I can't think of anything worse than being stuck in this boring old store for the rest of my life. There's no way I'm going to stick in a dead-end place like this. No way.'

He sacked me, and quite right too. I was an ungrateful wretch, but this ungrateful wretch had dreams of things far greater than McKenzie's and Whangarei.

Stan wasn't pleased.

'What are you going to do with yourself, then?' he asked. I shrugged.

'Something will come up,' I assured him. 'It always does.' And it did.

The news of my sacking reached Auckland and the ears of Joan. She rang Stan, and the news she gave him was to change my life.

'Tell Peter that I've got him an interview for a job in a restaurant here,' she informed him brusquely. 'If he wants to be a chef, he'll have to start somewhere, and it's certainly not going to happen up there on the farm. Two days. The interview is in two days and he'd better be here. It's very possibly his last chance. Tell him not to let me down.'

'You'd better take it, lad,' Stan told me, his voice sombre. 'Your mother could be right. You might not get another chance like this.'

'But I don't want to go to Auckland, and I certainly don't want to have to live with her.' The thought of even speaking to Joan filled me with dread. Moving into her house was bound to be a disaster. Stan's expression said it all. I had to go. I had to leave home and let my mother back into my life.

Chapter 5

All Joan and I needed was tumbleweed skittering between us to
complete the scene of two old adversaries facing off. This was the
duel at the Not-So-Okay Corral, and it was South Auckland in
1969, rather than the Wild West. Me, eyes narrowed, motorcycle
helmet in my hand, ready to jump back on my trusty Triumph
Tigress and head back to Whangarei. Joan, cigarette clenched
between scarlet lips, eyes like chips of polished aquamarine,
wearing impossibly high heels to show she had absolutely no
intention of running anywhere.

'You're here,' she managed to enunciate crisply, despite the
cigarette.

I nodded. Then silence. She looked me up and down. Two years
had passed since she had sold Pasadena to me. I had grown up
since then and she knew I was no longer an awed child, ready to do
her bidding.

I was determined to stand my ground, and braced myself for a
battle with my mother. But instead, she turned on one spiky heel
and went into her little house, calling for me to bring my bag in.
My breath came out in a slow, controlled, disappointing seep,
rather like a balloon going down after a party — and I hadn't even
been aware that I was holding it. We had an unspoken truce.

When I stepped inside the little two-bedroom flat I was
immediately enveloped by my younger sister.

'Ooh, you're here!' Kay echoed Joan's words, but her tone was
totally different. She was thrilled to see me and shadowed my
every step, hopping with excitement, as Joan showed me to my
room. I unpacked my belongings and little Kay sat on the narrow
bed, chattering away. Suddenly, she went quiet. I heard a man's
voice, deep and sombre, talking to Joan.

'Who's that?' I asked Kay.

'Bill,' she muttered. 'Mum's boyfriend.'

Then it all came out. Joan was drinking more and Kay was not
happy. There wasn't much I could do about the situation at that
moment, but I decided to sort it out as soon as I could.

I got the job that Joan had lined up for me. The head chef, a big, blond Dutchman, liked me for more than my cooking skills. Within a few days of starting at Auckland's Commercial Travellers' Club I realised that the only dish he was admiring was me. His other taste was for booze, and within a few weeks he was failing to turn up for shifts. While everyone was wailing and wondering how on earth we were going to feed the clients with no head chef, I got on with the job. The second chef, a young woman, saw I was onto something and went to her place at the grill. We were a good team. When the Dutchman returned and found out he was no longer needed, he sacked me. I didn't care. I had tasted responsibility and I liked it. With my newly bolstered confidence I felt ready to tackle anything — and that included the Kay situation. I rang my father in Whangarei and told him what had been happening.

'Come and get Kay, and don't worry about Joan,' I told him. 'I'll deal with her. Just get Kay out of here.'

Stan drove down between milking sessions, bringing a trailer to put Kay's bike on. She looked a small, forlorn, but very relieved figure as she waved goodbye. Joan, who was now working as a Community Baby nurse(Plunket), arrived home from work later in the day.

'Where on earth is Kay?' she demanded. 'Do you know anything about this?'

'Dad came and got her. She was unhappy here, Mum. She wanted to go to Dad's but didn't know how to tell you. She's gone.'

Instead of exploding, Joan suddenly went pale and crumpled. Flopping into a chair, she leaned forward and buried her face in her hands. I couldn't leave until she had cried herself into a soggy heap, and then I put her to bed.

Once the grief was over, anger kicked in. She told me she felt I had connived behind her back and told me to leave. I went to the YMCA for a week or two while I decided what to do. I had found another job, at a little tearoom, but had also heard that the Commercial Travellers' Club contract had gone to a new person. The Dutchman was gone and a short German bloke had taken over. I was welcomed back with open arms — and not just at the Commercial Travellers' Club. Joan had just bought a two-bedroom house with an attached granny flat in Papatoetoe, South Auckland, and wanted me to move back in with her.

'I know we parted on bad terms, Peter,' she said. 'But the fact is, I need someone to help me pay rent to help me service the mortgage and, well, it would be nice if it was you.'

I could tell she was relieved when I agreed. Not only did she have her mortgage covered, she also had someone to look after her. It was the guilt card, and I always fell for it. Whatever Joan did, deep down I loved her and she loved me. It seemed to work, living with Joan, at least for a while. Bill, her boyfriend, was a gentle, grey-haired man who genuinely adored her. He brought her sherry and she kept him company. In a way they had the perfect relationship.

I enjoyed being back at the Commercial Travellers' Club too, learning how to run a big operation smoothly. I worked hard, learned fast and was soon preparing the daily lunch smorgasbord for 120 people. Not bad for a 16-year-old lad from a farm. Ambitious and wanting to earn some decent money, I even took on an extra shift, working at night on the serving counter.

'You need something to help you stay awake,' Joan remarked one morning as I slumped at the breakfast table, utterly exhausted but about to set off for another shift. I frowned as she passed me a pill. 'What's this?' I said. 'I don't want this.'

'You certainly need it. It'll keep you awake and help you burn off some of those spare tyres you have, Peter. How do you think I keep my figure? Magic spells? Genes? Good luck? Oh for goodness sake, don't look at me like that. These pills are perfectly legal. The doctor gives them to me. They're a medicine.'

I shrugged and took the pill, too bleary and muzzy-minded to argue with her. Before long, the chemicals were perking me up.

'Told you they work,' she said, handing me another one the next morning. The pills, prescribed for dieting, were amphetamines, or speed: a legal version of a well-used illegal drug. I took them, raced through days and kilos, and before long I was as hooked as Joan.

However, I was careful to keep my pill-taking from Yvonne, who had recently moved down from Whangarei to go to school in Auckland. Dad and Bud had moved to a new farm that was beyond the school bus route, so Kay was boarding at Whangarei Girls' High School. It was now 1970 and Yvonne was a strong-willed young woman of 14. It wasn't long before she and Joan began to row.

Joan was becoming more and more unreasonable, mostly as a result of all the alcohol she was drinking. One evening Bill arrived as Yvonne and I were going out, and we met at the gate.

'Is everything okay?' he asked.

'Bill, listen,' I said, 'please don't bring Mum sherry. She's getting drunk and you know what she's like then.'

Bill blushed and hid the bottle behind his back. 'Better put this back in the car then,' he said sheepishly.

'Just don't bring any during the week, if you don't mind. She has to work. Weekends are fine.' I paused and looked up at the window, where I could see Joan peering out. 'On the other hand, Bill, she looks quite bad tonight; maybe I should stay.'

Bill's eyes opened wide and he hesitated.

'No, no, Peter, you go. I'll look after her. Here, here's $20. Take my car and go and have some fun.'

'I couldn't do that,' I said, feigning shock.

'Of course you can. Here.' The $20 was held out. I took it, and the car keys.

'Two hours,' I called over my shoulder.

'Two hours, fine,' Bill replied as he strode inside.

I know it was a cut-throat thing to do, but I took chances when they arose, and this was a chance for Yvonne and me to get something good from a difficult situation. Bill was happy, Joan was happy, and as we sped off in Bill's green Zephyr, with a whole $20 to spend, Yvonne and I were happy too.

Well, we were as happy as we could be living with Joan. Her drinking got worse, and occasionally she would slug down enough sherry to put her into a stupor. As I tucked her into bed after one of her binges, she seemed very vulnerable.

'I don't want to be like this,' she whispered.

'I know, I know, Mum,' I said.

'Sorry, sorry; oh Peter, I am so sorry.'

As she dropped off to sleep I knew that I loved her, no matter what she did. More than that, I felt needed by her again. But I was torn by the tension that was building between Joan and Yvonne. One night, as I was coming in from a shift at the restaurant, tired and ready to put my feet up for a while before popping a pill and heading off for another eight hours in the kitchen, I heard shouting coming from the house. In the kitchen, Yvonne and Joan were yelling at each other. I stepped between them and tried to calm them down, and then Yvonne walked out and went to a neighbour's house. I tried to soothe Joan, then, when I thought she had cooled down enough, I followed Yvonne to the neighbour's. She was sitting in a chair, still shaking from the shouting match. Gay, our neighbour, brought in a cup of tea. Her own mother Mabel was an alcoholic so she knew exactly what it was like. Suddenly the door opened, and Joan was standing there with a strange smile on her face. Wobbling slightly, she reached over and let several empty pill bottles fall onto the chair beside Yvonne. 'There,' she announced. 'You don't have to worry about me any more.'

I stared. Gay gasped, and Yvonne's head drooped like a tired flower. But Joan had gone, staggering up the hallway and back to her own house.

'What has she done?' Gay demanded, running her hand over the bottles. I picked them up, one by one, checking the labels. I had picked up the prescriptions for her the day before. I knew exactly what was in them. A month's supply of warfarin, which thinned her blood and stopped thrombosis, something she was prone to. There was another blood thinner and a diuretic because she carried fluid, and valium. Each one had been a month's supply, and now they were gone.

When the ambulance arrived, Joan was in a bad way. She wanted Yvonne to go with her in the ambulance, and I followed in her old Anglia. As we sat in the waiting room of the emergency department, huddling together, Yvonne and I could hear Joan screaming in distress as the staff tried to save her life. Finally the doctor came to see us in the waiting room.

'The drugs your mother has taken . . . well, one of them is warfarin, which is actually an ingredient in rat poison. It's a very powerful poison,' he explained. 'She is bleeding internally and the situation is pretty serious. We've pumped her stomach, with some difficulty as you may have heard. We've given her vitamin K to help counteract the warfarin. All we can do now is wait. Would you like to see her?'

We shook our heads in unison. She had got through the worst. That was all we could face at that moment.

Later that evening we came back to the hospital to see her. She looked terrible. The blood vessels in her eyes had burst, giving her completely bloodshot whites, and bruises covered most of her body. Sitting in the hospital bed, surrounded by soft pillows, she seemed tiny and fragile. Nothing was said, but I think she was glad to be alive.

Chapter 6

Joan was in hospital for months recovering from her suicide attempt, and I resigned my job at the club so I could look after Yvonne. But I'm never one for sitting still, so I made other arrangements for my sister and tried a move to Wellington. I was lonely and fed up there, and within 10 days I was back in Auckland.

'I knew you wouldn't cut it,' Joan sighed when I turned up at her bedside at visiting time.

For all her hard words at times, I did feel a need to look after her. Whatever she did or said, she was still my mother, and at this point she needed as much help as possible. So I found a flat and took a job at the hospital.

As a special orderly on the spinal unit, I learned quickly how lucky I really was. Just walking to work through the late summer sunshine, then going into the ward, filled with people who would never take another step, was a humbling experience. One woman had been incredibly house-proud, and had polished her wooden stairs so well that she had slipped on them and broken her neck. She was a tetraplegic and would never pick up a duster again, let alone get to walk around her sparklingly clean home. Both she and the house she had loved were now gathering dust.

Sometimes I would sneak a few of the male patients out to my flat for a party. They would down endless beers, but never need to rush to the toilet — one of the few bonuses of having a catheter and bag. On the ward, there was one young woman who caught my eye. Karen was feisty, beautiful and stylish, even as she lay in bed after an accident had left her paralyzed from the neck down. Her cutting wit kept me smiling, and we soon became good friends. Then one day, as I was tucking in her sheets, she leaned towards me.

'Peter,' she whispered. 'I have to know.'

'Know what?' I asked, expecting a witty quip.

Her beautiful face grew grave and she leaned so close her breath rustled in my ear like autumn leaves.

'I need to know if I can still feel. If I can still want and be wanted. I need to feel desire again, Peter.'

She blushed slightly, but I knew what she meant. We arranged to have some private time together, supposedly to discuss her rehabilitation, but in reality to touch each other and kiss.

Afterwards she smiled and lay back, her eyes closed.

'Thank you,' she whispered. Nothing more needed to be said, and it was never repeated. Later she married a downtrodden, weak-willed sort of bloke, and I went to the wedding. As she left on her honeymoon, I bent forward to kiss her goodbye and she leaned close, that breath in my ear again.

'It should have been you,' she murmured. I knew better. I was still only at the start of my journey.

Gary, another of the hospital orderlies, seemed to have the same ideas as I did about pursuing a better future. 'You know, we need to get out of this place,' he would often say.

Eventually I replied, 'Why don't we then?'

What was keeping me? By now Joan was well and back working, this time as a midwife. Yvonne and Kay were in boarding school. My father was happy with Bud. I was just filling time pushing wheelchairs and lifting patients. A new challenge was needed and I was itching for change.

'Sydney,' said Gary.

'Okay; Sydney it is.' Sometimes that's all you need to do to make a big change in your life: just say it, then do it.

Joan and my sisters saw me off at the airport. I was 16, still big at more than 13 stone, but dressed in the height of fashion — white flared pants, white jodhpur boots and a pale-blue bri-nylon knit shirt. As I watched Auckland become smaller and smaller through the window of the plane, all I felt was relief.

Gary and I moved into a small hotel in King's Cross, and that's when I realized I didn't know my travelling companion quite as well as I thought. I knew he was gay, but I didn't realize he was in love with me until I saw a letter he had written to his mother and left sitting out in our little hotel room.

'I love Peter, but there's no way he will love me back. I just know it. It tears me to pieces,' he had written, the ink smudged with tears.

I knew Gary had tried to commit suicide twice before and the letter worried me. I had to talk tough.

'Look, it's not working out,' I said. 'I know you have feelings for me, and I just don't feel the same. I'm sorry.'

Gary looked utterly devastated. 'I can't see you every day, knowing I can't have you. Please think again Peter,' he begged.

But I couldn't feel what wasn't there, and he knew he had to leave.

'Where will I go? Should I just go home? Oh God, this is awful, Peter.'

I felt bad for him. He was so mixed up and troubled. I knew I had hurt him, but it was better to do it at that moment than further down the track when he was more dependent on me.

'Maybe you should head back to Auckland,' I told him, one hand on his shoulder. He crumpled beneath my touch, but he knew I was right. He found a Russian boat that was heading to Auckland and got a place on board. I went to say my final goodbye and found him slumped in the tiny cabin, looking completely bereft of hope.

'Here, take this.' I gave him $20. 'You'll get through this.'

Gary didn't know that without that $20 I had just 20 cents left in my pocket. But there was no way on earth I was heading back to Auckland, money or no money. Sydney was where I was determined to stay, and make my life. I wandered into a pub on Pitt Street, bought a glass of beer for 18c and sat at the bar, trying to get my brain around the situation.

'Where are you from?' A deep voice broke into my thoughts.

'Auckland.' I wasn't in any mood to talk.

'Ah, Auckland. I hear it's a lovely city.' The man was very neatly dressed, in a suit and tie, and was sipping a beer.

'It's okay.'

Few are the times when I have very little to say, and the man, who turned out to be the manager of a menswear store, soon had me chatting. Having had too many brushes with men looking for a thrill, I felt quite guarded when he asked me to stay the night at his place in Manly, across the harbour. Although I had moved out of the hotel and had nowhere to stay, I was going to say no; I had the word on my tongue, but held it back. The thought of a lovely trip across the water, looking at the lights of Sydney from the best viewpoint in the city, was too good to miss. Even so, when we got to his house I fully expected him to lunge at me, and braced myself.

'Here. You can have the couch. It's quite comfortable. I've put out a couple of blankets in case you get cold, and a feather pillow,' he said, yawning and heading to his own room. I waited for a while in case he returned, but no, this man was genuine and wanted nothing in return. In fact, he had more to give. On the return ferry the next morning we leaned on the rail and watched the boats on the water.

'Can you sell?' he asked.

'Sell? Me? Sure. I'm good at selling,' I bluffed.

'Okay. I suppose you could start at the shop pretty much straight away then?'

I grinned.

Back in the city I went straight to the train station to get my bag from the locker where I had left it. In the men's toilets I unearthed what I was looking for — my slightly crushed blue suit, the best item of clothing I owned. I showed up at the shop and started work fifteen minutes later, only taking a break at lunchtime to use the phone and find somewhere to live. I rang the Methodist Mission refuge.

'Look, I don't have any money, but I do have a good job. If I stay there, can I pay at the end of the week?'

I put on my most polite, persuasive voice and hoped for the best. The manager agreed, and for $9 a week I had a roof over my head. The room was tiny, with a single bed squeezed in, and the food was basic at best, but I was there, safe and warm. Of course, I wasn't satisfied for long. Maybe even then I sensed that my time would be limited and that I needed to make the most of every chance I got. Within three months I decided I needed a change, and I got a job as a theatre orderly at St Vincent's Hospital, living in a flat with a couple of hippies.

This was the time of turning on, tuning in and dropping out. We painted wildly imaginative murals in the flat, and sat around on cushions smoking marijuana. Some people took LSD, but I didn't. I felt crazy enough, and high on Sydney. At nights we would go to the Cross and dance in the street. Life was bizarre but good. Yet although I felt at home in this colourful, dangerous city, I soon decided it was time to move on once more. Two of the guys from the flat were driving to Cairns in Queensland, hoping to sell some marijuana and have a wild time. Would I like to go? Of course I would. How could I resist? We didn't know it then, but taking dope to Cairns was like taking coals to Newcastle. Naively we set off, full of dreams.

We got as far as Mackay, a town on the coast where the Great Barrier Reef begins, and I found a job as a waiter. I had never worked as a waiter before, but I bluffed my way through the interview. Within three days I was told I had one more chance to improve or I'd be out on my backside. That was all the motivation I needed. I stuck at it, learned what I could, and was soon in a secure job. During my three months there I learned a lot about the other side of the hospitality industry, the front of house. I could have stayed in the job longer but my itchy Kiwi feet got the better of me. I went to Roylan Cruises, a company that sailed from Mackay around the reef.

'Hi,' I announced with my brightest smile. 'I'd like to be a deckhand? Any positions going?'

The manager looked glum. He'd obviously had lots of approaches like this from landlubbers with no idea what seafaring life was about. Just as my smile started to lose some of its glimmer, he sighed.

'We need a cook. Can you cook?'

The smile turned up to full wattage. Could I cook? Did Jackie Kennedy have a little black dress? I could cook like an angel, I told him. I could create food that would leave him weak at the knees. Name a dish and I could cook it, not just well, but so fantastically that the punters would be sobbing with sheer delight when they tasted it. They would have to be forced down the gangplank after the cruise, determined to stay and have more of my heavenly cooking. I was the cook he had waited all his life for.

I finally paused for breath and looked at him. It was a pause so pregnant it was about to go into labour at any moment.

'Okay,' he said, looking a little relieved that I had stopped my ranting. 'Be ready to leave tomorrow for a five-day cruise.'

I was going cruising. Could I be any further from my life on a Northland farm? At that point I didn't think there would be a more exciting moment in my life. I was wrong, of course, but I didn't know that. As I stood outside the office I wanted to fling my hat into the air like Mary Tyler Moore, but I had no hat, so I settled for visualising a good old hat-throwing session. I was on my way again.

If cruising brings to mind an image of that dreadful TV show The Love Boat, throw it overboard immediately. The ship I was on was a narrow Fairmile boat, 112 feet long, and used in the war as a support vessel. During its war days it was called Ajax. Now it took 25 guests around the reef and had a crew of nine. The bunks were tiny, two to a room, and the skipper and engineer kipped in the wheelhouse. As soon as I arrived at the ship I started work, loading food ordered by the previous cook. I had no idea what was ahead, except that I had to avoid box jellyfish. That little gem of advice came from a book I had read about Australia's most venomous creatures. Apart from that, I was absolutely clueless. Kitted out in my uniform — white shorts, white T-shirt, long white socks, and a white dress shirt for arrivals and departures — I looked very cruiseworthy indeed. What a pity my first meal wasn't.

Lunch was a disaster. The corned silverside took too long to cook so I rustled up some crab sandwiches, using tinned crab, and served them with soup. Soup in the tropics wasn't my idea. It was company policy, and a silly one at that, but it went down a treat. The dessert of banana custard was also welcomed by the guests. I don't know if they were just being polite but I wasn't happy with myself, being something of a perfectionist. I vowed to do better.

Cooking conditions weren't ideal, so doing better was tricky. The galley was so small I could touch the oven and the benches at each end just by holding my arms at full stretch. The assistant cook was a hippy, and when I saw his long locks I realised I had to get rid of mine. There was just too much hair in too small a space. Anyway, I was well over the hippy look, with hair held back with a leather band, and I was too hot.

The first two weeks were a case of mucking in. I had to find a system that made it easier to produce great food in difficult conditions. The guests ate constantly — biscuits and tea served in their cabins at 6.30am, followed by a full breakfast, morning tea, lunch and afternoon tea, cocktail nibbles, dinner and finally a late-night snack. I was surprised they managed to get out of their cabins at the end of the cruise, they ate so much.

For an adventure-hungry 17-year-old it was an unforgettable experience. I was in a position of responsibility, and I had gained the respect of the captain. I trusted him as well, knowing that when storms brewed and rain began to pelt down on the increasingly frightening seas, he would keep us safe. I saw the reef and all its wonderful islands: Brampton, Lindemann, Daydream, Paradise, Hook, Hayman. At Whitsunday Island we got off the ship and stood on a beach covered in the most incredible fine white sand. I began to walk up to the treeline when the captain stopped me.

'Don't go near it, lad,' he said.

'Why?' I asked, just as I realised other people were running from the bush, followed by clouds of black sandflies.

'We warned them too,' the captain said. 'Nasty buggers, those sandflies. You've never seen anything like it.'

I shuddered. Little did I know it then, but it would be a sandfly just like one of those that would later change my life.

No matter how often I saw the reef from a glass-bottomed boat, sailing over the busy coral with its neon fish, the wonder didn't fade. Sometimes I would fish with some of the crew, one of us always keeping a look-out for grey nurse or white pointer sharks, which would snap the catch off the line.

On a day that remains etched in my memory, the boat stopped for lunch over a particularly shallow reef. Three hours from any land, it seemed perfect and safe, until we became 'glassed in'. This is when the sea and sky become exactly the same colour and there is no wind to move the surface of the water. It becomes like being inside a giant spherical mirror. Your eyes can't see through the oily reflection and your brain struggles to interpret what is there. Even more frightening, the horizon simply disappears.

The captain stood on the deck and looked around. I could see he was worried. 'The tide's about to change,' he said in a low voice when I asked him what was happening. 'We've got to move from this anchorage before then because there's no room to turn with the tide. There's no way we can see what's under us. It's not good, Peter.'

At that point two deckhands got into a small dinghy, dragging the end of the hose we used for washing down the decks. They sprinkled hose-water on the glassy surface of the sea. I watched in wonder as the reef appeared before our eyes, the mirror surface shattering under the beads of water. Then, just as the anchor went down in our new position, the water exploded as more than a hundred sharks began a feeding frenzy. All the passengers crowded to one side of the boat, cameras snapping, causing it to lean dangerously close to the hungry sharks. I threw cabbages to the sharks, watching them leap and thrash as they tore them apart. Any slip and it would be over, I thought, as I craned out as far as I could and hurled another cabbage. One shark was gashed by the teeth of another and the heaving, bloody mass turned on him, ripping him to pieces. When the sharks had finished, all that remained was a slick of oily blood and tiny shreds of fish.

During cruises that summer of 1970–71 I would sometimes ask the skipper to stop at Dent Island so we could visit Ruth, a fat, jolly Queensland silversmith, and her American husband. They had a huge colony of peacocks, which looked beautiful, although I soon discovered how utterly vile they could be. When I cooked a barbecue for everyone the birds would hang about, lurching forward to peck sausages straight off the grill. If I waved them away with the tongs they would peck my legs. If I stepped away to avoid their sharp beaks, chances were that I would stand in a peacock dropping and go for a skid. Then, while I tried to regain my balance, they would raid the tray of cooked food. I went off peacocks for life.

My time cooking on the boat was wonderful, the only down being when the kitchen assistant had a major epileptic seizure in the kitchen. It was the worst place to have a seizure. He thrashed around, taking up all the available space, one foot burning against the oven door. I was cooking fish in beer batter and there was a pot of boiling oil on the stove. I jumped onto the counter to give him more room.

'Put a spoon in his mouth to bite down on, or he'll swallow his tongue,' shrieked one of the hostesses, who had walked in on the scene. I edged myself off the counter, armed with a wooden spoon, and managed to stick it between his jaws.

Later I learned he had not taken his medication. 'Don't ever, ever do that again,' I told him. 'It could have caused a fire, pushed me into the oil or tipped the whole lot on top of you. Or you could even fall overboard, and you know what those sharks can do.'

He promised to take his pills, but two weeks later he had another fit, thankfully without injury, and was dropped off at Hayman Island to be choppered back to the mainland.

The arrival of the cyclone season meant the end of my seafaring career. But the experience seemed to have settled my mind. Three years had now passed since I had left school and I was aware that I needed some qualifications. Yes, I had a talent for cooking, but I wanted to know how to do it properly. I also wanted to go beyond just being a chef. Management was my new goal. I had saved some money while on the boat, and it would be enough to pay for a course at catering college. I was sorted.

That is, until Joan reappeared in my life, with a phone call that changed everything. She seemed to have an uncanny knack of knowing when to pop up and cause maximum disruption. This time, she said she was getting married to Bill, the accountant she had been seeing when I was living with her.

'Mum, that's great,' I said, feeling genuinely happy for her, and a little relieved.

'Oh Peter, there's just one thing missing, darling,' she crooned. I held my breath, because I recognised the tone of her voice. The 'do something for me or I won't love you' tone.

'Yes, what?' I tried not to sound as guarded as I felt.

'I want you to give me away. Say you will. It would mean so much to me.'

I bit my lip and summoned all my mental strength.

'No, Mum, I can't. I don't have the money.'

'What about your savings?' she answered.

'Once I've paid the fees for my studies I won't have enough left to come to Auckland. Sorry Mum, I can't.'

'Well, your sisters are going to be bridesmaids.' I could visualise her pouting as she said this. 'They are putting themselves out for me. I don't see why you can't too. It's my wedding after all. Don't you care?'

So I dutifully hitchhiked to Brisbane and caught a plane to Auckland. It was two weeks before Christmas. It only took me two days to work out that Joan had conned me. She had cancelled the wedding — possibly even before she contacted me — and had rationalised her demands by thinking I would still want to see her. My college fees were gone, and my mother was not marrying Bill. I was full of anger. She hadn't changed. But I had. I returned to Australia and started at catering college in Sydney a week later.

'I'll sort out the fees later,' I told myself as I signed up for the three-year hotel and catering management certificate course. There was a bigger issue, however. I had lied on my application form, saying I had passed six subjects in School Certificate and five in the University Entrance exam. In fact, I had passed nothing. I'm usually an honest person but at that point my desire to do the course, and my determination to succeed, overwhelmed everything. And the problem was, I had to present my certificates. Fortunately I was offered an out by the New Zealand postal workers, who decided to go on strike about then. I was very grateful to them, as their action gave me a valid, if unlikely, excuse for the non-appearance of my papers. After a while the college stopped asking for them, and I breathed a sigh of relief.

I was in college, and I was staying.

Chapter 7

'You think this looks easy, eh? Just shaking it up a little bit for the
punters, and tipping it out, eh? Easy-peasy, no?'
I shook my head as I watched the stream of golden tequila being
poured into the cocktail shaker from a great height, not a drop
spilling.
'It's not easy. I can tell you that. But you will learn, Peter. And if
you don't, you are out.'
It was 1972. At the age of 19, I was in the presence of Peter
Zorbas, the best cocktail barman in the whole of Australia, and he
was giving me a personal lesson in the art of creating the perfect
cocktail. His flamboyance was legendary, and every drink he made
was virtually a show in itself. I was in awe of his skills.
My job as Peter's trainee barman, at the Paradise Bar in Sydney's
famous Chevron Hotel, couldn't have come at a better time. I was
at college and living in a rooming house on Flinders Street.
Sharing a bathroom with 18 other people was gruelling, to say the
least. The beds had bugs, but at least the sheets were changed once
a week, giving a couple of nights free of bites until the nasty
creatures worked their way up from the mattress again. I was so
broke I had to pretend I wasn't in when the landlady knocked on
my door for the $18-a-week rent. I would pinch an apple off a fruit
stand on the way to school just to fill my grumbling stomach.
Any savings I had left were used to buy my books and chef's
whites for the college cooking classes. I needed a job on top of my
40 hours of study a week, and I was very lucky to get the one in
the Paradise Bar. This was the time of the Vietnam War, and
soldiers on leave would come in to drown the memories of warfare
and spend lots of money. One thing they wanted to splash out on
was drink;
the other was sex. While the ordinary soldiers drank in public bars
and picked up street girls, the officers wanted cocktails and high-
class prostitutes. The Paradise Bar had both.
'A scotch on the rocks for me, and something for the lady,' the
officers would say to me.

At first, when the girls asked for vodka and tonic, for example, I gave them exactly that. Then one of the girls, a beautiful woman in her thirties, took me to one side.

'Darling, don't actually give us the drinks we ask for.'

'What do you mean?' I was baffled. They ordered a drink, I served them. It was as simple as that, or so I thought.

She chuckled and shook her head.

'No, don't put alcohol in it. God knows, we need all our wits in this game, honey. Charge the punter the full cost, put the money for the mixer in the till, and keep the rest.'

I blushed. It was obvious now that she had explained it. They always ordered drinks like gin and tonic, vodka and orange, rum and Coke — anything that didn't show it had no booze in it. Peter hadn't explained that part to me, of course. But then, did he know? I wasn't sure, and I certainly wasn't going to ask him.

Just to complicate matters, there were times when the girls did want alcohol, usually at the end of a long shift or on a quiet night. A subtle wink, a flick of the hair, a raised eyebrow, that was all they needed to do and I would know they wanted a strong drink.

I grew fond of the girls who worked there, and gradually I learned their stories. Anna was in her late thirties and worked during the day as a marine architect. Her husband had died three years earlier and her children were away at college. She was desperately lonely but still unready to commit to one person. Instead of dating, she became a high-class hooker. 'I might as well get paid for it,' she said, with a sad smile.

Then there was Maria, a curvaceous, dark-haired woman from Budapest. 'My leetle darlink,' she would say, patting my cheek, when I brought her favourite drink, a warm cola. The other working girls didn't like her because she undercut their prices. Even more annoying, she took the clients home, instead of to a hotel room, and cooked them a steak meal.

'Then, darlink, I cross myself in front of my Jesus on the cross in my bedroom and do my duty,' she told me.

I loved the atmosphere of sexual tension in the bar. There was other tension though, between Peter Zorbas and me, during my second week there.

'That's only half of what I put in the tip jar. Where's the rest?' I asked when he handed me $5.

'That's how it goes in here,' he replied. 'Look, you can take the rest in booze. Take $5 of drink. You can do that instead. I'm a fair man.'

I knew he was running a scam with the tips and stood my ground. 'I don't need alcohol, I need money,' I said firmly. He sighed, realising that I wasn't going to back down. Another $5 was pressed into my hand, and that's how it was from then on. I did three months at the bar and Peter Zorbas liked me so much he asked me to continue. I think it was partly because I was so discreet, but I was also good at my job. It was fortunate for me, because I needed the money for more than just my keep.

The phone call came one afternoon.

'Peter?' My heart sank. It was Joan.

'Oh. Hello. How are you? How are the girls?' I asked.

'I don't have time for that. Just listen. My money is about to run out on this phone. I'm in Sydney. I need your help.'

It turned out that Joan had found God and had moved to Sydney to work in a hostel helping pregnant Aboriginal girls.

'It's a charity so they pay nothing. I don't have a penny, Peter. You have to help me.'

I winced at her words. She had virtually nothing, and I couldn't bear to think of my mother being in that state. I started giving her money every week for essentials. It was hard, finding enough cash for us both to survive on. One source of income was out-of-hours events that course students were sometimes asked to work at. As I was the poorest but keenest student in the class, the lecturers would often pick me to work at these events. These included the incredibly sumptuous feasts held by the Food and Wine Association, where you might find such things as truffles, oysters, caviar, 1923 champagne, stilton soaked in 1918 port, and French coffee. I absorbed the atmosphere and ate the scraps, savouring these totally new flavours.

And yet, my usual day would start with me pinching that apple on the way to college. I was cautious about the apple, so it was quite a risk when I decided to up my booty to a yoghurt instead. One day the owner appeared just as I was about to leave. He peered at me over the top of his glasses.

'Try the hazelnut one. I hear it's delicious.'

I blushed. He had caught me and I was horrified.

'I'm so sorry. I just — I didn't — I don't have any money.' The words came out as a terrified babble.

'No, it's okay. Take one.' He nodded towards the fridge. I hesitated and looked back at his face.

'Go on. I know you're hungry. You've been doing it for weeks.' He was so kind about it that I felt utterly horrible. I took the yoghurt, blushing furiously, but I never went back in the shop again.

Even though I was poor, I still kept my weight on. I guess I was eating any old junk that I could get my hands on, and most of it was fatty, starchy stuff that filled me up. Then I caught the flu. By now I had turned 20, and I had moved from the Paradise Bar to a seafood restaurant called Laddies At The Spit. College now took up only 14 hours a week and we had to work 40 hours each week in the industry, so the job fitted well. The owner, Laddie, was a little fat bloke and I was horrified when I was mistaken for his son.

'Ah, don't worry about it,' laughed Laddie, slapping me on the back. 'Think of it as a compliment. I would.'

But I didn't. Then the flu kicked in and Laddie suggested fasting. 'It's the best way, you know. You just fast, drink nothing but water, for three days, and you'll be cured.'

I did exactly as he said, and amazingly, it worked. It was so easy to fast that I decided to carry on, fasting for 48 hours and then going vegetarian for 24 hours. I lost 46 kg in three months, and after nine months I was a total of 46 kg lighter. I looked good and felt better, but I still had an image of myself as 'the fat boy'. It took another 20 years before I could shift that mindset once and for all. I never binged again, and I weaned myself off sugary foods. The relief I felt at casting off one legacy of my awful childhood, the comfort eating, was unbelievable.

I also managed to get Joan back to New Zealand and rid myself of another burden. Yvonne had now finished school and had also come to Sydney, because she missed me so much. I was thrilled that my best friend was with me again. Then Joan caught Yvonne in bed with a boyfriend, and was so outraged that she got on a plane and went home.

A year later, Joan reappeared in Sydney. She was living at another hostel, I heard, and training to be a counsellor. I phoned the hostel to speak to her but got the man who ran the place.

'It's so good to hear that she's training,' I said cheerfully.
'Training? What do you mean?' He sounded confused.
'She's training to be a counsellor there. It's a good move for her, don't you think?'
'I'm afraid you've got the wrong idea,' the man said. 'She's not here to train; she's here drying out and on our drug detox programme.'
It was a shock, but also a relief. Finally she was doing something. I went to see her, to tell her that I was proud of her decision. She was in the garden when I arrived, a tiny figure, bending down weeding a large vegetable-bed.
'Mum.'
She turned her head and looked at me, surprised.
'What are you doing here?'
'I came to see you. I know why you're here.'
Her head drooped.
'I see. Well, it's not like it was a big problem for me or anything. Just a small one, and there's no harm in stopping it getting bigger. You know how it is.'
She was still in denial, but at least she was doing something. During her time in detox she was kinder and more involved with Yvonne and me than she had been for years. She cooked a beautiful meal for my 21st birthday, and was happy to meet Simon, the boy who would eventually become Yvonne's husband, without making a single snide comment. When she was well enough, Joan left the hostel and went back into nursing.
My last year at college was a good one. I flatted with Yvonne, I had a gorgeous Italian girlfriend, and my course was going well. I left Laddies and went to work for a posh French provincial restaurant called La Perouse. There, among the garlic and tomatoes, I learned some important lessons about this kind of food, and these I would take with me back to Auckland. My friend Tony Adcock and I even set up a student union at college, and it was a huge success. I felt as if the world was really my oyster when I graduated. I wanted to prise it open and scoop out everything that was good, to savour and devour.
Then one day Tony made a suggestion. 'We'd better make the most of our student status and get a cheap flight home,' he said. He

was right. I looked at my bank balance and saw I had $165. The ticket was $123.

'Right, let's go,' I told him.

Sarah Davidson was another student we both knew, and we all met up in Auckland. It was wonderful to be back. Of course, Auckland was tiny, almost a small town compared with big, colourful Sydney, but I was happy to be home.

'You've got to go to Clichy,' friends kept telling me.

'What on earth is Clichy?' I asked Tony and Sarah.

Sarah laughed.

'Just the hottest thing since sliced bread and only opened this month, Peter. It's the place to eat, the place to be seen in. Anybody who is anyone is going there. There's not a chicken in the basket or a pineapple ring in the whole place.'

'Oh my God, that sounds fantastic. Let's go.' I was virtually heading for the door as I spoke.

We walked into the restaurant, three students full of enthusiasm and confidence. I immediately cornered the owner and asked if he could show us around. Later we sat at the table, nursing our coffees and whispering.

'We could do this,' I insisted. 'It's easy for us. We can't leave it a moment longer or someone else will do it. Come on. Let's go for it.'

The other two were just as excited. We were barely out of our teens, but here we were, three young people with an amazing idea and lots of cheek.

And that's how Le Brie was born.

Chapter 8

'If I have to stitch one more of these bloody tablecloths, I swear I'll go mad!'

I was virtually buried in a pile of checked material and my fingers were raw from edging the tablecloths that Sarah was cutting out.

'Oh quiet, only another six to go,' she chided.

'But I'm seeing checks, and not of the monetary kind,' I wailed. 'I never want to see a checked thing again in my life.'

Tony was fixing hessian pelmets over the fluorescent lights, cursing each time he hit his finger with a hammer.

'Hey, at least you don't have to do this. The blood is draining from my arms. I'll never be able to cook — my arms will have withered and dropped off.'

Up on his ladder, he mimicked an arm falling off and a miserable face. Sarah and I laughed. None of us really disliked being there. In fact, we loved it. This dingy little dungeon of a place was being transformed into our own restaurant and we couldn't have been more excited.

After our visit to Clichy we had sat down and worked out how much we would need to open our own place. The total was $12,000. Then we each went to our parents and asked for a loan to start our company. I asked Stan, Joan being as penniless as ever. He was happily farming in Northland, and the idea of investing in a French provincial restaurant was not something that had ever crossed his mind. A new bull, possibly. A fancy eatery, never. Still, Stan saw how enthusiastic I was and happily gave me the $4000 I needed, at the same time wishing me luck. I hugged him warmly.

'Thanks. You won't regret it,' I promised him.

We looked at lots of possible venues. Some were too expensive, some too disgusting, others in terrible locations. Just as we were about to give up we found a little place that had been a health-food café, on the corner of Chancery and Warspite Streets in Auckland's city centre.

'I think I'm in love,' I sighed, as I walked through the cosy but character-filled little shop.

'I think I know where my hammer is,' sighed Tony.

'I think we need to sign immediately before someone else snaps it up,' said Sarah, always decisive.

The owner let us have the place for no rent until we opened, and we got it cheap after that.

'What colour should we paint it?' Sarah wondered. 'Red?'

'No, not red, every restaurant is red. It's overdone.' I hated red anyway. It was too garish. We needed something fresh and new.

'Yellow and green,' Tony said, and we loved the idea. Yellow and green it was, with green checked tablecloths and curtains, and hired plants for greenery. I got old photos of Ponsonby Road from an op shop for the walls, and painted the words Le Brie on the window. It was small, simple and barely noticeable from the street. While working on getting Le Brie ready we all had other jobs. I was cooking for a crew of carnival workers. I spent the mornings dishing out meals and the afternoons playing on the dodgems. Life was so exciting. I was letting off steam before settling into Le Brie. Opening day was May 19, 1975. We had just $200 to buy produce and stock the kitchen. Nobody would let us have anything on credit as we were total unknowns. As the lunchtime opening loomed we all stood in the restaurant and took a deep breath. We were a tiny team, but we were ready to take on all that Auckland could throw at us.

I opened the little front door and a few people looked over. Then one or two trickled in. Our nervousness dissolved as the orders came in and we got into our stride. There were a few hiccups, but nothing major, and we finished our first lunch with a glass or two of wine to celebrate.

'We can really do this!' I said. And everyone agreed.

It didn't take long for word to get around and the trickle became a flood. We had a winning recipe: the menu — four entrées, five main courses and three desserts — was changed monthly. There was always garlic bread and French onion soup, a terrine or pâté, and a hot or cold dish of offal, such as sweetbreads or kidney, done in different ways. Steak with a sauce, and some kind of casserole, as well as seafood, were always among the main courses. The desserts were simple. I made literally thousands of crème caramels, and my cream tart filled with juicy plums became one of our biggest sellers. I came up with ideas like feijoa mousse or fresh figs soaked in boozy orange juice. The emphasis was on country produce cooked simply, so the flavours were not overpowered. We also took chances with the menu, from time to time introducing local ingredients such as eel. A nice Maori bloke from Port Waikato would bring us a sack of live eels, for which we paid him a dozen beers. One lunchtime he came in late and was clearly the worse for wear.

'Hey, mate, here's your eels,' he slurred, dropping the sack on the kitchen floor. The sack was open and the eels saw their chance, slithering out and across the lino floors into the kitchen and storeroom. Waitresses came in to find eels slithering around their ankles, and a few plates went flying. Everyone who could face touching the slimy creatures was wrestling the eels into buckets. The kitchen was filled with screams, giggles and shouts of 'There's another one, quick, grab it!' Once we had the eels trapped in buckets, they went into the fridge. Eels go into hibernation when they are chilled and the trick is to get them while they are still snoozing, chop off their heads and skin them. I discovered how important it was to keep them cold when one day I thawed them by accident and they came round while I was trying to behead them. Despite the goriness of their demise, the eels were delicious and certainly didn't pass into eel heaven in vain. I sautéed them in a little white wine, onion and tomato, and served eel à la provençale as an entrée. There was also whitebait and even rabbit, which we called 'baby hare'. Occasionally Stan would come down from Whangarei with a home-killed milk-fed pig. It was a lovely day trip for Stan and Bud, and our customers liked the pork so much that we had a list of people to call when it was available.

Our reputation grew beyond all expectations — except those of the three of us who had started it. We had always believed it would be big. Sometimes I looked in the mirror and stared. I was 22, a kid from the back end of Whangarei, and here I was, executive chef and co-owner of one of Auckland's best, most innovative restaurants. One day a salesman came into Le Brie and asked to speak to the owner. When I said, 'Yes, I'm the owner,' he didn't believe me, because I looked so young. I loved that. Sarah, Tony and I worked well together, and we knew we were changing eating habits in New Zealand for ever. Le Brie stayed open for 24 years, an amazing achievement for a restaurant.

We had a hatch between the kitchen and the dining area, so the customers could see us cooking, and even that was new. We saw other restaurants changing their set-ups and menus, inspired by our success. But nobody quite matched Le Brie. A year after opening, we were on a high. At the end of each night the staff would sit down at a cleared table and eat, drink and relax. It was the time when disagreements were settled, ideas pitched, thanks and praise given, and a few dashes of gossip thrown in.

We started each day at 8am and finished at 1am. I became expert at grabbing a quick nap on the floor, but Tony found it hard. He got stressed in the kitchen, lost weight, and could only do six weeks in one go. In the end, he took some time off. I would step into his shoes, which meant a more front-of-house role, and go between the two areas. I loved it and thrived on the buzz, the energy and the sheer thrill of Le Brie.

At one point Larry Quickenden, another friend from college, stepped in to give Tony a break. He was good, and it let us all having some breathing space. After a while, I knew even I was in danger of flagging a little too. I was tired, and I didn't want my enthusiasm for the business to flag. I needed a new challenge.

On my one day off each week, Sunday, I had started horse-riding again. It had been a very long time since I had ridden, and that was down to a secret I carried. What nobody knew when I left Whangarei was that I had actually lost my nerve. My pony had thrown me too often and I no longer wanted to get back on and try again. For a long time, the last thing I wanted to do was to ride. After eight years I thought it was time to try an experiment. Could I still ride? Would I quake with fear? Could the horse sense I was apprehensive? Eight years was a long time to go without riding. I joined an adult riding club, and found that the years away from horses had actually healed my nerves. I got back on, gritting my teeth, and was almost surprised when the horse didn't throw me. That moment was all I needed to make the memories click back into place, and for me to remember how much I loved riding. Before long I had bought two horses and was riding regularly, enjoying the fresh air away from the garlic and onions of Le Brie.

Our instructor was Karl de Jurnack, and he liked to be fed and filled with alcohol rather than paid money for teaching the group. Karl seemed to keep a close eye on me, especially when I bought my third horse, a big gentleman called Havana. One morning he called me over after a lesson.

'Peter,' he said. 'I know you have talent. It's plain to see. But you are wasting it just pottering around here. You need to train more. You should go to the National Equestrian Centre.'

'The national what?' I had never heard of the National Equestrian Centre. I had no idea such a thing existed. 'Karl, I can't go anywhere. I've got a restaurant to run; a business depends on me. For the first time in my entire life, I'm actually making decent money. I can't give all that up just at the drop of a riding hat, for goodness' sake.'

I had also been offered a beautiful cottage on 80 acres by an uncle in Whangarei, and although the price of $80,000 was beyond my reach at that moment, I was determined to explore ways of buying it. But Karl was dangling a big carrot in front of me. I loved horses, and I wanted desperately to learn more. I had always been the kind of person to follow my passions, even at a cost, rather than stay safe and static. It is an attitude I still have to this day.

The thought took root in my mind. Tony had taken a break from Le Brie, so there was no reason why I couldn't. I went back to the restaurant, discussed the possibility with Sarah and Tony, and arranged to take a six-month break. Then I rang Karl.

'Karl, you'll never guess what,' I said, barely able to contain my excitement. 'I can go to the National Equestrian Centre. What do you reckon?'

I had to hold the phone away from my ear to prevent his hearty response bursting my eardrums. However, it wasn't quite as simple as I thought. I would have to take a test.

'What kind of test?' I asked the secretary at the National Equestrian Centre in Taupo. 'Nobody mentioned a test.'

Apparently the test — to ride before the national coach — was compulsory, and in addition there was a three-year waiting list to get into the centre as a student. I had jumped before I had checked the facts, arranging leave from the restaurant without a thought of not getting into the course.

I was told to report to the Papatoetoe Pony Club's grounds at Alfriston, in South Auckland, with Havana. My mouth was dry and I felt nerves buzzing in my stomach as I arrived and made sure Havana was okay and safely tethered. Then I went to look for the national coach, a well-known dressage expert called Lockie Richards, who would test me. There were a few people milling about and I had no idea who to look for. So I waited instead.

'Morning,' said a wiry, dark-haired bloke in his forties, opening the gate to a flat paddock.

'Oh, hello there,' I said, recognising the man from the National Dressage Championships a couple of months earlier. I had gone with a friend, Linda, who was competing. As I watched her go around the ring, performing all the complex moves in perfect order, the same man had been resting on the fence beside me. His sharp eyes didn't miss a single move.

'Nice horse. Nice rider,' he had muttered.

I mentioned that we had met at the championships, at the same time wondering what he was doing at Alfriston and where Lockie Richards was.

'That's right. I remember,' the man said gruffly.

'Well, nice to see you again. I'm just waiting for Lockie Richards, the national trainer. I have to do a test. Wish me luck.'

The man didn't blink or smile.

'I'm Lockie Richards,' he said.

I blushed, hastily thinking back to the dressage contest, hoping I hadn't said anything silly to him.

'Oops, sorry.' I gave him a grin that I hoped was endearing. That had blown it.

'So, what are you doing here? What is it that makes you want to do this?' he asked.

'I'd like to do three-day eventing.' This was the triathlon of equestrianism — cross-country, dressage and showjumping — in which New Zealand had achieved medal glory at the Olympics several times. 'Havana is great when it comes to jumping. He's a good hunting horse and can easily clear a four-foot wire fence,' I gabbled on, my nerves showing through.

Lockie looked at the paddock. It was empty.

'Nothing to jump in there, Peter.'

'Well, there's a few wire fences there, and a ramp. I'll give it my best shot.'

I got Havana and trotted into the paddock, trying to look bold and confident. Havana skipped over the fence, jumped into the next paddock, back over again, and then hopped over the ramp. I cantered over to Lockie.

'That's it. There's nothing more to jump in there,' I said.

Lockie was smiling.

'That wasn't bad,' he said. 'Can you do dressage?'

My face fell and he noticed. I didn't like dressage. It was extremely disciplined and the horse couldn't put a foot wrong. There was no room for creativity.

'I won't lie to you, Mr Richards. I don't know anything about dressage, except what I've seen, but I will certainly give it a go.'

I did my very best, turning, circling, trotting, walking, halting. Lockie watched me like a hawk. When I had finished, he came up to me.

'You do realise that it's hard work at the centre. There's no room for slackers.'

'Mr Richards, I have a restaurant that seats 70 people. I work six days a week, and 16-hour days. I know all about hard work.'

'There's not much money in it. Just $12 a week from a scholarship. Nothing more.'

'I have savings, Mr Richards. Money isn't an issue. I want to do this. I'm the son of a dairy farmer, I can drive a tractor, I can lift bales of hay, I'm not afraid of getting my hands dirty. I can do this.'

Lockie listened and was silent. I waited, barely daring to breathe. What would his decision be? Was my dream within my grasp?

'I'll put you on the list and let you know,' he said finally, and walked away without another word.

So I went back to Le Brie, putting my leave on hold. Two months later I was in the kitchen, chopping a huge pile of onions, when the phone rang. 'Can someone get that? God, why is it that when you need someone to do something simple, there's never anybody there.' I grumpily wiped my hands on a tea towel and picked up the phone.

'Hello, Le Brie. Peter speaking,' I sighed, mentally working through what else needed to be prepared for the night's menu.

'It's Lockie Richards. You can start in eight weeks. Take it or leave it.'

Chapter 9

The fat little chestnut horse definitely had hiccups, and I had absolutely no idea what to do. It wasn't like I could give it a fright, get it to count to 10 or suggest it stood on its head and drank a glass of water, as you did with humans. Did horses die of hiccups? It didn't look too distressed but it sounded terrible, the great belching burps coming from the pit of its stomach. As I stood in the horse's stall at the National Equestrian Centre trying to work out the best solution I heard a voice behind me.

'What is it now?'

I turned to see Sheryl, the centre manager, looking very fed up. A no-nonsense horsy type from a rural background, she had decided I was a waste of space when I turned up at the centre with a double bed, a dog and a cat in tow.

'It's very odd,' I said. 'Cuddles seems to have, um, hiccups. I went out to get him and he was making these weird little burping noises. It can only be hiccups. What should I do?'

Sheryl rolled her eyes.

'Horses don't get hiccups. He's been wind sucking, that's all.' I swear she muttered something about city slickers knowing nothing as she trudged off down the stable yard, shaking her head.

Wind sucking, as I found out when I looked it up in a horse book, is something horses do to comfort themselves when they are bored. It turns into a habit and can give them stomach pain. Basically, they hook their top teeth to something and gulp down air. The noise I heard was the air popping out again.

'Thanks a lot, Cuddles,' I groaned to the horse, realising that I had once again annoyed Sheryl. I hadn't been able to do anything right since I had arrived a few days earlier, in my V8 Kingswood, with a horse float on the back. Havana was safely installed on one side of the float, and my bed was on the other. In the car I had my stereo, my Doberman–Labrador cross Barrabas, and my tortoiseshell cat Motley.

If Sheryl took a wee while to thaw towards me, her dog Daisy, a blue heeler, fell in love with Barrabas immediately. The fact that they were mad about each other, constantly wanting to be together, meant that Sheryl saw me much more often than I think she would have liked in those early days. But I was determined to win her over, and slowly but surely she began to see that, despite being as green as could be, I was keen to learn and respected her knowledge of horsemanship.

Lockie wasn't at the centre when I arrived. As the national dressage coach he had a demanding job that took him all over the world. He had also been the leading three-day event rider in the United States during the 1960s, and that's where he was when I arrived. A week later he returned and it was straight into the hard graft.

During my first morning in the ring, as we worked through various moves, I spoke to him from the heart.

'Lockie,' I said, using his first name now that I was on his home turf. 'This is a hobby to me at this point. I love riding and horses. If I have talent, real talent, I'll willingly continue on this path. If not, just tell me at the end of the first month and I'll go and play tennis or something instead.'

It was difficult for me to say this, but I couldn't bear the thought of ploughing on at something I had no real talent for. The longer it went on before that harsh news was broken to me, the worse it would be. Lockie nodded, and nothing was said for a month. I worked hard, putting in long hours and giving it everything I had. But deep down I wondered if it would all be worthless, and if he was going to tell me what I dreaded to hear. At the end of a month, Lockie called me to his office.

'You have talent. I want you to continue. Do you want to continue?'

I wanted to hug him.

'I'd love to,' I said. 'I feel this is right for me. Thank you.'

He nodded.

I threw myself into my work even more vigorously, riding up to six horses every day. Sheryl always seemed to give me the weird, wild or wacky ones. They bucked, reared, even sat down on their bottoms. I was given Cuddles the wind-sucker to ride and he liked nothing better than to lollop along with his nose in the air, not paying attention and tripping over his feet. The only time Cuddles and I really clicked was when I galloped him through the 20-acre paddock, within sight of the mighty Waikato River. There were fragrant pine trees on one side and rolling hills on the other. The paddock was dotted with cross-country jumps, there were long flat areas for cantering, and hills to trot up for stamina and endurance. We would swim the horses at a dam near a geothermal station, and Barrabas would run at heel, his tongue lolling out, never giving up no matter how far we rode.

This was 1978 and New Zealand was about to send its first team to the International Three-Day Event in America: Mark Todd, Nicoli Fife, Joanne Bridgeman and Carol Harrison — still big names in the world of horses. I met the team, and hoped that one day I would be going with them.

Lockie was a wonderful mentor. He died in 2004, after a long illness, and his loss will be felt for a long time to come. For his time Lockie was an unusual man. He believed strongly in discipline, meditated and stuck to a healthy diet, and neither smoked nor drank. His perception was incredible. He would get me to move my hip just slightly, or my leg a little higher, and my riding would improve tenfold. More than anything, he taught me to feel as the horse did, to put myself in its position and realise what was needed to achieve the best performance.

Lockie had a unique way of thinking and I admired him for that. He put together that first team and had endless faith in the riders he taught. It was an honour to be taught by him, and to be asked to take over as manager when Sheryl married a racehorse trainer and quit. It was such a relief not to have to leave when my six-month scholarship was over. After talking with Tony and Sarah, I decided not to return to the restaurant.

The position of centre manager involved teaching, and one of my pupils was the owner of the posh Huka Lodge. Harland Harland-Baker wanted to be part of the hunting set and was desperate to ride well. He was a pretentious man, who drove a 1920s Lagonda sports car and always wore goggles, a leather hat, and wonderful shiny riding boots. He had such faith in his ability as a horseman that he was pretty shocked when he fell off in the ring and dislocated his shoulder. I managed to get a very sore and cross Harland into the tiny Triumph sports car I was then driving and take him to hospital. All the time I was driving, he was ranting about not being able to host dinner at Huka Lodge that night. 'Don't worry,' I said, trying to comfort him and drive as fast as possible at the same time. 'I've got lots of restaurant experience. I can do it for you. Now, just lie still. Not far now.'

We finally reached the Taupo hospital, where I left him, then I drove back to the centre and got into my black and white before going on to Huka Lodge where I was met by Harland's wife Diana. She was chef for the evening and beside herself at the thought of Harland being hospitalised.

'It's only nine for dinner, thank goodness,' she said, fanning her face with a napkin. 'Oh, Peter, you are an angel. There's one other thing though. Can you do breakfast too? Harland usually does breakfast and I can't cope with it. The hospital says he will be in for a few days. What on earth would I do without you?'

Harland's injury turned out to be worse than first thought, as he had also torn some ligaments. And so I added Huka Lodge to my list of responsibilities. What a timetable I had. I would get up early, the students would feed the horses, then I would go to Huka Lodge to do breakfast and be back at the centre by 8.30am to ride the horses, organise the management side — whether it was worming or slashing back paddocks — then return to the lodge to host the evening meal.

Two weeks after I started helping at the lodge Diana contracted brucellosis from a piece of venison. She was also taken to hospital, and Harland's brother came over from Australia with his wife to run the lodge. It was a relief to be able to cross Huka Lodge off my daily schedule, but unfortunately the relief didn't last long. Harland's brother snapped his Achilles tendon playing tennis. I had been selected for the North Island eventing team in a competition against the South Island, but with all the Huka Lodge management in hospital I had to pull out and go back to my hospitality role again. It was a hard decision to have to make, but I knew I would get another chance. I had worked too hard not to make it happen. Meanwhile, Havana, my big beautiful horse, had become lame, so I sent him up to Stan's farm for a month's rest. My girlfriend at the time was Amanda, whose father was my vet. He was a taciturn man, not given to many kind words, and as a result his daughter was one of the kindest, warmest people I knew. She had been waitressing at Le Brie, a job I had given her when her father mentioned she needed some extra money to help her through her arts degree. There were two things I noticed immediately when I met this amazing girl. First, she had a smile and laugh that were so infectious it was impossible to be grumpy around her. Secondly, she had the thickest pair of spectacles I had seen on a woman, and she didn't feel self-conscious about them at all. She had been fine until a few years earlier when a fall from a horse had left her with a head injury that affected her eyesight. The lenses made her enormous blue eyes look even more huge, and I adored her. While Havana was resting his leg Amanda lent me her horse, Little Joe, and although he was a good jumper he wasn't a patch on Havana. Fortunately Havana's leg healed well, and he came back to the centre like a new horse. I broke Amanda's heart around the same time.

It was all down to Kate. We called her the Ice Maiden because she seemed to have a glacial heart, as well as Nordic good looks. With white-blonde hair and pale blue eyes, she was petite, gorgeous and aware that she could twist men's hearts at will. I knew her through her husband. When they split up she decided to do something different with her life. She was a good rider, and when I heard she was coming to the centre to improve her horsemanship I didn't feel it was right to let her stay in the bunkhouse. Not for a single moment did I think she would lure me in. I thought Amanda was everything, but I hadn't bargained on Kate's determination.

'I've got a two-bedroom cottage. You're welcome to use the spare room,' I told her. The other men around the centre winked when they found out, but I just shrugged.

'Not my type,' I said. 'Besides, I'm taken, don't forget.'

But within days I noticed the Ice Maiden had warmed to me. There were cakes and stews on the table when I got home, and soon she was in my bed. I knew I had to do something, but her icicles had worked their way into my heart. I told Amanda I no longer wanted to be her boyfriend, and felt like the worst person in the world when she cried.

'Never mind,' purred Kate. 'You've got me now.'

I nodded solemnly. This wasn't what I wanted but I had made my bed, and Kate was in it. I had to live with the situation.

Soon Lockie told me it was time to start competing. Havana and I went to a one-day event in Nelson, and he was a dream to ride. I felt as if nothing could go wrong as I sat on this huge horse, ready to wipe out the opposition in the jumping arena. But they say pride comes before a fall, and although I stayed in the saddle, my smugness took a hard knock. I cantered in and headed the horse towards the first fence. The crowd was quiet and I got ready for the jump. To my utter amazement, Havana stopped. He skidded to a halt and I cringed inside. It was entirely my fault. I had been cantering him at a dressage pace, rather than a jumping one, and he wasn't ready to take the jump. I gently stroked his neck to let him know that I took full responsibility. He went on to jump a clear round, but that first fence put me into third place. I had learned a humbling lesson from Havana and I was grateful for it.

I loaded up my old horse truck and set off for Christchurch, where we were to compete in a three-day event. Kate was with me, as she had now moved to Taupo. It was a relief to have her out of the cottage. I felt as if I couldn't breathe with her around. She wanted to know everything, any little change, particularly if it had anything to do with money or my career. She didn't feel much like a partner, more like a business development manager. I'm sure she saw me as some kind of investment. I certainly felt like cold currency, as she measured my worth constantly. On this trip we were barely talking, following some row over a bill or something. The truck was also playing up, and it coughed to a halt on a country road.

'Give it a minute. It'll start then,' I said, knowing how temperamental it could be. Kate sighed, clearly annoyed, and went into the back to check on the horses. Immediately, I heard her shout.

'Quick, Pete, something's wrong!'

Havana? I felt sick as I scrambled around the side of the truck and peered inside. It wasn't my horse. It was Fairy Legend, one of the others we had taken to the show. Her face looked like a basketball. She had her eyes shut, and her tongue was puffed up and poking out. Worst of all, her breathing was erratic, meaning her windpipe was affected. It looked like an allergic reaction — and it was: I hadn't known it but this very expensive horse, which belonged to one of Lockie's top clients, was allergic to the wormer I had dosed her with just before we left.

I had put a prize horse in mortal danger through my choice of wormer. Fairy Legend was very sick indeed.

'What the hell have you done? This is all your fault,' shrieked Kate, her face pale and terrified. She knew as well as I did what this might mean. I bolted to the nearest house, which thankfully had a phone, and called a vet in a nearby town.

'Come quick. The horse is dying. If it kicks the bucket, it's big trouble,' I gasped down the phone. The vet came just in time, giving Fairy Legend a shot to reduce the reaction. I sat with her, watching her breathing settle and her face deflate, and felt utter relief.

'Close one. You were lucky this time,' Kate muttered as we set off again.

'Yeah, tell me about it,' I mumbled back. On the plus side, at least we were talking again, for an hour or two.

The competition in Christchurch was my first three-day event, so I competed in the novice class. Havana was fantastic. He cleared the cross-country section with ease, sliding down muddy banks and cat-jumping through difficult combinations, so that all I had to do was hang on. He was the driving force that day. The dressage was good too, and he barely put a foot wrong. I was a little nervous in the showjumping and one rail was knocked down, meaning we came third, but I was as proud of Havana as if he had won the whole thing.

Before heading for home again we had to pick up five yearlings from an Arab stud, to take up north for one of Lockie's friends. Unfortunately, as I drove around Christchurch a little white dog ran out in front of me. I swerved as best I could in the clumsy truck but the dog was hit and died immediately. I parked the truck, feeling sick to the stomach, and tracked down the owners. They were upset, but not angry. The dog was prone to rushing out at trucks, they said, and it had only been a matter of time, but they thanked me for telling them. I left their doorstep with a heavy heart and gave my own dog an extra big cuddle that day.

Back at the centre Havana went back into work, still on a high from his competitions. It was a sad day when Lockie pointed out that maybe he wasn't quite as good as he used to be.

'I don't see it,' I said, although I did. He was just not the same, and he was getting on in years. But I didn't want to admit it. 'He's fine, he truly is.'

Lockie shook his head.

'Time for a new horse,' he told me. Deep down I knew he was right. Havana had to retire. I sighed, and Lockie patted me on the shoulder.

'Besides,' he added. 'You've got the talent to be an international rider. Someone like that needs an international-standard horse.'

And that's how Fez, the horse that broke my heart more than any lover would, came into my life and turned it upside down.

Chapter 10

I could barely contain my excitement as Lockie and I travelled to a sheep station near Dannevirke to view some horses. Even so, I believed it was going to be virtually impossible to find one as good as Havana.

Lockie was determined. 'You're going to be an international rider, Pete, and that means you need a horse of an international standard. Believe me, Havana's time is done. He's taken you this far. Let him go and move on.'

Moving on meant trailing around endless bloodstock yards searching for that elusive creature, the perfect horse. We made the trip to the Dannevirke station in the summer of 1979, and I really hoped they would have something worthwhile. As we pulled up at the farm an elderly man came out. He had a weather-beaten face and white hair, tousled by the wind that came sweeping down from the hills. I noticed he also had the wiry, lean, slightly bent form of a jockey, only not so small. Lockie and he shook hands, and then he shook my hand too. His palm felt like saddle leather, and his eyes took in everything about me.

'This is Mr Robinson,' Lockie said. I never found out the man's first name, and he had such presence that I would never have used it to his face anyway.

Mr Robinson bred Cleveland Bay crosses, which are usually carriage horses, being bigger and stronger than thoroughbreds, the horses I normally rode. Cleveland Bays are built for endurance and stamina. Mr Robinson took us around the paddocks and stables, pointing out the horses that were available. Lockie and I shivered in the chill wind, nodded, and took in all the details he gave us in his gravelly voice. After seeing 30 or so horses I was starting to get bored and was ready to go home. It was obvious there was nothing there. I tried to catch Lockie's eye to give him the hint, but he was engrossed in a mare Mr Robinson was showing him in the stable yard.

I sighed and kicked at a stone. As I looked up to have a second go at attracting Lockie's attention I suddenly became aware of a horse watching me from a nearby stable. You know how those romance films have the couple's eyes meeting and that soaring orchestral movement. Well, if this book ever becomes a film, this is the moment for that sort of music. I fell in love with the horse in that split second, and I am sure he felt the same about me. He was brown, his forelock fell over one eye, and he had a duck-egg-sized lump on his nose. We gazed at each other across the stable yard.

'So what do you think, Pete? She's a good mare, right enough. Got stamina, plenty of scope. Pete? Pete? Are you listening?'

Lockie's voice broke into my thoughts and I turned to find the two men staring at me, looking puzzled.

'What? Oh, sorry. I was just wondering about that horse over there, Mr Robinson. The one with the lump on his face. Can I have a look at him?' The words rushed out faster than a sprinter on race day.

Mr Robinson frowned slightly.

'No. That one's mine. I bred him to steeplechase. Now, about this mare . . .'

I wasn't going to give up that easily.

'Can I just try him?'

Mr Robinson shook his head and Lockie was giving me a funny look, as if to say, 'What are you playing at?'

'He's not for sale,' Mr Robinson said firmly, and he turned to look at the mare. I walked quickly over to the box, aware that I wasn't supposed to be doing it, but feeling the pull of this unusual horse. His dark brown eyes were twinkling at me as he breathed through his flared nostrils into my hand and then onto my face. I blew at his nose gently from my mouth, mimicking the greeting that horses give each other.

'You're beautiful, aren't you,' I whispered, stroking his nose. The big lump on his face didn't matter to me; I thought he was splendidly handsome.

I was now even more determined to get on this horse's back, and I strode back across the yard. Lockie had an 'oh no, what now' look on his face, but I tried not to let it affect me.

'Sir, I'd really like to ride this horse . . .' I began. Mr Robinson had a deep frown now and was about to give me the 'not for sale' line again, when I suddenly asked, 'What's his name?'

'Name?' His craggy face softened. 'His name is Fez. My daughter was in Fez, in Morocco, when he was born, right here on this property.'

I asked about the horse's parentage, realising I had struck a chord with this taciturn old man.

'He's by a first-class racehorse called Bulenshar, who is by Nearco, out of a great Irish steeplechasing mare. He's been bred for one reason and one only. To race.'

'Wow,' I said, genuinely impressed. 'Can I ride him? Just one quick ride?'

Mr Robinson hesitated, then he said, 'Tell you what. I'll ride him and you have a watch. See if I can put you off wanting the damned thing and stop you pestering me.'

He went to get Fez out of the stable, leaving Lockie and me standing in the yard. Fez had only been used on the property as a shepherd's horse, ridden by a 15-stone shepherd using a stock saddle with a sack underneath. This was basic country riding and nothing more, with no fancy bits or martingales. Mr Robinson walked Fez into the yard where we were standing. It was a large space, with two 44-gallon drums toward one end. He got us to put an old plank between the drums and went to the opposite end of the yard. Fez trotted proudly, his eyes flashing with interest and excitement.

We stood back as Mr Robinson, sitting like a monkey on Fez's back, cantered to the jump. Bang! The horse's front legs hit the plank and down it came, almost bringing him down with it, but he managed to stay upright and keep Mr Robinson on his back. I felt a sinking sensation. Maybe I was wrong about Fez? Mr Robinson looked as if he might dismount, as if that was the end of it, but instead he trotted back to the far side of the yard again.

'Put it back up. We'll give him another go,' he said.

Fez's front legs cleared the plank this time, but his back feet clipped it and knocked it down. I must have looked pretty disappointed because Lockie put a hand on my shoulder.

'I'll take him in tighter,' yelled Mr Robinson as he trotted Fez around in a circle. 'Put the fence up again.'

We did as he said then watched, breath held, as he urged Fez into a controlled canter and faced the fence. This time the horse flew over it, looking every inch a champion. I wanted to whoop and yell. He could do it. Fez had that special ingredient that I needed in a horse. Lockie smiled. 'You could be right about this horse, Pete,' he murmured as Mr Robinson, his expression unchanged, took Fez back to his stable without offering me a ride. I was convinced he would sell Fez now. He had jumped him for us, shown us that he had what it took.

'How much?' I asked Mr Robinson when he returned.

'I've told you, Peter. He's not for sale.'

But I wasn't going to give up. I would choose my moment and ask again. We all went into the farmhouse to have lunch, but I couldn't eat the lovely home baking Mrs Robinson had prepared. I desperately wanted this horse, but Mr Robinson wasn't going to change his mind. He had made that clear, even though I wasn't prepared to accept it. I had come too far in the horse game to give up on the best horse I had seen. Mr Robinson chatted to Lockie and I stared out the window at the paddocks, planning my next move.

'What would you do with that horse anyway, Peter?' Mr Robinson asked, breaking into my thoughts.

'I would event him, sir,' I replied.

He looked at me, took another bite of his scone, chewed slowly, had a sip of tea and swallowed, all without taking his eyes off me.

'Two thousand dollars,' he said finally.

The realisation that he would sell Fez was immediately overshadowed by the price he had quoted. Two thousand dollars was a lot of money for such an inexperienced horse. I could have bought an A-grade showjumper for between $1600 and $1800. I had put $1600 away, expecting to spend only a portion of it, and here I was, not even near the amount he wanted.

'I'm $400 short,' I said. 'But I can save the rest and get it to you. I really want Fez, Mr Robinson.'

'Will you train with Lockie?' he asked.

'Absolutely, sir. I can't imagine training with anyone else.'

Lockie nodded, to show he was happy to train me. Another bite, chew and sip followed, then Mr Robinson said, 'Right, you can have him. It's still $2000, but you can save the rest and come and get him when you have the full amount. Is it a deal?'

I almost broke a cake-stand as I jumped up and leant over the table to shake his hand.

'I can do this,' I said to Lockie as we drove home. 'I've still got some income owing from the restaurant. It might take a few weeks, but I'm not going to let this horse slip through my fingers.'

About eight weeks later, I rang Mr Robinson.

'Is Fez still with you, sir?' I asked, praying that nobody had bought him and Mr Robinson hadn't changed his mind.

'Of course he is. I stick to my word,' he replied. 'He's yours. Have you got the money?'

'No, I've got $1900 so far, but I'll get the extra hundred pretty soon and then I can collect him.'

'Right you are then,' Mr Robinson said, and hung up.

Another four weeks went by, then I finally went down in my truck to pick up Fez. I arrived at night and was greeted in the yard by Mr Robinson. As country people they went to bed early, so all I had time for was tea and a quick chat before being shown to the spare bedroom for the night.

'It's still not all cut and dried, mind,' Mr Robinson told me as we were saying goodnight.

'What do you mean, sir?'

'You ride him in the morning. I want to see how you get on riding him, and if you get along okay, you can take him. If not, the deal's off. No point in wasting a horse with someone who doesn't go well with him.'

I didn't sleep at all well that night, thinking of his words. But in my heart I knew Fez and I already had a bond that wouldn't be broken. I just had to prove it to Mr Robinson.

The next morning I was woken at 6am by Mr Robinson standing over me with a cup of tea. He had probably been up for ages.

'Are you ready, boy?' he said gruffly. 'Time to ride your horse and see how you go.'

Fez was already standing in the yard, tethered, and I saddled him up. Beyond the yard the paddocks stretched as far as I could see. I had brought my saddle with me, and I wondered how the horse would take to a different feel on his back. Not a muscle flinched as I tightened the girth and got onto him. Something just seemed right about him, and I felt as if I had been sitting on his back forever. Mr Robinson opened the gate to a huge flat paddock that stretched right down the valley, and I walked Fez in, getting him up to a canter slowly. Then I tried to urge him to a gallop but he kept to the more leisurely pace.

'He doesn't know how to go faster,' I thought, realising that he simply hadn't learned these basic things in his job as a shepherd's horse.

Mr Robinson beckoned me back to the top of the paddock, and by shouting through his hands and gesturing he got me to walk, trot and canter Fez in circles. Fez did everything with ease. 'I can almost feel him grinning,' I thought. 'He loves this as much as I do.'

Finally, Mr Robinson waved me back to the gate. I got off Fez and stood there, a determined look on my face. I was not going home without this horse. No way.

'Well,' he said. Then silence. I waited.

'You look pretty happy; he looks pretty happy. Go on. Take him home.'

I grinned.

'Thank you,' I said.

I was keen to get on the road quickly, as it was a long drive. But it dawned on me that Fez might not have travelled in a truck before and would be afraid. In all my excitement I hadn't thought about that before.

'He's been once, when we took him to the Dannevirke show. He'll be right,' said Mr Robinson.

'But my truck's pretty low,' I pointed out. My horse truck had previously been a bread delivery van, and it didn't have the high roof of the ones made specifically for horses.

'It'll teach him to keep his head down, is all,' said Mr Robinson, as if it was the simplest thing in the world.

The old man was right too. Fez never moved during the six-hour drive. When we arrived in Taupo I went to get him out and discovered that a little gate at the back had come undone and must have been flapping near his leg all the way. Most horses would have kicked their way out of the truck if something like that had happened. But not Fez.

Chapter 11

I stood beside Fez proudly. 'What do you reckon?'

Kate looked him up and down, then her icy blue eyes focused on his nose.

'That lump is gross,' she said.

I rubbed it and smiled. 'Maybe it's his lucky lump? Give it a rub and wish.'

She didn't laugh; just shrugged.

'Well, I suppose he's reasonable, although he's not going to win any beauty contests,' she said.

'He's not supposed to win a beauty contest, my darling. He's going much further than that. This boy is bound for the Olympics.'

Kate raised an eyebrow and almost smiled.

'He'll need that lucky bump then.'

I had a good look at the lump and remembered a woman telling me that she got lumps off her horses' legs by using a heat-rub-type ointment, which was supposed to be for people. I tracked it down at a pharmacy in Taupo and gently rubbed it into the swelling every day for six weeks. It seemed to work.

'You know, Fez, if I put your noseband just here, you can barely see it at all,' I told him. I'm sure he knew what I was saying. He had that look, thoughtful and intelligent. If he could have spoken I'm sure he would have asked for a mirror, just to check the evidence for himself.

The bump was barely there by the time he was to compete in his first competition. It was just a hack class at the Rotorua show, nothing fancy, and only an hour away from Taupo, so he wouldn't be stressed out by the travelling. As I led him out of the horse truck I could see heads turn. Fez seemed oblivious, like a truly beautiful person who is used to being the centre of attention when they walk into a room, even if they are wearing a ripped old boiler-suit and gumboots. Fez had never looked so good. His rich brown coat was gleaming, and he picked up his feet well, striding out. The other horses looked tired and dishevelled beside my Fez. I felt so proud of him, my humble shepherd's horse. He competed like a champion and won the title of reserve champion hack. It wasn't a gold medal, but it was the first tiny step on the path I was sure he would take.

Our next event was a cross-country competition in Tokoroa. Fez jumped perfectly, never faltering or knocking a bar. I had never been so sure of a horse in my life. Soon after the Tokoroa event Lockie and I came to a decision. We were going to leave the equestrian centre and go out on our own. Well, when I say 'on our own', it meant Kate coming too. We decided to buy a property at Clevedon, south of Auckland, and set up our own training centre. There was a little cottage for Kate and me, a larger house for Lockie to live in, a beautiful white-washed stable block, cobbled courtyard, dressage arena, paddocks and 50 acres speckled with flowering cherry and apple trees. To raise my portion of the money I finally sold my share in Le Brie. Although the restaurant had been a labour of love, I didn't feel sad to give up my interest in it. It was time to move on — I had bigger goals now, goals that the restaurant didn't figure in. Horse sweat and leather meant more to me now than garlic, onions and tomatoes.

It was June 1979 when we moved to Clevedon. Lockie brought his horses from the centre, as well as seven brood mares that were in foal to warm-blood stallions imported from Germany. But as our venture took off and interest in our warm-blood breeding project grew in New Zealand horse circles, Kate and I rapidly began to cool. The Ice Maiden was showing her frosty side more than ever. Although her horse Mono was going well, she saw Fez's continued success as a gauntlet thrown down. The relationship dragged on, but it was clearly in its death throes.

Around this time, a man approached me wanting to buy Fez. I don't want to use his name, but he had formerly been a well-known international rider. When I saw him for the first time it was hard to imagine he had ever been an athlete of any kind. Portly, with a face reddened by booze, he was loud, obnoxious and more dangerous than I could have imagined.

He turned up at the centre unannounced and offered me $6000 for Mono and Fez together. I was surprised that he even asked. It was clear that Kate was still pushing on with Mono, and Fez was in the early stages of a career that would go places.

'Well, sir, Kate's horse is her horse, and you would have to deal with her directly about Mono,' I said politely. 'As for my horse, well, he's worth $4000 alone, but he's definitely not for sale, so there's no point in discussing it. Thank you.'

His piggy eyes bulged in his purplish face, and he looked as if he was about to burst. I carried on grooming Fez and he hovered at the stable door, trying to persuade me to sell. I just shook my head and kept repeating, 'Fez is not for sale, thanks.'

Eventually he left, but I hadn't seen the last of him. A short while later he came back to the centre and tried again. 'I want them both. Come on, every horse has its price. I'm paying you good money.'

'Sorry. A sale of my horse is not going to happen, and you'll have to discuss any possible sale of Mono with Kate. He's not mine. That's all I have to say on the matter.' It was an awkward moment, and I was glad when he drove off, muttering furiously to himself.

A month later I had Fez in the Horse of the Year Show in Gisborne. He went like a dream, winning two supreme championships, as well as two dressage classes, and was upgraded in the showjumping. I sat on him in the line-up in the middle of the ring, waiting for the grand champion to be announced, my heart in my mouth. When our names came over the loudspeaker I could barely hear them as they were drowned out by the roar of delight from the crowd. The judge stepped forward and placed the big tri-coloured supreme champion sash around Fez's neck. I trotted out, feeling that nothing could spoil this moment. And there was the man, at the gate, waiting for us.

He paused for a moment, while a number of well-wishers patted Fez and congratulated me, then he walked up.

'You know, I don't like you jumping my horse without permission,' he said smoothly.

'What are you talking about?' I couldn't believe this approach. Would the man never give up? 'He's not your horse, he's mine. End of story.'

'No. I've bought your horse.'

'How can you have bought him? I haven't seen a cent. I never agreed to a sale and I told you, very clearly, that he wasn't for sale anyway.'

His pug-face turned even uglier and he reached up for the reins.

'Wrong, mate. This horse is mine. He's mine now. Get it into your head. Believe me, you don't want to make this difficult. Right?'
I moved Fez away from his podgy grasping hands.
'You're off your trolley,' I said, shaking my head. 'You'd better leave me alone or I'll be taking legal action.'
Back at the truck, I tried not to let his threats take away my happiness at Fez's win. I was giving the horse a final check-down for any soreness when another competitor came up. I didn't know him well, although I knew his name was David and that he was Australian. He shook my hand, then lowered his voice.
'Pete, I've heard some whispers about a certain person wanting your horse. I think you'd better know. He's in cahoots with . . .'
David named another horse person from the area. I wasn't too surprised. This was someone I had known for a long time and he had never been very trustworthy. I thanked David, and realised the problem wasn't going to go away.
A week later I woke suddenly in the night, hearing a car engine revving outside. A big four-by-four vehicle was coming up the road, fast. It crashed through the gates, drove up onto the lawn, did a huge wheelie that left deep gouges in the grass, then hared off down the road. I ran out and caught a glimpse of the driver. It was the younger brother of the man David had warned me about.
As I mended the fence and gates Kate wailed, 'You can't just leave it. The lawn is a mess.'
'No,' I said patiently. 'I'm not going to rise to the bait. It was just a childish prank.'
A few nights later Barrabas, my dog, kicked up a huge row down at the stables. I knew he only barked for a good reason, and I ran from the cottage in time to see a vehicle leaving the yard. I'd heard gossip that there were plans to set fire to our stables. I recognised the car too. It was my neighbour. But no damage had been done, and it seemed pointless talking to the police. I just hoped the affair would die down in its own time. I didn't want to get Lockie involved either, so I kept my reaction low-key, even though I was extremely worried about the situation.
Two days after the midnight visit another car pulled up in the yard. It was a sleek, dark-blue sedan and the man who got out was wearing a suit.

'Are you Peter Taylor?' he asked. I walked across from where I had been cleaning saddles, wiping my hands on a cloth.

'That's me. How can I help you?'

He handed me an envelope.

'Consider yourself served.'

'Served? What for?' I was totally baffled. He got back in his car, ignoring my questions, and drove off. I opened the envelope and found a legal document relating to the supposed sale of Fez and Mono to the pug-faced man. I was completely taken aback. He was suing me for thousands of dollars. As I read further, I was amazed to see that he had on-sold the horses to the Italian national event team and was suing me for loss of profit, as well as the cost of airfares for the horses from New Zealand to Italy.

I was furious. This was crazy. I read the words over and over, trying to understand how someone could be so vindictive to another human being. It meant I had to counter-sue him, and that cost big bucks, bucks that would have to be taken out of the business. It was time to call an end to his stupidity. I didn't want Lockie or Kate getting upset about the man's personal vendetta, and had deliberately kept the seriousness of the situation from them, playing it down if they asked me about the rumours. I was the target of this nasty piece of work, but not for much longer.

I rang some of his former teammates in an attempt to get his telephone number. They were all overseas, so they didn't know why I was keen to get hold of him. The gossip hadn't yet gone beyond New Zealand, and they were happy to give me a contact number, knowing I was a horseman too. I called him at his farm, where he apparently lived. I hadn't even known that about him.

His voice was shocked when he realised who it was on the line.

'Now it's your turn to listen,' I said, my voice steely with anger. 'You are wasting your time and money. I don't even have the horse any more. Call off your wolves. There's nothing for them to get hold of any more. The horse is gone.'

He spluttered with outrage but I just put the phone down. I made one more phone call, to secure Fez's future safety, then I went out to the stables. Fez stuck his head out of his box, recognising my footsteps.

'Time to go, mate,' I whispered. We had a small horse float at the centre, and I loaded Fez into it. He looked around excitedly, thinking we were going to an event.

'Not this time,' I told him. 'Not for a while, I'm afraid.'

It was dark and lights were going off at farms around the centre. I didn't want anyone to see us leave. I drove under cover of night, just keeping my mind on one goal. I had to get Fez to safety. I had to hide him.

Chapter 12

My good friend Beth Fife was waiting for me as I drove up with
Fez in the horse float. She hugged me warmly. Nothing else
needed to be said.

'You know he can stay here for as long as you want,' she said after
we had got Fez settled and were sitting in her farmhouse kitchen
having a cup of tea. Although Beth was connected to the horse
world she was very discreet. She also had a sheep farm, so for the
second time in his life Fez would be just another shepherd's horse.

'It won't be for too long,' I said. 'I'm getting out of the centre,
going overseas. I'll let you know when I'm ready for him to come
over.'

'Can't you keep him in New Zealand?'

I shook my head.

'No way. It's too dangerous.'

I had explained the situation to Beth when I had phoned to ask for
her help. She was aware of how treacherous the equestrian world
could be, and I knew Fez would be safe with her. When he had put
on a little weight, let his belly drop and got used to trotting lazily
after the sheep, he would be unrecognisable.

I took a deep breath of cold night air and went to say goodbye to
Fez. 'See you soon,' I promised, pressing my face against his. His
nostrils flared and I felt his warm breath on my cheek.

I drove back to Clevedon with a heavy heart. Lockie had just come
back from a three-month teaching trip to the States, and now I had
to break the news to him that I wanted out.

'Do you have to leave, though? Isn't that a bit drastic?' he said
when I told him what had been happening. 'You know, I met some
people in America who were very interested in Fez. They'll give
you a good price, Peter. It might be a better idea than doing all this
undercover stuff.'

But my mind was made up and there was no way — no way on
earth — that I was selling the horse. Lockie read my expression,
and selling Fez was never mentioned again. I was giving up

everything, and that included Kate. She barely blinked when I told her I was leaving.

'You two can buy me out,' I said. 'It's doing well now, it's turning over nicely. You'll get it back in no time.'

'Are you absolutely sure, Pete?' Lockie was frowning at me, still worried. I nodded.

'I am.'

Kate sighed and Lockie saw his cue to leave.

'So, that's it for us too, I suppose,' she said bitterly.

'Come on, Kate, it wasn't working out. You know it as well as I do.'

'I suppose so.' She said the words grudgingly but without an ounce of sadness. I saw her as she was, the Ice Maiden, cold to the core. I was glad to be leaving her behind.

'Where are you going?' she asked eventually, as I was packing my bags.

'England.'

She looked surprised. 'Why on earth are you going there?'

I shrugged. 'No idea; probably because it's as far away as I can get from all the crap going down just now.'

With the money Lockie and Kate paid to buy me out I was able to put away a nest egg so that I could bring Fez to England when the time was right. As I left the centre I felt relief — relief to be leaving Kate, and the place where I had almost lost Fez. But I also felt incredibly alone as I flew across the world to make a fresh start. It was October 1979.

When I arrived in England I contacted my friend Mark Todd, who was one of New Zealand's best-known riders, and would go on to achieve Olympic glory. He was happy to have me stay while I got settled.

'No worries, Pete, you can stay as long as you want. It'll be a laugh,' he said. And it was a laugh. Mark loved to party, and for two days we drowned my sorrows many times over. I didn't have time to wallow in sadness or self-pity, or even really register the fact that I was now in England, thousands of miles from everything I had known. But after a couple of days I told Mark I needed to move on. There was something I had to face up to, I told him.

'Something or someone?' he said knowingly.

It was the latter. I wanted to see Amanda, the girlfriend I had ditched for the Ice Maiden. I had never come to terms with the guilt of finishing with this funny, exuberant, charming girl, with those big thick spectacles and huge blue eyes. If I was honest with myself,

I hadn't wanted to finish with her, but circumstances pushed Kate and me together, and sometimes distance is an obstacle in a relationship.

I wanted to say sorry, properly this time. I knew that Amanda was living in Dorset and I tracked her down through friends of friends. She was astonished to hear from me, and touchingly happy. If she had called me the worst names under the sun and then slammed the phone down, I wouldn't have blamed her.

'You must come and stay,' she said cheerfully. 'Come on, it'll be wonderful to see you again. We have so much to catch up on.'

'We certainly do,' I admitted.

Mark agreed to pick Fez up from the airport once I had arranged for him to be sent over from New Zealand, and to keep him for me until I got settled. Then I headed to Dorset, where Amanda was working as a chef at a stately home called Hyde House. The house had been bought in a rundown state by a very wealthy man from London, who employed travellers from all over the world to work on renovating it. When I arrived there were 20 people there and an instant job for me, helping Amanda in the kitchen.

I was worried about how she might feel, working alongside me again. It had been some time since our days at Le Brie, and I knew I had hurt her. But she wasn't fazed at all; she bubbled with enthusiasm at having me in the kitchen. From the moment I arrived at Hyde House it was clear she had forgiven me.

'Don't even think about it,' she said warmly. 'It's the past. This is now, and it's lovely to see you again. Silly thing.'

The property was incredible. The house had been started in the twelfth century, added to in the fourteenth century, and then again 200 years later. There was a rose garden in the grounds, and even a trout hatchery. The previous owner was an elderly woman who had lived in just the kitchen and one other room. The other 50-odd rooms had remained empty and neglected until the house was purchased and the big renovation project began. When it was finished, the idea was that the property would become a country retreat for the owner and his highbrow friends.

I understood why Amanda was so happy there. The working day started at 8.30am and finished at 1pm. We had the entire afternoon free to do what we wanted. We cooked on a big old Aga oven, which guzzled coal, and cooked for 20 people at each sitting. After the nightmare experience I had gone through in New Zealand this was exactly what I needed. I also found that I wanted to rekindle my relationship with Amanda. I could barely believe that I had put her to one side to be with Kate. What had I been thinking? I must have been crazy, I thought, watching Amanda as she sat in the beautiful sunny gardens, laughing with some of the others from the house.

Most afternoons we would head off on an adventure in the big old Land-Rover that was available for the staff to use. Loads of us would pack into the vehicle and head off to places like Salisbury Cathedral or Cheddar Gorge. We were given £3 a day for food, more than enough to buy a ploughman's lunch and a beer in a pub. Amanda and I became closer, although it was a slow process, for which I didn't blame her. I had hurt her badly and she was tentative about being involved in more than a friendship with me. Eventually we became a couple once more, and I was proud to having this smiling, warm-hearted girl part of my life again.

As with any Kiwis on the big OE, there were wild moments, such as the night Hamish, another New Zealander, found some magic mushrooms. We held a backgammon tournament that night and I won nine games in a row, just knowing what every move would be, or at least thinking I did, in my hallucinating state. We spent nights down at the local pub, the Silent Woman, or visiting Norman ruins in the moonlight, imagining what it must have been like all those centuries ago. I learned to grass-ski and was actually quite good at it, although cowpats were a hazard I didn't dodge often enough for my liking.

When work on Hyde House stopped for the winter, Amanda and I needed to find jobs. Amanda was offered a job in London and decided to take it. I went to an employment agency that found people for the equestrian industry, and told them I wanted to be somewhere with snow at Christmas. The company offered me three jobs, one in France, a second for a Countess in Rome on the site of the 1960 Olympics and another in Belgium. I said I wanted a day to decide, went to the nearest library, found a map of Europe and closed my eyes. A swirl of a finger in the air then down it went onto the map. When I opened my eyes the tip was in Belgium. Amanda and I knew we were once again on different tracks in life, but we parted as good friends this time.

On Christmas Day 1979 I built a big snowman in the paddock of the showjumpers' yard in the town of Eupen, just across the border from Germany, in the southernmost part of Belgium. Then I pelted my snowman with snowballs, whooping with happiness. I couldn't speak a word of German or Flemish, and I had to make my own fun.

I worked for Christof and Denise, an affluent couple with a two-year-old daughter. Christof was tall and handsome, with a mop of black hair, while Denise looked like a living Barbie doll: tall, slim, tanned and platinum blonde. There was also an elderly housekeeper, Rita. Christof had 13 of his own horses in the yard, along with 18 others that were stabled for people who lived across the border in the German town of Aachen. Germany was notoriously expensive when it came to having horses, and it was a lot cheaper to keep them over in Belgium, just a 10-minute drive away.

The property was sumptuous, and was run as a riding club for the elite. There was a lounge with red carpet and green velvet upholstery, an open fire, leather couches and a bar that also served strong coffee. Christof spoke English and Denise got by with a few phrases. Rita, I found out, had had an affair with an American soldier during the Second World War and also knew some English. It was she who taught me some German, so I could at least stumble along. I had the job of managing Christof's barn, and I quickly learned how to say 'broom', 'water' and 'oats' in German. I wanted to know more. In addition to my work with the horses I helped out in the bar, working there at night, mainly to improve my German. Within a week I could count, and two weeks later I was able to shop. I bought the best saddle I had ever owned while I was there.

I travelled a lot with the horses from Christof's stables, riding the less capable ones at shows to bring them along for the owners. After the huge spaces of New Zealand I found it bizarre to ride inside most of the time, and to have to fight for a chance to go to the practice fence with 40 other riders all waiting their turn.

But I also had goals in Europe, and a time limit for achieving them. Two years ahead was the World Championships, and I wanted to be there, with Fez. Two months after I arrived in Belgium, I heard from Mark Todd. He was returning to New Zealand and would be bringing his horse Southern Comfort back to England to compete at Badminton. This is one of the biggest three-day events in the world, held on the Duke of Beaufort's estate in Badminton, Gloucestershire. Mark said he would check how Fez was going and arrange to bring him over with Southern Comfort.

I knew from Beth that Fez had been doing a little bit more than shepherding. Two young girls who were friends of the family had ridden him at pony-club events, walking over the competition, of course. I didn't mind. A pony-club class or two wouldn't attract too much attention, and it would help keep his fitness levels up. The next time I heard from Mark he told me that Fez was in wonderful shape, and that arrangements had been made to bring him to England with three other horses. Excited at the prospect of seeing Fez again, I took a train back to England so that I could be at the airport to meet him, and to arrange transport for all four horses. The other three were to stay in England, but Fez was coming to Belgium with me.

When I saw him trot off the plane I was shocked by how little he looked. Had those wee legs really taken me over those huge cross-country fences? I was so used to the big showjumpers in Belgium by now that I had forgotten how pint-sized my boy was in comparison. After arriving in England he had to spend three weeks in quarantine, then he was able to cross on the ferry to Belgium. I had to pay an enormous amount of duty for him, and it was a procedure to hot-brand his little hooves. I couldn't wait to get through all the paperwork and bureaucracy so that I could take him to Eupen. Every moment I had, I would stroke his face and talk to him, relieved to have him with me again. The love we had was as strong as ever. He nuzzled and chattered to me, in the way that horses do, through breaths and whickering noises. It was February 1980 and freezing cold, but Fez wasn't concerned about the chill. His ears were pricked and his eyes bright as he took in everything around him.

Eupen was a magical, topsy-turvy place, and I hoped Fez would be as happy there as I was. It was a place that was full of surprises. On Armistice Day the town was closed to men until 2pm. Only women were allowed, and they partied hard from 11am. Between 2pm and 5pm the men were allowed in, but even then the tables were turned and women took the dominant role. This was still quite a conservative society and women asking men out was not the done thing, except for those three hours each year.

When I had first arrived, I had been horrified to find that the horses were kept in the stables all the time. In New Zealand horses had the run of paddocks during the day and were stabled at night in deep beds of shavings or sawdust, and only then if they were champions. But in Eupen the horses were born in boxes, lived in boxes, and died in boxes. If you put one in a paddock alone it would panic and want to come back inside. Space was something these horses didn't know about, and weren't comfortable with. They rarely went to the paddock, preferring the indoor arena, where they were given time to roll and play and gallop for short periods of time each day.

The stables were right on the edge of a huge forest that stretched right across the border into Germany, and I knew Fez would love the rides through there. When you ride in snow, there's hardly any sound, just a slight crunch as the hooves crack through the crust. Sometimes the snow was a couple of feet deep, but the horses didn't mind. From time to time I would ride horses into Germany to save the owners paying huge importation taxes at the border. It was a good way of making a bit of extra money and I enjoyed the excitement of taking the horse through the trees and snow, to be met by a truck at the appointed place. I would be given a little moped to ride back along the cleared trails.

The first day Fez was in Eupen I kept him in a stable, but I could tell he was getting restless. 'Let me out, I want to stretch my legs,' his eyes seemed to plead.

'Okay, okay, but behave yourself,' I said, leading him out to the paddock. I thought he would just amble around, as he was still getting over the journey and was in a new place, but no, he immediately launched into an excited canter around and around. I felt a bubble of joy in my throat. He looked beautiful. Then, suddenly, he jumped right out of the paddock and into the next one.

'Fez,' I called, looking around to see if anyone had spotted his flying leap. Then, before I could get hold of him, he had cantered to the other side of the paddock and cleared another four feet six inches of fence, and disappeared into the forest. It was time to get help, and soon we were all searching for him. At least he wouldn't be hard to spot. Much smaller in the leg than the big, rangy European horses — oh, and running loose, of course. I didn't know whether to laugh or be angry about his great escape. All I am sure about is that when I got a call about a strange horse down by a deer-skinning factory, I was very relieved. When I went to collect him he was standing in a paddock, nuzzling a horse on the other side of a fence. I was just glad to get my beautiful boy back unscathed, and forgave him instantly.

'Your horse is naughty,' Christof laughed, ruffling Fez's mane, when I got him home. 'He must be a good jumper to get out of that paddock.'

'He is, and he knows it,' I said.

'Do you mind if I try him, maybe over a fence or two?'

At that point Denise butted in, wagging a manicured finger at her husband.

'You are too big for him. You will, how do you say, squash him?' she chided.

I laughed. Although he seemed small in comparison with the Belgian horses Fez was actually 16.2 hands, a reasonably large horse by most standards. He was just a different shape to the ones Christof usually rode.

'No worries,' I said. Fez popped over a four foot six fence no problem, and I was full of pride.

'Can we try five feet?' Christof said as he trotted back to me. Fez had never jumped that high, but I was keen to see if he could do it. I nodded and the pole was raised. Fez eyed the fence and gathered himself to jump. His feet flew over it, with space to spare. Christof was breathless with delight.

'How much?' he gasped, before he had even dismounted.

'Sorry, he's not for sale,' I said, not for the first or last time in my life.

'Ah, come on.' He named a price. It was the equivalent of almost £30,000. I didn't hesitate.
'No. Fez is not for sale. He's my best chance of getting to the World Championships and the Olympics.'

Chapter 13

Why is it that the words 'I will put you on hold' are so irritating?
It's even worse when you are making a call across the world in the
middle of the night and every second is costing you several dollars.
I gritted my teeth and waited for the woman from the New Zealand
Horse Society to get back to me with the answer to a very simple
question. Could I have an international riding permit, please?
'The thing is,' she began, her voice a nasal whine, 'you really
should have got it before you left New Zealand.'
'I didn't know. I had to leave in a hurry. Otherwise, I would have
done, believe me. So can you get me one, as soon as possible? I
need to be at this three-day event in Holland. Surely it's just a case
of stamping a piece of paper and popping it in the post.' I was
desperately trying to be patient.
'You appear to think my job is just about stamping bits of paper,
Mr Taylor. If only it was. It's much more complicated than that.'
'How can we simplify it then?'
It was now May 1980 and Fez had done well at a one-day event in
France earlier in the month, winning easily. The three-day event at
Hooge Mierde, which was only a couple of weeks away, would be
his first international three-day event and there was no way I was
going to miss it.
'You can't simplify it,' the woman said tersely.
'Can't you try?' My patience was now wearing very thin, as was
the amount of money I was willing to spend on this useless
telephone call to the society's Hastings headquarters. 'I have a
guest licence already, so surely it's just a question of making it
official? Please.'
I was quite willing to plead with this obtuse woman. I was not
going to forgo this event, not for some feeble paperwork. I had
entered it, telling the organisers that the international permit would
follow, but that the mail from New Zealand was notoriously slow.
It was an excuse that had worked before so I thought it was worth
another go, and it had so far kept the questions at bay. But when I
actually attended the three-day event, the permit would need to be

sighted. There would be no 'it's in the mail' then. If I didn't have it, I wouldn't be competing.

'Well, it will take at least 10 days ...' the woman began.

'Ten days! I don't have 10 days.'

I realised then that I simply had not brown-nosed the authorities in New Zealand enough, and was now feeling the consequences. I hung up, feeling despondent, although I hadn't lost hope entirely. The secretary of the International Equestrian Federation was in Belgium to supervise the measuring of the Belgian team's uniforms for the upcoming Moscow Olympics. He could sign the permit for me. I knew this lovely, rosy-faced little man was a gin-drinker, so I went along to see him, taking a large bottle of gin.

'You have come, what, 14,000 miles and they won't give you the permit? They are mad,' he said cheerfully, stamping the permit for me. It was as simple as that — and I didn't even need to give him the gin until after he had done it, and then simply as a thank you. The Hooge Mierde event was a big one, with a full advanced international course. I had no idea just how important it was until I actually got there. Every other rider had a groom, a manager, the best equipment and a place in a top hotel, courtesy of the show's organisers. I was small fry and on my own, doing all my own grooming, with just the gear I already had, and bedding down in my sleeping bag in the announcer's caravan. But I didn't care. Fez and I were there, at least partly thanks to a Belgian rider who had given us a lift.

Before we left for the event I had had Fez shod by a blacksmith who came over from Germany regularly to shoe all the Belgian showjumping horses at the stables. It was the second time he had shod Fez. The following morning I noticed my horse was a little sore in his left front foot.

'What's up?' I said softly, lifting his hoof and inspecting it closely. I felt it with my fingers and it was hot, which indicated pain. One of the shoe nails had gone in quite high through the hoof so I took it out to relieve any pressure. That seemed to help. The other problem I had to deal with before we went to Holland was a watery one, and something I hadn't even thought about until the Belgian rider brought it up.

'Are you okay jumping water, Peter?' he asked a couple of days before we were due to leave.

'What do you mean?' I was puzzled. In New Zealand it's rare to have water jumps. Instead, we have pebbled streams or shallow rivers as obstacles on the cross-country courses. Nature provided, and there was no need to build any special structures.

'You need to know how to jump water because there will be many like that at Hooge Mierde,' the Belgian explained. 'Okay. We do not have long, but I will teach you, yes?'

'Yes!' I was grateful that he had pointed out this lack in my experience.

The Belgian took me to a property nearby that had a big pond with a log along one edge of it. He taught me to canter towards it, then jump, letting the horse stretch his neck and keeping the reins loose for longer than usual so he could find his footing in the water.

After two or three tries Fez and I had it down to a tee. In fact, Fez seemed to enjoy the new experience of water jumping, and I felt confident we could get through anything the Hooge Mierde course threw at us. Finally, we were ready.

On the first day Fez and I went into the dressage ring looking our best. I didn't have a fancy double bridle, like the other riders, but I was proud of how smart we both looked. Fez's bay coat gleamed like mahogany, in contrast to his black legs, mane and tail. He was so excited he let out a little squeal as we walked in, then we waited on the X that marked the starting point. Dressage is like a ballet, a strictly choreographed series of movements designed to show off a horse and rider's abilities. I felt completely in sync with Fez. We moved as one, with rhythm and grace, as if our muscles were bonded. The thrill of knowing that Fez was loving every moment, proudly showing off his presence, made it all the more special for me. We came 21st out of 87, which is fantastic for a first-timer at an international event.

The cross-country part of the event was on day two. Mark Todd wasn't there, but he had told two of his friends who were competing, Virginia and Clarissa, to look out for me at Hooge Mierde. I was walking the course for the third time, astounded by the sheer size and complexity of some of the fences, when I heard crisp English voices nearby. I was very excited, as I hadn't come across many people to chat to. I walked over and said hello to the two girls. They turned out to be Virginia and Clarissa, and we carried on walking the course together.

'I thought this was going to be an intermediate course, but some of these fences are pretty advanced,' I said in passing.

Clarissa stared at me. 'You do know that this is the final qualifier for the Moscow Olympics, don't you?'

This was news to me, but I hid my surprise. 'Yes, of course,' I said, in my most convincing voice.

Fez couldn't wait to get going at the starting point. As the countdown began he was eager to be off, trotting on the spot and straining forwards. Full of confidence, he cleared the first few fences without any trouble. This was what he was made for, I thought, as he cantered towards the water jump. We were well within the time limit set for the course, and he was bowling along at his own pace. I should have reined him in a little but I felt confident that he could get over anything. Up he went, over the brown rail and down the other side, hitting the water at full pelt. Too fast, too fast, was all I could think, as I felt Fez crumple beneath me. We both went under the muddy water, right under. I gulped a mouthful of the foul liquid and Fez squirmed to get his head above the surface. I felt myself parting company with him in the murky blackness. We both stood up at virtually the same time. Water poured from my helmet and Fez shook his head to clear his ears, drenching me, although I was already pretty waterlogged. My brand-new saddle was soaked through. Even worse, I had worn leather gloves and they now had the texture of slippery soap. The leather reins were like seaweed. I put my foot in the stirrup, getting ready to remount. Water gushed out of my boots. I hopped back on, desperately trying to keep my hands from slipping off the reins. 'Fez, it's all up to you now,' I whispered.

He pricked his ears and cantered on as if the fall had never happened. With no way to get a firm grip on the reins, it was like driving without brakes. All I could use was my voice. When he came up too fast to a fence I knew I couldn't pull him back with my hands, but when he heard me say, 'Whoa, Fez, easy now,' he slowed enough to pop over it without any trouble. I was breathless with excitement as we cantered over the finishing line. The fall cost us 60 penalties, and there were time faults because I had had to remount, but apart from that it had been a dream ride. I was ecstatic, patting the horse's neck and ruffling his mane, grinning from ear to ear.

As he slowed up I noticed an uneven quality to his movement. The vet, who checked each horse as it finished the course, noticed it too. 'He seems a little lame. I'll come to the stables within the hour and check him over,' he told me.

At the stable block I took off Fez's gear, hosed him down, put his rug on, and walked him, looking at every step he took, hoping my eyes were deceiving me. He seemed a little sore, but not that lame. 'Might just be a stone giving you a wee bruise, Fez. Maybe you've twisted something in that fall? It could just be cinders from the cross-country track in that nail hole.' I was chattering away to him, trying to convince myself that it was nothing, when the vet arrived. I told him about the high nail and he checked the hole. It was crammed with cinders and we washed it out using soda water, as the bubbles helped clear it.

'What do you reckon? Will he be okay for tomorrow?' I asked. The vet thought about it for a moment, then sighed. 'The hole is the reason he's sore, but it's been flushed out now. Perhaps he will be okay for you to show jump him tomorrow. See how he is at the vet check before the event.'

Another vet, from the Belgian team, said he would take a look at Fez's leg first thing the following morning. I got up early, rolling out of my sleeping bag at the crack of dawn, to walk him out so he wouldn't be too stiff.

This vet noticed an infection in the nail hole. 'He's sore, but I can give him an injection of strong painkiller. That might be enough to get him through today so he can complete his first three-day event.'

The drug was so powerful it made Fez wobble a bit, but he jogged it off and seemed fine for a few steps, before the lameness returned.

'It's up to you, Peter. You can present him at the pre-event vet check if you like. I've done all I can,' the vet said.

It wasn't just Fez's first three-day event; it was my first international. This was about completing it. I bit my lip, trying to work out what to do.

An hour later, Fez went up before the vet committee. I knew he looked sleek and fit, but would the vets feel he was too sore to compete?

'It's a nail injury,' said the vet who had examined the hole the day before. 'In my opinion, the horse is quite capable of jumping the course.'

A few heads nodded, but my eyes were fixed on one face, that of the English judge, Joanna Hall. She knew Lockie and I trusted her judgement. She spoke.

'Peter, I know you've come a long way to be at this event, but I have to say this. I don't want you to compete. There is something wrong with Fez and it's my responsibility to make sure he is safe. The horse's safety is of the utmost importance.'

She was right.

'Ma'am, I would never put my horse in jeopardy. I'll withdraw him from the event.'

I took Fez back to the stables, and started to undo the plaits in his mane. Then I got a poultice for his foot, to draw out the pain. As I was applying it I heard a soft cough, and looked up to see a slim, dark-haired woman at the door. I wasn't in the mood to speak to anyone, but she just stood there, waiting until the poultice was on. Then she said, 'You're trained by Lockie Richards, aren't you. I can tell. I saw your style of cross-country and you rode it like a New Zealander. Any New Zealander who can come this far and ride that well must have been trained by Lockie Richards.'

I frowned. 'Who are you?'

'My name is Selma Brandl. I'd like to buy your horse.'

'He's not for sale,' I said sadly. 'He's lame.'

The previous night I had been approached by six different people with open chequebooks, making the same request as Selma. One had offered me £40,000, enough to buy an entire farm in New Zealand. I had told them all the same thing.

'I know what it's like to have your horse in agony and not be able to complete an event you have set your heart on. I feel for you,' Selma said.

'Thank you.' I didn't want to talk about it.

'Do you have a trainer?' she asked suddenly.

I told her I didn't. Selma told me that she and Lockie had trained together under Robert Hall in England. He was the husband of Joanna Hall, the judge. As Selma spoke, in her calm, strong voice, I was reminded of Lockie and his caring but down-to-earth way.

'You know, I really would like to train you,' she said. 'What is your goal?'

'My goal? To get to the World Championships in 1982. Fez and me, together,' I replied.

'Well, I can train you for that,' she told me. 'I live in Germany, near Dusseldorf, and I've got seven international horses that a young girl called Claudia von Brautisch rides. The facilities are excellent. I think we would get on very well, you and I.'

I shook my head.

'I live in Belgium, and after this I'm going to work for a woman showjumper in northern Belgium. It's all agreed. Thanks anyway.'

Selma smiled and handed me a card with her contact telephone numbers on it.

'Let me know by the end of the week,' she said. 'The offer is still open.'

Chapter 14

The next day I wrapped Fez's legs in thick bandages and loaded him in a truck for the trip to Keerbergen, where the Belgian woman, Hilde, lived. I was already wondering if I had done the right thing by taking the job. My new employer and I didn't appear to be on the same wavelength. She seemed cold, tight with money, and to see the horses as mere commodities, rather than living, breathing creatures. Selma's card stayed in my pocket. My concern for Fez was so great that I hadn't given a second thought to her offer of training me. Everything was about Fez and making him well again. It was unbearable to see him suffering. The third day after our arrival at Hilde's place, his leg was swollen and hot. The local vet had a look at him and I knew from his face that Fez was in a bad way.

'Your horse has a major infection. He needs to be in a clinic. This is very serious,' he told me.

Hilde was listening in on the consultation, and recommended a vet who had trained in Switzerland. After initially grumbling because it meant taking time away from her own horses, she agreed to drive us to the clinic. I stayed with Fez in the back of the truck. He couldn't even stand on the foot any more. He was dangerously unstable, trying to balance on three legs as Hilde swerved around corners, keen to reach the vet clinic, drop off the horse and return home for her dinner. Fez curled his lips back in a grimace of pain. I felt every jolt, every bump and every swerve of the woman's dreadful driving, and I desperately wished I could take Fez's pain from him.

At last we arrived, to my huge relief, and the vet inspected the horse. He then said that he would run some tests. I didn't want to leave Fez, but Hilde was my employer and her face told me she was keen to get back on the road.

'Make sure he has pellets or soft food, not oats,' I told the vet. 'He's just been competing so he needs building up. Not oats, okay?'

'What's wrong with oats? That's what my horses get and it doesn't do them any harm,' grumbled Hilde. I climbed back into the truck with a heavy heart.

The next day I rang the clinic and was told more tests were needed to find out if it was a bacterial infection and, if so, what kind. The results would come through in two days. When I went to see Fez after those two days I could barely believe how dreadful he looked. He was on a thin bed of straw and his feed bin had straight oats in it. Pus was oozing from the fetlock joint above his foot and his leg was as swollen and tight as a fence post. The pain was so bad he had ground his teeth on the concrete wall of the stable until the roots and nerve endings of several of the teeth were coming through. I was horrified and heartbroken to see my friend in this state. I stroked his neck gently, seeing in his eyes relief that I was there, but also another emotion: a desperate hope that I would help him and stop the agony. All I could do was press my face against his and will him to get better.

When I finally saw the vet I managed to hold back my anger at Fez's condition. 'You told me on the phone that he looked like he was getting better,' I said coldly.

'I took an X-ray and that's what it looked like to me. The tests have come back and there's no infection.' He shrugged.

'What are you talking about?' I snapped. 'There is pus coming out of his leg. That doesn't happen unless there's an infection, anyone can tell that. Your tests are wrong. You're giving him a painkiller but it's not working. Have you seen his teeth? They are ground to the nerve endings because he's biting the walls in sheer hell. What kind of a vet are you? I'm getting him out of here.'

The vet shook his head.

'Not until you pay the bill. The horse stays here until I get my money.'

I felt sick. He didn't care one jot about Fez. The only thing he wanted was cold cash. I paid him and found someone with a horse float in the town to take him to the University of Liege in Brussels. A friend had suggested taking him there because the attached veterinary college was one of the most advanced, on the cutting edge of animal medicine. I bandaged Fez's leg over and over to make sure it wasn't bumped on the journey.

'Stay with me, Fez,' I whispered. 'We'll get this sorted out. I promise you.'

I phoned the vets at the college before we set off, and there were three of them waiting for us when we arrived. It took all four of us to help Fez down the ramp and into a stable filled with soft, deep straw. The chief vet told me they would run some tests.

'I know there is a massive infection there. I just know it,' I said. I hadn't slept properly for days, and my face was pale and drawn. The vet put a hand on my shoulder and I sagged under it, even though I was determined to stay upright.

'We will do everything we can,' he said gently.

'Thank you. I want to go to the World Championships with him. He's special. He's not just a horse. He's my best friend.' I left then. I couldn't speak any more; the anguish had drained me to the point that I was beyond words.

The next day I went back and the chief vet sat down with me in his office. He cleared his throat and spoke to me in German.

'Peter. I don't know what you call it in English, but Fez has a problem called osteomyelitis. Do you know what that is?'

I winced and closed my eyes. Yes, I knew exactly what it was. The word was the same in English. It meant an acute bacterial bone infection.

It seemed the nail injury was the probable cause. The nail had pricked the pedal bone, which is the big main bone in the sole of a horse's foot, letting in bacteria that were now eating right through his leg bones.

'So what next? What can we do? Can we drain it? Don't you have any stronger antibiotics? You could start him on them now, right now. We can't waste any time.'

My garbled words faded away as I looked at the vet's expression. He shook his head.

'Peter. It is incurable. I cannot save him. Nobody can.'

The words hurt like blows to the guts. I couldn't catch my breath. This couldn't be happening. It was surreal, like a horror film. What did he mean: he couldn't help Fez, that nobody could? But I knew, I knew exactly what he meant. Fez couldn't go on. It was over. When I eventually found my voice through the pain, I asked him if he would do it.

'I will put him down for you, Peter,' he said quietly.

'There's one thing. It's really important. He's had lots of painkillers and antibiotics. Don't let him be used for meat.' I knew horsemeat was very popular in France and Belgium, and the thought sickened me.

'No, of course not. The furnaces are going here just now.'

'Will you do it soon, so he doesn't suffer any more? Please.'

'I will do it in 15 minutes. Just as soon as I get the gear together.'

'Good. Let me have that time with him. I need to say goodbye.'

I made my way to the stable and went in. Fez was down in the stall, resting in the soft bedding with his front legs tucked underneath him. He was facing the corner but he turned his head when I came in. His ears flickered forwards. He was pleased and relieved to see me.

'Hey, mate,' I whispered, fishing out a chunk of carrot from my pocket. I sat down beside him, as close as I could get. His eyes were glazed and the soft part of his muzzle was crinkled from the pain. As I stroked his face, his mouth relaxed and he seemed to know I was there to help him. I knew it was the right decision to let him go. It was time.

'I love you, Fez. I love you so much that I have to let this happen,' I whispered.

World Championships and the Olympics, we could have been at them all, I thought, feeling his warm breath on my hand as he took the chunk of carrot. His beautiful long eyelashes brushed my face as I hugged him gently, a last hug as I knew the 15 minutes was almost gone.

'Goodbye, Fez,' I said. I know he watched me as I stumbled from the stall, and I think he knew that his pain was about to end. I have always regretted not staying with him as the vet put the needle in his neck. But I couldn't bear seeing his body being winched into the furnace.

For me, there was no end to the suffering. I wanted to feel Fez's pain, and I believed that I should be punished for what had happened. I wanted to die too. I went into the city centre and tried to drown my sorrows, not caring if I humiliated myself. I couldn't go back to Hilde's and face her stupid questions, so later that evening I went to the house of one of her grooms and collapsed into bed, crying until I fell asleep.

The next morning I knew what I had to do. After paying all the vet bills I had £20 left. The ferry to England cost £12. I could track down some friends there and make a fresh start, earn some money and eventually head back to New Zealand. I would sell my horse rugs, my water buckets and my saddle if I had to. In a strange moment of clarity, I had it all decided in my mind. Of course, it was the grief that fired my decision. I was running away but I didn't care. The further I got from this place where Fez had died, the better my chances of rebuilding my life. I told a disgruntled Hilde that I was leaving, started packing, then suddenly realised that I hadn't given Selma my final decision. It was a week since we had spoken. I found her crumpled and soggy card in my pocket, picked up the phone and dialled her number.

'My circumstances have changed. My horse has been put down,' I said flatly. 'I'm not coming, but thank you for your offer. I'm going to England.' Then I hung up on her.

I thought Selma would just leave it after my abrupt message, but I hadn't bargained on this feisty, strong-willed German woman. She rang me back 10 minutes later.

'You're not going to England. Why would you want to go there, for goodness sake? You are coming to me in Dusseldorf and that's all there is to it. You will come and ride my horses and I will train you. It's as simple as that.'

'No, ma'am, it isn't that simple, I'm afraid. I can't do it. I don't want to ride anymore.' I meant it too.

Her voice softened.

'You will come, Peter. I have lost a horse too. I have lost my husband too, in a riding accident. I know what it is to grieve for someone who has been taken away from you. You can't go to England.

'There is a train leaving Brussels today; you will stay overnight in Cologne and you will be in Dusseldorf on Thursday. I have checked all the times and I will be there to greet you.'

'I'm sorry, ma'am. I can't do it. I'm not coming,' I said.

'Yes, you are.'

A silence. I thought about what she had proposed. What else was I going to do? England was just a place to run away to. I couldn't escape the reality of my situation by moving from one country to another. My dreams were already shattered. There would be no

Olympics, no World Championships, and no Fez. I had nothing to lose, apart from a £5 train fare. I took that train.

Chapter 15

The emptiness of losing Fez was still there, but I felt a numb sense
of safety as I lay in the comfortable single bed. And it was thanks
to Selma. I was in a little flat at the seven-acre property of the von
Brautisch family, near Dusseldorf in Germany. It was 1980 and I
was 27. Selma trained the daughter, Claudia, and had spoken so
highly of me to her parents that they had offered me a place to stay
and full use of all facilities and horses during my training.
Selma met me at the station in Dusseldorf and drove me to the
property. The first thing I noticed was the huge wire fences, with
three layers of barbed wire along the top. They circled the whole
seven acres. We were let in through a huge gate by a security
guard, and drove along a beautiful tree-lined road, with an
immaculate dressage arena on one side and the stable complex on
the other. Selma parked outside a little cottage a short distance
from the palatial mansion where the family lived. After I had
unloaded my gear she left me, and I went outside and walked
around the property. As I saw all the facilities I felt a buzz of
excitement break through my sadness. I walked back to the
cottage, ate some food I found in the fridge, then collapsed into
bed, falling asleep almost immediately.
When Selma returned the next morning I was full of questions.
Who was Claudia von Brautisch, and why did her family need all
this security? 'This place is amazing,' I said. 'What do they do?
How can they afford all this? It's perfect.'
Selma patiently explained. Claudia was now 22 and had been in
the junior German three-day event team, winning a silver medal at
the European Championships. She was clearly a promising rider,
but had needed more training to make it to the adult division (for
ages 21 and over). Her father was the managing director of a huge
chemical company, one of the largest firms in Germany,
employing 72,000 people.
'But why all the security? It's like a prison,' I said.
'To keep people out, not keep people in, so not a prison as
such,' said Selma. 'This is a dangerous time to be rich in Germany.

The Red Army Faction has been kidnapping the children of wealthy industrialists. Herr von Brautisch has lost a good friend, the head of Mercedes-Benz. They kidnapped him and killed him. He has a son older than Claudia and another daughter, younger than her. There is no way he would risk losing them. You will be given security clearance so you can get in and out, but you will always be checked. There are police and guards on duty every hour of the day and night. Don't worry. You're in the safest place in Germany.'

She wasn't kidding either. But once I got used to the constant surveillance and being shadowed by guards, I hardly noticed it. I loved the luxury of the place. It even had a heated tack room. Selma came every morning to train Claudia and me. Our goal was to become top riders in the European circuit, taking on the best, and winning. If anyone could get us there, it was Selma.

At the end of a long day working the horses, Selma finally told me the story of her life, and the hardship that had shaped her into the person she was. We were leaning on the fence at the dressage arena as she started talking. She told me how her husband Albert had trained her, and she had been chosen to compete in the 1976 Montreal Olympic Games. She was the first German woman allowed to compete in the dressage competition, as until then the sport had been completely dominated by men.

'I went to the stable to check my horse, just to see how he was, you know,' she said softly, staring into the distance. 'It was a week before we were going to the games. I was so excited. There were no signs, no signs at all, that my horse wasn't perfectly fine. I went to the stable, and there he was, lying in the straw. He was dead. Just like that. It was all over.'

I felt the ache of loss, not just for Fez, but for her horse too. She knew what it was like to have a special friend taken away for no reason, and just when you needed them most. But she hadn't just lost her horse. She and her husband Albert had been running a large and successful stable. One day Albert took a four-year-old horse out to train and it came back without him.

'I went looking. I felt in my stomach that something terrible had happened, but I could not believe what I found,' she said. 'Albert must have been crushed or kicked in some way. My Albert passed away a few days later.' She caught her breath at the memory.

'Not a day goes by that I don't think about him and wish he was here to share every moment with me.'

Then Selma turned to me.

'You see, I was speaking from the heart when I said I know what it is to lose someone you love. That's why I knew how much you were hurting and why it was so important for you to come here.'

I felt humbled by this strong-spirited, determined, sensitive woman. But before I could get a word out to say all that, she smiled.

'Right, enough of this, let's settle the horses and get some dinner.'

Training in Germany, among the rich and elite, was so far from my life in New Zealand that it could have been another planet, not just another country. There were moments when it would suddenly hit me that I was among some of the most privileged individuals in Europe. For example, there was another estate we went to for an event, and as we drove through the huge gates there was a black panther prowling inside a cage, with a diamond-studded collar around its neck.

There was a darker side to having access to that kind of money though. One owner developed an automated feed system so he didn't even have to employ people to feed his horses. Selma and I were both horrified when we saw this. At certain times of the day a flap would open in each horse's stable and a set amount of feed would drop into the bucket below. The owner was very proud of it and showed it off to us. But our reaction was far from positive.

'How disgusting,' Selma whispered when the man wasn't listening. 'Feeding a horse yourself creates a bond; it's like a mother and child.'

I knew exactly what she meant.

'Maybe he is afraid of the goat,' Selma added, nodding towards the grumpy-looking white billy in the corner of the stable. 'I hear he is the horse's companion and they are inseparable. The horse pines without it but it's a bad-tempered beast, apparently.'

We held in our giggles, but underneath we were shocked at how something so personal and special could be turned into an automatic process without an ounce of humanity.

For all her empathy with equines, Selma was no soft, animal-loving pushover, particularly when it came to training humans like me. I found this out a few weeks after I started with her. One morning I was feeling homesick and out of sorts. Selma always appeared with a beaming smile, no matter what kind of day it was. 'Good morning, Peter,' she said cheerfully, as usual. I mumbled a greeting back to her, not even looking up from the jumps I was setting up in the indoor arena.

Now Selma always carried a long dressage whip. It was one of the tools of the trainer's trade.

I heard her say, 'Can you say good morning properly please, Peter?' I felt annoyed. What on earth was she on about? 'Yeah, yeah, good morning, Frau Brandl,' I sighed sarcastically. Whack! She flicked me with the whip, catching me on the back.

I turned around immediately, furious at what she had done. 'Don't you dare hit me, ever,' I spat.

Selma stood her ground, her face stony, and she flicked me again with the whip, catching me on the leg.

'And don't you ever speak to me like that,' she said.

I was rigid with rage. We stared at each other.

'Peter, pick up that showjumping rail and do ten push-ups with it, above your head,' she ordered.

I didn't break her gaze as I picked up the rail, pushing it above my head and counting. When I got to ten, I dropped it, glaring at her.

'Hmm, you still haven't caught on, have you,' said Selma. 'Right, run around this arena five times.'

The arena was sandy and it was like running on a beach. In my long riding boots it was an ordeal to run in the sinking substance. But with each circuit I cottoned on a little bit more to what Selma meant. Panting after the five circuits of the arena, I looked at her more softly. I know she read in my eyes that I wanted to know what this was about, and why she needed to teach me this lesson.

'I am here to help you, Peter,' she said. 'You have talent, but unless you respect those in authority, you will go nowhere. How can you learn if you don't listen, and listen properly? This is not about becoming a submissive person. It is about accepting that someone else is the authority figure, making yourself available to learn from them.'

I understood. I apologised and told her that I appreciated her frankness. It taught me that there was a difference between arrogance and confidence, and I still carry this in my heart today.

Selma taught me that discipline is not always a bad thing as it helps focus the mind on the task required. She also taught me to smile.

'Greet me with a smile, because if you're not happy then I don't want you riding the horses and making them unhappy too.' It was a simple lesson and an apt one. Misery is infectious, so carry joy in your heart and on your face. It will make other people, other living things, just as joyful.

Claudia followed Selma's rules too. The two of us often laughed away together as we worked, something her mother, Frau von Brautisch, a typical German, loathed. She would yell at us to shut up, but we would soon be giggling away again. One day she marched up to me.

'You laugh too much,' she shouted. 'You must not be working hard enough. Working people do not have time to laugh.'

'Sorry,' I said politely, trying not to catch Claudia's eye because I just knew I would start laughing again. Frau von Brautisch picked up the signals that we weren't taking her seriously. She gritted her teeth, got into her beautiful new Mercedes, slammed the door, and screeched out of the stable yard. The main house was only 200 metres up the road and she was so angry that she roared into the driveway and didn't brake soon enough. The front of the car hit the garage and damaged it. Claudia and I stood open-mouthed in the yard, watching her. Frau von Brautisch got out of the car, shrieking in German and kicking the wheels. That was all it took for Claudia and I to collapse into gales of laughter until tears ran down our cheeks.

There was never any romance between the two of us. We were good friends, but our focus was on the horses. I think Selma knew that my Kiwi cheekiness would be good for this young, staid German woman. And though Claudiea sometimes didn't find that all-
important emotional connection with a horse, her self-discipline was good for me. Claudia was an accomplished, textbook-style rider.

Earlyboy, a feisty little horse, had never gone well for Claudia, particularly when jumping. But the two of us had clicked well. His strength was cross-country, but he had to be pushed. We were competing in a small event one day and I was confident we would go clear during the cross-country. As we approached one fence he began to hesitate and I knew he was going to stop. That incurs twenty faults and I knew he could get over it if he tried. So I resorted to good old-fashioned New Zealand tactics. 'Go on, you mongrel,' I roared, giving him a slap on the rump with my whip. It worked. He flew over the fence. But a couple of the other fences were a little tricky and we finished in seventh place. I was a bit disappointed, but Selma was happy, especially when Claudia went clear and finished fourth.

'You are both doing so well,' she said, beaming her big smile at us both. 'I loved the "mongrel" technique. It certainly works.'

I smiled back, but felt I could have done better.

Later I was standing at the car, just about to leave, when a man approached me. I knew he was important, and also a good friend of Selma's. A former champion showjumper, he was now the chief trainer of the German event team, based at the national training centre.

'Peter, I would like to say congratulations,' he said warmly, holding out a hand. I shook it, but was puzzled.

'Thanks, but why are you congratulating me? I haven't won anything.'

'Ah, it's for your outstanding ability in cross-country. How would you like to train with me, and ride with the German team? I would like you to show them how to ride cross-country. Come and train with me.'

I was utterly gobsmacked, and almost dropped the sausage roll I was eating. You had to be German to ride with the German team. It was like the Holy Grail of European riding. I looked down as I thought about his words, and when I looked up again, there was Selma. She had heard what the man had offered me, and had walked directly up to him. Her eyes were filled with tears. I remembered then that this man was one of the people who had helped her when Albert had died. He was her good friend and he had tried to poach me.

'How can you do this?' she said. 'I have just found this rider and he is working well with me. He is very talented and a good person, and you want to take him away.'

The man looked slightly sheepish as Selma walked away. I knew what I had to do.

'Sir, I'm extremely flattered and thrilled to be asked to ride with the team, but my loyalty lies with Selma. She's my trainer and will stay my trainer. Thank you.'

As he turned and walked away it dawned on me just what I had given up, and for a second I wondered if I had done the right thing. But then I saw Selma, and I knew I was following the correct path. She was teaching me so much more than better riding techniques. She gave me insight into how horses thought and what made them tick.

Shortly after this, Claudia took a break in Switzerland with some of the horses, to get them fit in the high altitude. The time was drawing close for a three-day event to be held in August 1980 at Luhmulen, a top equestrian venue near Hannover, Germany.

Claudia's mare was in great shape as we rode out, me on Earlyboy and Selma watching us. As the mare stepped up on a grass verge the ground gave way and her leg went down a big hole, twisting badly. Claudia managed to stay on, but the mare was very lame. All the tendons were stretched and broken. In fact the injury was so bad that the mare had to be retired and spent the rest of her days as a brood mare. Claudia was devastated.

'What will I ride now?' she asked sadly. 'We worked so hard to get to this point, Peter. It is so unfair.'

As I comforted her I had a sneaking suspicion what the decision would be. Essentially, Claudia's family owned Earlyboy, and he was the best horse for the event.

'Claudia will take Earlyboy to Luhmulen. You will be her groom,' Selma told me.

I didn't allow myself to feel disappointed. I wanted the best for Claudia and this event was important to her. Luhmulen was where the World Championships were to be held in two years' time. I had hoped to be there with Fez, and getting there was still a goal, although I wasn't sure that I would be able to achieve it. Even being at Luhmulen as a groom and getting the chance to look around was an opportunity too good to be missed.

On dressage day Earlyboy was his usual arrogant little self and made a few of his own decisions, making Claudia's final placing quite far down the list. Cross-country was next and I walked the challenging course with Claudia, looking at each jump and deciding the best way to get over it. At a big ditch, Claudia paled.

'Earlyboy doesn't like these much,' she said.

'Oh, he's just being pig-headed. Honestly, he can get over them when he wants to. I've seen him do it.'

'How? I have tried everything with him. If he doesn't want to go over, he won't.'

'You know what you haven't tried.'

'What? Tell me.'

'Okay, when you head for the ditch, line him up and go for it straight, so he doesn't think he can duck out. Then, when he is just about to either stop or jump, you are going to yell at him "Get up" in a growling voice. Try it.'

I demonstrated the very Kiwi roar. Claudia looked a bit startled and gave it a shot. It was like a kitten purring.

'Louder. Roar at him. Make him know that you are not going to tolerate anything but a big jump out of him.'

'Get up!'

'Louder.'

'Get up!'

People were staring but we didn't care. Claudia grinned at me.

'It's not a very German thing to do, you know,' she warned, thinking of her mother.

'Maybe, but it will get you over that fence.'

And it did. Earlyboy came in with just half a time fault, putting Claudia in second place to an American rider who had competed in several Olympics. In the showjumping Earlyboy went clear, and Claudia finished third overall. It was a tremendous result. We were ecstatic, hugging each other and patting Earlyboy over and over. Claudia was beside herself with delight.

'I can't believe it. Get up! Get up!' she whooped.

'Well done, my darling,' boomed a deep voice. Her father came striding across the grass towards her. Two security guards, dressed in what they obviously thought were 'horse people' outfits, shadowed him, failing miserably at blending in. They were both about six foot seven in height and looked bizarre in tweed and jodhpurs. Herr von Brautisch had arrived in a police helicopter, which had dropped him near the lorries so he was out of sight of the main area.

Claudia embraced her father and he dropped a kiss on the top of her head. He then came to me, put his arm around my shoulder and gave me a squeeze. I'm not that tall, just five foot five inches, and he was a good deal taller, not to mention bigger in build. I felt like a small teddy bear being hugged by this huge bloke.

'You've done a wonderful job with that horse. Thank you,' he boomed. 'Come and see me later, when you get back. I wish to talk to you. But now, you all must celebrate.'

We went into the town centre and had a huge drinking binge, knocking back little glasses of grapefruit and apple schnapps until we couldn't keep our eyes from crossing. It was a wonderful night. Back at the estate it wasn't long before Herr von Brautisch caught up with me, taking me aside one day.

'I would like you to compete in the World Championships,' he said.

Even though I had hoped for the chance to go to the championships, I couldn't imagine being there without Fez or a horse as good as him. And to me, that was virtually impossible.

'So, I will buy you a horse,' Herr von Brautisch said when I explained the situation. 'There is a good one available. I am happy to pay the money for you.' The price he quoted was the equivalent of £30,000.

What an opportunity to advance my career. My dream could have come true, but it wouldn't be because I had found the perfect horse. It would be because another person had bought it. I didn't want the obligation, or the tie. In essence, I didn't want to be bought.

'Thank you. Let me think about it,' I said politely.

'You know, Peter, if I buy it soon, you can compete for New Zealand. All I ask is that you keep Selma and Claudia, and the horses, happy.'

The offer was generous. It was also full of obligations to the family. I would have to compromise my way of life and fit in with the von Brautisch way. That would delight the rigid Frau von Brautisch, and I couldn't bear that thought. It was too far removed from my independent nature. I asked him to give me two days to think about it. Right on time, he appeared at the tack room and we sat down together.

'What is your answer, Peter?' he asked.

'I appreciate your offer and I love being here at your property, Sir, but I can't commit to being here for another two years.'

I told him he couldn't buy me, although I didn't put it quite like that. If I went to the World Championships, it would be on my own terms, and through my own efforts. Getting there because the way was paved with someone else's money was no achievement in my view. Herr von Brautisch understood, however, and left, saying, 'You are a man of integrity, Peter.'

As the end of the eventing season approached, I knew it was time for a change. I had learned much from Selma, and I had healed the raw wounds left by the death of Fez. Now it was time for new adventures.

I had stayed in contact with Amanda during my time in Germany. She had gone from England to the famous Spanish Riding School in Vienna, where she had been working in the stables. She had experienced her own fair share of adventures, including one in which a stallion attacked her. Stallions are usually quiet but if a female is menstruating they can become dangerous. This one grabbed Amanda's hair in his mouth and lifted her off the ground so that a lump of hair was torn from her scalp. That released her from his grip and she was able to crawl across the floor, trying to avoid his hooves and teeth, and reach the door. Just as she opened it and rolled out into the walkway one of his feet crashed down just centimetres from her.

In her latest letters Amanda had talked of heading back to England, and of missing me. I missed her too, so I arranged for her to come to Dusseldorf, then we would set off to England together. After a couple of days we left from Dusseldorf station. Selma came to say goodbye. I never feel sad about farewells because they mean the start of a new adventure. I like to keep in contact with the special people I meet, and I knew I would be staying in touch with Selma. 'I am proud of you,' she told me on my last night. 'You know I will always be here if you need me. I don't think this is a "Goodbye" for ever. Wait and see.'

The train journey was followed by the ferry trip across the English Channel, a long, dull voyage. Amanda and I snuggled together on a seat by the window, looking out at the steely grey sea. I could feel her warmth through our coats, and I pressed her closer to me. I had missed her so much. I loved her. It all seemed so right. My brain shouted down to my mouth, 'Say it, for goodness sake, just say it.' The connection finally got through.

'Amanda,' I whispered. She looked up at me and her big blue eyes were quizzical.
'What?'
'Will you marry me?'

Chapter 16

The rest of the ferry trip passed in a blur. We made plans for our wedding and talked about the life we would have together. It made perfect sense. Both Amanda and I loved horses and wanted to work with them. We speculated about what might happen, where we might go together in life. The wedding, we decided, would be held at her parents' home in Albany, near Auckland.

Then I remembered.

'I'll have to go and tell my mother. I haven't heard from her for a bit and this is something to say to her in person, not by letter or phone,' I said.

Amanda agreed. Once in England we would go back to Hyde House, which was still undergoing renovations, I would stay for a week, then I would head off to see Joan. She had moved again and was now in the United States, of all places, living in Little Rock, Arkansas.

'I just have this feeling that she needs me,' I said. 'It's weird. I don't hear from her for ages, and then suddenly, I just know.'

Amanda understood totally. 'It's fine. You go and I can start making plans,' she said, hugging me warmly. 'We can meet up in six weeks in Auckland.'

A week later we had a farewell party at the house and one of the lads pressed a little goodbye gift into my hand. I opened my palm and found a small lump of hashish, the size of my thumbnail.

'That'll keep you going,' he said with a wink.

In those days everyone smoked dope. It was the culture of the time, the drug of choice, and there was no stigma attached to it. I thanked him and put the piece of hashish in my pocket. The next day I headed for London, stopping off on the way to break the journey and see my old friend Mark Todd. Mark was pleased to see me and we had a bit of a party. A couple of grooms from Princess Anne's stable came over. I was still a bit wrecked when I hugged Mark goodbye the next day and left to hitch to Gatwick Airport.

I was flying with Freddie Laker, one of the early budget airlines, and as I walked into the terminal I noticed a sign directing passengers to purchase a meal voucher for the trip. I put my hand in my pocket, looking for the right change, and found the remains of the block of hashish in among the coins. My first instinct was to throw it away. Then, before I could change my mind, I popped it in my mouth and swallowed it. Well, it was a shame to put it to waste, I thought.

On the plane, I was seated next to a quietly spoken Singaporean girl. When the cabin crew announced they were coming through with the meals for those with vouchers, she looked stricken. She had forgotten to buy one. By this time the effects of the drug were coming on strongly and I was very stoned. Eating was the last thing on my mind.

'Ah, have mine,' I said cheerily, and handed her my voucher. Then I promptly fell asleep and when we woke the plane was landing in New York. Still stoned, I booked into a motel near the airport and slept off the hashish. Not surprisingly, I just kept on sleeping, right through the night, and when I woke it was the next morning. Time to track down Joan.

A woman answered the phone when I rang the number I had for her.

'No, Joan isn't here, she was in Miami Beach last week. I guess you know the good news,' said the woman, who was Joan's flatmate, and another nurse.

'What good news?'

'She's getting married to a guy she met there, just a week ago. But hey, who am I to judge. If it makes her happy, I guess that's all that matters,' she said.

I almost fell over. Married?

'Where is she now?'

'I think she is in Williamsburg in Virginia.'

'Have you got a number for her?'

The woman went and found the number, and I wrote it down with a shaking hand. Then I immediately dialled it. Joan was surprised but pleased to hear from me.

'Oh hi, darling,' she said. 'Where are you?'

I told her, trying to cut through the bland pleasantries so I could get to the bottom of the situation.

'What on earth is this about you marrying some man you met a week ago?' I blurted out.

'It's wonderful, darling, absolutely wonderful. He's a dear man, an aristocrat, you know. He has three names and has a number after them, you know, the third. Imagine that.'

'Don't you think it's a bit rash to marry him so soon?'

'Not at all, Peter. He's delightful. He's said lots of lovely things to me,' she replied in a sing-song voice.

'They all say nice things, Mum. Look, do not marry him. Wait until I get there, okay?'

I flew to Williamsburg that afternoon and took a taxi to the address she had given me. Joan met me at the door of the house. When I say 'house', I really mean 'hut'. This man might be an aristocrat, but his castle was a shack on the edge of town and so ramshackle it looked as if one decent shove would knock it down. Joan hugged me. She was 50 now, and still beautiful, in a blowsy kind of way.

'What is this place? You can't possibly be living in this . . . this shed, Mum. I thought you said he was rich?'

Joan shrugged.

'Darling, he has a bit of a booze problem, you see. But he comes from such a good family.'

I sighed.

'You are not getting married, Mum. It's a crazy idea. Have you got any money left?' She shook her head. 'Credit card?' She nodded.

'Right, you are coming back to Arkansas with me.'

Joan pouted and sulked, then she said, 'Oh, I suppose so. Come in and meet him anyway. Maybe you'll change your mind. He's very charming.'

I went in through a rusted door and saw how down-at-heel the interior was. It was like one of those documentaries about poverty that you see on television and wonder how anyone could live in such a state. There were one or two pieces of furniture that were very grand and would have been more at home in a mansion than a shack, but apart from that it was clear Joan's suitor was at the end of his luck.

Despite that, he was very genteel, well-spoken and dressed in a beautifully cut suit. I told him exactly what I thought of the situation.

'You cannot marry my mother. It's crazy. You have known each other for a week and you live in appalling conditions. You can barely look after yourself, let alone a wife.'

The man looked crestfallen and I almost felt sorry for him.

Joan was very quiet on the flight to Arkansas and kept sighing heartily. I ignored her. If I started to pander to her, I knew she would never snap out of this melancholy. I had to be strong for her. We went back to her apartment in Little Rock, in one of those typical American complexes, surrounding a tennis court and swimming pool. Her flatmate was still there. During the journey Joan had explained a bit about why she was in Little Rock. Basically, she had to work as a nurse in a place where there was a shortage of trained medical staff for one year, then she could get her green card. She was partway through that year and wanted to stay.

I had barely a cent to my name, so I found a job straight away, as lunchtime chef in a cute little Swiss bakery. But I also needed an evening job. 'I saw a sign in the window of Murray's Dinner Theatre in town,' Joan said. 'Try there.'

Murray's Dinner Theatre was run by a woma called Ginger McIntyre , and she was everything I expected from her name and profession.

'How yawl doin', honey,' she drawled. 'Ah'm Miss Ginger and that's what ah like to be called.'

I could have listened to her all day. She was overweight but voluptuous rather than fat, with bright red lipstick, lashings of mascara, and bright red hair in a bob, sprayed into a scarlet helmet so it didn't move one millimetre as she spoke. Miss Ginger's elderly father owned the dinner theatre and she managed it for him. She wanted me to work as a waiter, which would mean setting up the tables for dinner, then serving the diners who came for a meal and a cabaret show. I had an idea I would like working in this off-the-wall place, with its busty barmaid and her black beehive, and the Southern belle waitresses. Towards the end of the interview Miss Ginger asked me what I'd been up to and I told her about riding horses in Germany.

'What do you know, honey, my daughter rides horses too. She has just the most wonderful trainer, you must meet her. She's something else,' she purred.

'Thanks, it'll be nice to meet her,' I said.

Miss Ginger just glowed. 'Her name is Miss Karen Walder. The horse barn where she works is not too far from here. I'll get her to call in and see you, real soon. Oh honey, she is going to like you,' she said, a naughty twinkle in her eye.

I wanted to laugh. These people were so like the stereotypical Southerners you see on television and in films. I liked them immediately, but was also aware that this was a hard type of life, and things hadn't been easy for many people around there. I wasn't at all surprised to learn that the film Deliverance, with its backwoods, inbred, no-neck families, was shot nearby in the town of Mountain Home in the Ozarks Mountains.

Two days after I started at Miss Ginger's place, Miss Karen Walder walked in. I was just finishing laying the tables when this tall young woman with long chestnut hair and dark eyes walked in. I noticed she was wearing jeans and long boots.

'Hey, I'm looking for Peter Taylor,' she said sharply.

'That's me,' I smiled, putting down the cutlery and straightening up. She looked me up and down, and I stood my ground, noticing how high her cheekbones were and what flawless skin she had.

'I'm Karen Walder.'

'Hi, nice to meet you. I hear you train Miss Ginger's young daughter.'

'Yes, I do. I hear you can ride?' She was almost aggressive in the way she spat questions at me.

'I do, but I'm not here for that. I'm just visiting my mother, who lives here.'

'Do y'all want to come for a ride or what?'

'I'd love to, thanks.'

She gave me directions to her horse barn and strode out. I stood there, laughing quietly and shaking my head. I hadn't met anyone like this woman before.

The next day she picked me up in a bashed-up black car. 'Get in,' she shouted. I didn't hesitate. On the way out to her barn, she barely spoke.

'So, you say you can ride?' she said as we pulled up outside her place. I nodded. 'Let's see how well you can ride then, shall we? I've got a horse called Desi who'll show me how you can ride.'

Desi was a small horse with a determined glint in his eye. He wasn't easy and he didn't respond well to anyone trying to move him around. But I managed to get a good performance out of him, while Karen watched. After a few minutes I trotted Desi over to her. Her angular face seemed much softer.

'Man, you can ride,' she said grudgingly. 'You can stick around, watch me take a lesson, an' all.'

I leaned on the fence of the paddock as she took a class of teenagers. Karen had about 12 horses on the property, which was dominated by an old Southern-style barn. There were two paddocks, one with sand and jumps, the other clear, for class work. Even though Karen was absolutely gorgeous, I was determined not to become attracted to her. After all, I was engaged to Amanda and our wedding was imminent. But Karen was keen on me, and within a week she was picking me up most nights from the dinner theatre. I told her I was leaving in a few weeks to get married in New Zealand, so she didn't think I was interested in her. During the time we spent together I found out that her dad was Irish and her mum was half Cherokee Indian, which was where she had inherited her cheekbones and eyes from.

The more time I spent with Karen, the more I wondered about marrying Amanda. I loved Amanda, but was it simply for convenience that we were getting hitched? I was happy in Little Rock. I really didn't want to go back to New Zealand, as I still felt I had so much to do and experience. I had to face facts. I didn't want to get married. One night I picked up the telephone and dialled Amanda's number in England.

'Are you still okay about the wedding and everything?' I asked gently, after we had caught up with each other's news. The conversation had been strangely subdued, on her part as well as mine.

'I suppose so,' she said. 'Are you?'

'I think so.'

'Goodness, listen to us, we don't sound like a couple dying to get married, do we?' she said with a sad chuckle.

'No, we don't. Amanda, I want to say . . .'

'Oh, Peter, I can't hold this off any more. I don't want to get married. I'm sorry.' She blurted it out at the same time as I said virtually the same thing. We both laughed. We couldn't help ourselves.

'I think we are even more in tune with each other than we realised,' she said.

'You're right. Are you sad, Amanda?'

'A bit, but it's for the best, isn't it? I want to stay in England, you want to stay in Arkansas. Marriage is the last thing we need. It wouldn't work.'

She was absolutely right. I hung up feeling down at heart, but relieved. I told Karen about the decision the next time I saw her. We were at the little house where she lived, near the barn.

'Well, I'm not getting married. I'm not going home,' I said nonchalantly, trying to slip it into the general conversation. Karen stared at me.

'Are you serious? Does that mean we can hang out?'

'We were anyway, weren't we?' I was confused and still getting to grips with the slang.

'No,' said Karen, her eyes glittering like chips of jet. 'I mean really hang out, like this.' She curled her slender arms around my neck and kissed me. We woke up the next morning in her little single bed, curled up like kittens.

Even though I adored Karen, I had to be upfront with her about another part of my private life. For years I had been bisexual, occasionally having short-term relationships and flings with men. Don't forget, I grew up in the time of 'free love' and no barriers, so it wasn't unusual to be bisexual, and there was no stigma attached to it among my generation. Karen was fine about it, just as previous girlfriends, including Amanda, had been. It wasn't a big deal to them.

The only time it became an issue was when a man I was seeing would fall in love with me. And that's what happened in Little Rock. Having been in the US for four months, I had seen this young guy in town a couple of times and we had spent some time together. He was quite needy and demanding, and I soon realised he had fallen for me. When I told him I didn't feel the same, he was devastated. He knew where I lived and went to see my mother when I wasn't there, but I had no idea until the next day, when I came to pick her up for a trip to Tennessee. She was moody and sullen, which was not unusual. Not liking the idea of a two-hour drive in horrible silence, I asked her what was wrong.

'A man came to see me last night, Peter,' she said, sounding half-hurt, half-angry. 'He says you have been seeing him romantically. Are you gay?'

'Ah, I see. Well, I'm bisexual.'

Joan closed her eyes, as if in pain.

'Oh God, it's because of your father and I, isn't it? How we brought you up. I knew it. We . . . warped you, or something.'

'No, it's nothing of the sort,' I said. 'It's just the way I am and it's nothing to do with you or Dad or anyone. Don't make a big thing out of it, Mum. It's nobody's fault.'

'Do you love this man?'

'No, of course I don't. It was just a fling.'

'Does Karen know?'

'Yes, she does. All my girlfriends have known. Karen is the one I want to be with, Mum. Honestly, it's not an issue.'

Silence for the next hour. Then, just outside Memphis, Joan launched into an acidic tirade. I was a pervert, I betrayed women, I was sick, I was a failure, and I didn't deserve to have a normal life when I was so abnormal in my love life. Oh, and that chestnut, how could I do this to her?

I let her get it all out of her system. More silence, until we arrived outside the immigration office in Memphis. Joan had now completed her year working in the US, and she had to get her green card processed.

'I have an idea,' she said suddenly, as we were waiting in the queue. 'I'm about to get my green card, so I can sponsor you to live here. So, why don't you give me your passport and I'll take it in with me, and sort out getting you a green card too.'

It made sense. I handed her my passport and went to wait in the lounge. After 15 minutes a man came out and called me into an interview room. I assumed this was just part of the sponsorship process, but I was wrong. The man, who was in his fifties, sat opposite me at a large desk in a windowless room and looked at my passport, then up at me. His jowly face was grave. I smiled, trying to ease the tension that filled the small space.

'Son, I think you should wipe that there smile off your face,' he growled. 'You are in one heck of a lot of trouble.'

I had overstayed my entry permit by one month. On the way back to Little Rock, Joan was livid.

'Look, I'm sorry. I didn't know about the six-month thing, okay?' I said. 'I thought I was fine to be here as long as I wanted.'

She clenched her thumb in her fist, like she used to when I was a child and had annoyed her.

'How could you not know, Peter?' she wailed. 'It's terrible. How could you do this to me? Not only are you gay, you're an overstayer too. Oh, I am so ashamed of you.'

I tried not to let it get to me, but for that moment I was back in her little bedroom in Whangarei, five minutes late with her breakfast and paying for it with a piece of my soul. No matter where I went in the world, I couldn't escape the past, and Joan.

Chapter 17

Rectifying my illegal status in the US meant taking a 10-minute trip to Mexico. When I say 10 minutes, I mean this is how long it took to nip across the bridge to Mexico in a taxi, do a U-turn back across, and stop at the immigration office to get a new visa. I had actually had to take a train from Arkansas to do this, but once at the border I didn't even have to take my bag off the train. It stayed under my seat while I crossed into Mexico and back in the cab.

It was the early hours of the morning and all I had eaten since leaving Arkansas was two packets of M&Ms that Karen had given me. The woman in the office looked tired.

'Can I get the visa for 10 months, do you think?' I batted my big blue eyes at her, hoping I could win her heart, at least until she had stamped my passport.

'Nope, all I can give you is six months,' she said.

'But my mother lives in Arkansas and she needs me. You know what mothers are like,' I appealed to her parental instincts. She gave me a look that said, 'Heard that one many times before, honey.'

Six months was all I could get, despite my heart-wrenching performance. A few minutes later I was back on the train and heading for Arkansas. At least getting that precious stamp would keep the Immigration Department happy for a while, and that was all I needed.

But my trip to Mexico gave me itchy feet. Joan had found a new man, the revoltingly named Wendell Scroggins, a fat, pompous rice millionaire , a Southerner who adored her. I loathed him, but she seemed happy enough. I adored Karen and liked Little Rock, but I also needed to stretch my legs a bit and see some more of America.

'I've come halfway across the world,' I told Karen. 'It seems crazy not to see a bit of the country, don't you think?' She agreed.

I handed in my notice at the Swiss café and the dinner theatre, and took a Greyhound bus to Cleveland, Ohio. A friend of Lockie Richards' lived there, and he had asked me to visit. I spent a few weeks there, riding his horses in the snow. It was a quiet place but I soon made friends. It was when I was staying with one of them, Sean, that I began to think about my life. I lay by the fire in Sean's wooden house, the snow falling gently outside, as I thought about Fez, and the horror of losing him. A feeling of utter despair came over me and I cried for hours. Somehow the peace of Cleveland allowed the feelings I had bottled up to be released. When I finished crying, I knew my grieving had moved on a stage. I had put Fez to rest and was ready, at last, to move on.

The next morning I picked up a gay newspaper and idly scanned the job ads. One caught my eye.

'Hey, there's a great job in here for a B and B with horses, a housekeeping position. That sounds perfect,' I said to Sean.

'What's a B and B? Is that a bed-and-breakfast place?'

Sean raised his eyebrows and smiled.

'No, it means body-builder,' he said.

'Why on earth would anyone want a body-builder as a housekeeper?' I asked naively. Then I saw Sean's expression and almost blushed. 'Oh, I see. Something nice to look at, as well as to do the cleaning and cooking around the house. Ah well, no harm in going for it.'

I put a copy of my CV in an envelope, together with a photograph of myself standing in a paddock, wearing a tight T-shirt and jeans with leather chaps over the top, working with a horse.

'How can he resist you?' Sean joked as I put the envelope in the post.

The phone rang a few days later. 'Peter Taylor?' said a man's voice in a crisp, cutting tone. 'You must come to Boston for an interview.'

'Sir, I'm not really in a position to fly around the country,' I replied. It was true. I was pretty broke.

'No, I will fly you to Boston,' he told me, and gave me exact details of flights and tickets.

John Huber was tall, slightly plump, with a face that would have been quite handsome in his younger years. He was in his forties and had the strangest shock of blond hair, which was in fact real despite looking exactly like a toupee. It was hard to stop myself staring at it. Despite the weird hairdo, John was a quiet, shy type of man. He interviewed me at his apartment in Boston, then took me out for lunch afterwards. As we sat at a beautiful café in the business district,

a number of attractive and obviously affluent men and women came up to talk to him. He was clearly someone of standing and wealth.

I watched him chat and tried to work him out. Finally, as he drained his coffee, he nodded at me.

'The job is yours. You will come to New Hampshire with me now.'

He drove a beautiful, sleek sports car and I virtually had to lie on the pavement to roll into it, it was so low-slung. I subtly found out more details of his life as he drove. He was one of the top riders and breeders of Arab horses in America. Arabs are the poodles of the horse world: pampered, showy and a status symbol for their owners. Stallions can make two million US dollars each in the sales, so I knew John must have plenty of money. He explained that he was actually a lawyer, and that while he was at law school he had worked as a model. His most memorable assignment was as a horse rider in a KFC ad. He had also met his partner, Bob, at law school, he explained. They had formed a business partnership, as well as a personal one, and had made a lot of money by forming a share-transfer company. Millions of dollars, I learned.

Bob didn't live at the house in New Hampshire though, John explained. Then he told me that he bred English bulldogs at the property. I had to hide a shudder. I don't like English bulldogs and loathe puppies in the house, especially spoiled ones, which is exactly what these sounded like. I decided that if I had to pamper the puppies I would leave and do something else. I wasn't going to be pushed into tasks I disliked by this man.

We drove through a little town of pretty houses, then approached a big white electronic gate, breaking up a neatly trimmed but high hedge. I could see a majestic three-storey house beyond the gardens, with a huge columned veranda. John drove up the driveway and stopped outside the house. I followed him through the front doors and into a glass atrium filled with light.

'Come on, let me show you around,' John said graciously. He told me the house had been built in 1790, and that an American president had once visited it, staying in the front bedroom. We went up a huge staircase, and he showed me his own room, a vast space filled with the best furnishings. My room was on the next floor up and was dominated by an antique bed with a canopy over it.

The house was breathtakingly beautiful and I couldn't wait to explore it properly. I soon got my chance. After he had shown me around John said he was going to a conference for three days, and needed to be back at the airport in an hour. He had a little time before he was due to leave, so he showed me his horse barn where there were 12 horses. The groom was a woman called Judy, and I also met Stuart, the man who looked after his kennels. I could tell from Stuart's sullen face that he was an ex-boyfriend of John's.

'I have an Arab breeding farm up the road, where there are over a hundred horses,' John said in his quiet voice, ignoring Stuart's moody glances.

We went back to the house, and soon a driver arrived to take John to the airport. Before he left he handed me $600 in cash and the keys to a white station-wagon.

'You will sleep in my bedroom while I am away. There are all the video surveillance cameras for the property in there, and you can watch them. If you have any problems, ring this number. It's for Ben. He runs the breeding farm for me, and is also the police chief of the town.'

It was all very Twin Peaks with mega-bucks, and I was intrigued by the whole set-up. As he got into the car, John wound the window down and beckoned me towards him.

'By the way, when I am not in the house, you must never touch the antique telephone beside my bed. You may answer the other two telephones. One is my private line and the other my business line. But the antique telephone is neither of those. Do not answer it. Thank you.'

I stood on the gravel drive, with a wad of cash in my hand and the run of an amazing three-storey house. I wandered through the sumptuous rooms, admiring the antiques and artworks. There were so many rooms, and each one was decorated in an exquisite fashion. As I went through the atrium, I heard a voice shouting John's name.

'Hello?' I called.

It came again. 'John! John!'

I followed the sound and found a green Amazon parrot in a large cage at the other end of the atrium. Peering into the cage, I introduced myself, and the bird cocked its majestic head, studying me carefully.

'Hello, I'm Fred, hello, I'm Fred,' he said.

'Wow, this is weird, Fred. I'm in this incredible house, talking to a parrot. I don't know if I'm very lucky or going mad. What do you reckon?'

Fred bobbed up and down in response, and I laughed. What other surprises did this house hold?

I caught sight of another paddock outside the atrium and noticed two fallow deer and two little white goats, not far from the swimming pool. Whatever John was, he was definitely an animal lover.

By dinner time, as I made myself something to eat, I could hear Fred chattering away to himself. He was having entire conversations and laughing. I shouted from the kitchen, 'Hey, Fred, are you having fun?'

'Oh, Fred, ha-ha-ha-ha,' he chuckled back.

I said goodnight and went up to John's bedroom, flopped on his huge bed, turned on the giant TV and flicked through his videos.

'Hmm, porn, porn, Doris Day, Rock Hudson, My Fair Lady, porn, oh and what do you know, more porn,' I muttered to myself. It had been a long day so I decided to skip the TV and snuggled down for the night. At 11pm I woke to a phone ringing. Turning on the bedside light, I tried to work out which one it was.

'Ah, it's okay. It's the business one,' I said to myself. It was John making sure I had settled in.

'Yes, everything is fine, thanks. Actually, I wanted to ask you about Fred,' I said. 'How come he's so vocal?'

'So you've met Fred,' John sighed. 'My mother lived with me for a while in the house and she struck up a friendship with Fred. She was always shouting for me, and Fred picked up on that, as well as all the conversations she used to have with me. The thing about my mother is, well, she was getting on in years and kind of repeated things a lot. Fred couldn't help but pick up on them. Sorry. It's like having my mother in bird form. He's only 30, you know. Parrots live for about 90 years. I could have another 60 years of my mother's voice.'

I stifled a laugh. Well, at least Fred was explained. I went back to sleep until 2am, when a phone rang.

'Yeah, yeah, John, I'm coming,' I mumbled, then I realised that it wasn't the business phone at all. It was the antique phone. Now when someone says 'Don't' for no apparent reason, it provides an almost irresistible temptation. I picked up the phone.

'Hi. Are you naked?' asked a husky voice.

'Excuse me, it's 2am and I'm trying to sleep,' I replied, taken aback. I hung up.

An hour later, the phone rang again. The voice was different, but the question was the same. Was I naked? I listened for a bit to the stranger and then made my excuses. At least now I knew what the antique phone was for.

The next morning was sunny and warm. I walked down to the stables where I met the other grooms, Sam and Jenny, and Sylvia, a woman in her thirties, who was John's stable manager. I watched with fascination as Sam polished the feet of one of the Arab horses. First he polished it with floor wax, then he sanded it back with fine sandpaper until it was smooth and clean, then he applied wax again. A third time and the hoof was finished. It was as shiny as a conker by the end of the process.

In another barn there were carriages and traps for the horses to pull. Sam took me upstairs, and I was astonished to see a collection of dolls' houses in the loft, some large enough for a toddler to walk around in and all furnished with miniature sofas, rugs and tables. Nearby, the bulldogs were kept — 20 runs and lots of these snuffling bandy-legged canines, whose every need was tended to by Stuart.

Stuart wasn't pleased to see me but he showed me around, proud of the puppies and breeding stock. 'We have five bitches who are our top girls,' he explained. 'They're called the Famous Five. Pretty famous too, I can tell you, winning everything out there.'

'Why do you have lemon everywhere?' I asked. 'There's even some in the house. Is it for the smell?'

'The bulldogs do not smell,' Stuart snapped indignantly. 'They are perfectly fragrant, thank you very much. The lemons are to stop the dogs choking when it overheats. They can't stand heat over 70 degrees. The shape of their face and nose, and all the saliva they have, makes it impossible for them to breathe when it's hot. If a dog isn't breathing well, you open his mouth and squirt some lemon down there. It helps him breathe better. These lemons save lives.'

I made a mental note to remember that, since there were a couple of puppies that were supposed to come up to the house. Why they needed to come to the house at all was a mystery to me. They had all the mod cons in the kennels, right down to a pooper-scooper system, alarms and air conditioning.

'Wow, this is seriously high-tech stuff.' I was pretty impressed but Stuart just looked aloof.

'Of course it is. These dogs are seriously valuable. They only have babies by caesarean because their pelvic spaces are so small. Each bitch will have three litters maximum and is insured for $20,000. The pups cost a lot of money too. They deserve the best. John would not give them anything less.'

Later I went out and explored the little village, falling in love with it and its rows of cute wooden houses, just like a film set. I shopped for groceries in the local store, ready for John's return. He was tired when he came back, and was pleased with my organisation of meals and the household. After his return we shared coffee each morning in the atrium, and always included Fred in our conversations. One morning, John tried to kiss me. That threw me. I decided I had to lay down some boundaries.

'Sorry, but I need to know what the situation is here. I know I cook, clean and look after the home, and tend to your guests. What else am I supposed to do?'

John frowned.

'I think you know there is more to the job than that,' he said. 'But if you don't want that, then I understand. I am happy with your work here. I trust you will be discreet?'

'Of course, that's not a problem at all.'

And I certainly had to be discreet during my time at the house. At times it was like being in one of those strange B-grade movies, a gay version of a Carry On film, with naked men in unexpected places and cheeky situations. One day I went into the lounge to vacuum the floor and found John and a hunky young Italian man, both naked, watching a film.

'Will you join us?' John asked hopefully.

'I'm cleaning, for goodness' sake,' I muttered, getting them to lift their bare legs so I could vacuum beneath them.

Sometimes John would go to see his partner Bob in New York. I began seeing the police chief's son Tom, who was bisexual. This was early 1982, and everyone was very promiscuous. It was nothing serious, and I simply enjoyed the cheerful, normal company, away from the strangeness of John's lifestyle. I noticed that John wasn't exactly a forceful person, despite his financial success. Within a short time I realised that he actually wanted me to boss him about and keep him in check. After a meal in the village restaurant he took it a step further and let me sign the credit card slip with his name.

'I know it's not hard to copy,' he said simply. 'Besides, it's handy if you can do it.'

I wondered how far I could push this submissive streak in him.

'You drive the car,' I said firmly as we left the restaurant. 'But I want you to wear that hat and chauffeur me.' He happily popped the chauffeur's cap on and drove me where I told him to go.

I started to enjoy my time there, but I was aware that I was riding less and took up jogging to keep in shape. No way was I going to pile on the kilos again. John also gave me an Arab to ride. The one he chose was a shy creature and I thought he might be a waste of time until I paired him up with one of John's pets, a llama. The two fell madly in love and the horse became full of confidence, although he was never to shape up as anything impressive. But the exercise kept me fit and I was happy with that.

I wasn't happy about the puppies in the house though. They lasted two days then I told John to get them back to the kennels. As I had come to expect, he complied. I think he liked to have someone take control of his life and remove some of the huge responsibility he had, for businesses, people, money, dogs and horses.

I also had to pick up the pieces when tragedy struck the bulldog kennels. It happened when John was at a conference. Stuart, who was an alcoholic, had fallen asleep without checking the air conditioning. That afternoon an alarm went off in the kennel building. Sylvia, the stable manager, and I arrived at the same time.

'It's for the air conditioning,' Sylvia said. 'The alarm means it's bust. God, let's hope Stuart is in there, keeping the dogs cool.'

But no, Stuart was drunk and sleeping in his room, and the dogs were desperately overheated. One at a time, Sylvia and I picked up these surprisingly heavy creatures, which were panting and near-death, and took them to the swimming pool. Ben, the police chief, arrived with Tom, and they helped us splash water on the dogs. We all stood in the pool, drenched but desperate. In the end, eighteen of the twenty dogs died, including four of the Famous Five.

Stuart panicked when he was woken up. 'John will go mad, he'll attack me, he might even kill me!' he wailed.

I told him to leave and come back in a couple of days, when and if John had cooled down. I was worried about how John would take the news about his dogs. He was due back that day, and there was a pile of dead dogs beside the pool. It was a terrible sight. I decided to ring him before he arrived.

Amazingly, he was calm and simply said he would see me later. I could tell he was absolutely shattered when he arrived at the house. His ashen face gave it away as he stroked the two dogs that had survived the terrible event. Later he admitted, 'I think I would have killed Stuart if he had been here. How could he let my dogs die like this? My poor babies.'

When a sheepish Stuart did come back, two days later, he was told to leave immediately. He didn't even get to take the nice little sports car John had given him as an ex-lover.

Once that episode was over life settled down for a bit, until Bob, John's partner, came to visit. As soon as the impending visit was confirmed, John's mood changed.

'Look, things are tricky with Bob. We fight, and I mean a lot. It will be ugly and if you want to go out, I understand. Just take my credit card and stay out as long as you want.'

He was nervous and upset, and I half-expected to find that Bob was some vile monster. When I finally met him, he was a tall, quite charming man, who shook my hand warmly. But the tension between John and Bob was almost palpable and I didn't like being around the two of them.

Later I made dinner for them, then I went to bed early. When I got up the next morning I couldn't find John anywhere. A strange, menacing mood hung over the whole house. 'Hmm, I don't like this one bit,' I confided to Fred, who ruffled his feathers in sympathy. None of the other staff had seen John either. I was about to ring the Boston apartment, to see if he had gone there, when Bob appeared. He was glowering at me.

'Peter, you work for me now,' he said. 'John is gone.'

I shook my head. 'No way, Bob. I work for John. It's that simple.' The first chance I got, I went to the garage and got out the sports car Stuart had been made to leave behind. Then one of the grooms appeared.

'The horses are gone,' he said, his face pale with shock. 'They've been taken away in the large truck. It must have happened in the night. Bob's going nuts.'

I was determined to get to the bottom of the situation. I phoned the apartment in Boston and a wave of relief washed over me when John answered. At least Bob hadn't done something sinister with him and the horses. He asked me to drive to Boston and that's exactly what I did, taking the sports car.

A miserable, tear-stained John answered the door to the apartment. 'Bob has a string of other lovers and I can't bear it. I know I'm just as bad, but for him to tell me that he's doing that too, it's just so terrible. I've left him, Peter. It's over.'

He also revealed that Sylvia had moved the 12 Arab stallions and 92 mares during the night. They were hidden in Florida, safe from Bob. It was going to be a complex break-up.

'You don't know the darkest parts of it,' he warned me. 'I can't tell you just now. Take the car, and here's some cash. Go home to Arkansas. I will contact you soon.'

It was a strange situation, but I was happy to head back to Little Rock and see Karen again. We hugged until our arms almost went numb.

'Tell me about your adventures,' she asked, delighted to have me back.

'I don't think they're quite over yet,' I said, and my feeling was right. A few days later I heard from John again. He asked me to drive the sports car back to Boston. I was happy to do the long drive, as it was a chance to have a road trip and see some more of America. When I arrived a very thin and tired John told me the latest developments in this weird saga.

He had found out that Bob was milking cash from their business accounts. One of Bob's lovers had committed suicide, adding to the scandal, and Bob had fled the country, taking millions of dollars and important documents with him. He had also poisoned the remaining horses at the farm before fleeing. It was a sad, bizarre situation. I guess it's true what they say: money can never buy you happiness, and the more you have, the more you want. The whole situation had imploded on these two men, leaving a string of tattered lives in its wake. I was glad to leave the apartment and head back to Arkansas on a Greyhound bus, back to the safe, ordinary life I suddenly longed for.

For a short time, I was happy. But I was still unsettled. I had missed my chance to compete at the World Championships later that year, but there was a bigger goal ahead, the Olympics in 1984. As if my thoughts had travelled across the Atlantic, I suddenly received a phone call from Selma Brandl. It was wonderful to hear her warm German voice again. We swapped news, and then she delivered a bombshell.

She had moved to another stable and was training a rider called Marc for eventing and showjumping — and ultimately, she hoped, for the Olympics. Would I come back and be her assistant? I bit my lip. It was too good an opportunity to miss — but how would I tell Karen I was leaving?

She took it badly.

'Why? Aren't you happy here with me? I can't believe you would do this. Am I nothing to you?'

I tried to comfort her, but she pushed me away.

'No, don't touch me. Just leave me alone. You should have told me you had no intention of sticking around. Then I wouldn't have done this.'

'Done what?' I asked, distraught at her fury and anguish.

'Fallen in love with you,' she said angrily. 'You know, you've never told me that you love me. Not once.'

I hung my head. It was true. I was in love with horses, not people, at this time in my life. Damaged by my childhood, I couldn't face any kind of conditional love, the kind that humans apparently need to give each other. There are always strings attached, expectations about the future, and at that point in my life I wasn't ready for all that. I wasn't able to love anyone or anything except horses, which gave absolute, unconditional love. But I couldn't tell Karen that. Three years ago I finally wrote to Karen and apologised. By that stage I was well into my illnesses and had a different perspective of my life. In 1982, I couldn't see into the future and I didn't know how unfair I was being to this strong, fiery, passionate young woman.

It was a sad farewell, but as I boarded the plane I felt a pang of excitement. This was it: the biggest challenge of all. My work for Selma, with all her expertise, would be my gateway to the Olympics. I would get to the games, whatever it took.

Chapter 18

I had gone to Germany in March 1982 with my heart still aching from hurting Karen. Maybe it was karma for this deed that made this time with Selma so difficult. It wasn't Selma herself who caused the problems. She was her lovely, positive, vibrant self and very happy to see me again.

Claudia had given up riding and become a physiotherapist, and Selma had quickly been snapped up by another German rider's family. Marc was a quiet, blond 18-year-old whose father had made a fortune from neon lighting. He had already excelled in the junior classes and was now expected to go on to the senior league with just as much success. As if that wasn't a big enough burden for a young man to carry, he was also a top pianist and studying for exams. The pressure was etched into his prematurely grown-up face.

'That boy should be out partying and letting his hair down,' I told Selma. 'How on earth can they expect him to cope?'

Selma shrugged. 'It's the German way, Peter. You should know that by now.'

She was right. During my time training with Claudia I had seen how much German parents expected of their offspring. Children started school at 7.30am and finished at 6.30pm. They had copious amounts of homework and had to be the absolute best in their field, leaving little room for fun. I wondered how many went off the rails in a big way.

Marc was doing his own little bit of rebellion, I soon discovered. He had a girlfriend who was 24, a full six years older than him, and from a family with not quite as much money as his. These were two terrible sins in the eyes of his parents, who viewed the young woman as a gold-digger. I felt sorry for Marc, having to put up with this kind of bias, but as I got to know his father I realised that this man had come from the hardest background imaginable and prized hard work above all else.

Heinrich was a short, round man with grey hair. 'I was a peasant boy and very poor, you know,' he told me one day, his face filled with emotion. 'At the end of the Second World War, I was with my mother. My father was dead, killed in the fighting, and she had hidden me from the Nazis, who wanted me to join the Hitler Youth movement. She knew it was a bad thing. We lived in the Black Forest area, near Munich. The day after the war ended, we walked out of our house, thinking everything would now be okay. An American soldier, who didn't know the war had finished, shot my mother. She died in my arms. I was 13.'

Heinrich told me how he had moved north and found work in a factory making neon lights. He worked his way up until he managed the company, and eventually bought it, turning it into one of the biggest neon lighting companies in the world. I could tell from his son's face that this was a tale everyone in the family had heard many times. But I was impressed by this little man's fortitude, and began to understand why it was so important to him that his son should succeed in life.

'Marc has it so much easier than I did,' he said, while Marc's lips thinned a little at his words. 'He doesn't know how lucky he is.' We were at the beautiful main house on the property that Heinrich owned, having Sunday dinner, a meal he cooked every week without fail. The fare was always the same too, following a recipe his mother had taught him. White sausage and cauliflower were boiled until they became a mushy stew, then potato and onion were added. It looked awful but tasted delicious. Heinrich and I drank beer from steins; Marc was considered too young.

Marc's riding was going well, even if his family life was a little difficult at times. He was competing on horses owned by Germany's rich elite, which also added pressure. The owners expected good results. One of the horses belonged to a diamond dealer whose girlfriend was a willowy international model, always dripping with jewels. After one event where Marc had done well on their horse, this couple held a celebratory party. I have never seen so many dead animals worn by so many rich people at one time. While the rest of the world appeared to be turning against fur, Germans couldn't get enough of the stuff, and the type of fur you wore spoke volumes about your status. Marc's father was in a bearskin coat, the dark brown pelt reaching almost to the floor. His mother was in black mink, shaped against her tiny svelte body, and had her hands tucked into a fat mink muff. Marc came in wearing a red fox fur-coat that went to his calves, and his girlfriend was in a beautiful grey mink coat.

'Wow, she looks gorgeous,' I commented to the diamond dealer's girlfriend, who was in silver fox. The woman sniffed indignantly.

'She looks crass and under-educated,' she spat. 'It is inappropriate for a woman of her age and low standing to wear mink. She should be in seal or marmot. Mink is for women of achievement, not trashy gold-digging girls. Wearing that coat simply shows everyone her ignorance.'

Marc and his girlfriend didn't stay long at the party.

And I didn't stay as long as I had hoped with Selma. I learned a lot while I was there, and enjoyed working with Marc and his family. In fact, Heinrich was so pleased with me that he gave me tickets to the World Championships, the ones I had hoped to attend with Fez. I was very touched by his kindness. The thorn in this bed of roses was Unn, a Swedish woman who was the head groom. On reflection, I don't think Selma really ever explained my position to this rather grumpy woman. When I made suggestions to improve something, such as the feeding system, she went into horrific moods, making waves with the other staff about me. I tried to be friendly, but she wouldn't have one bit of it. I was onto a lose-lose with this woman, that was certain.

Selma liked a peaceful, happy environment, and still insisted on smiles, just as she had previously. There were few smiles from Unn and none when I was about. She manoeuvred the situation so that I was left with just Marc's horses to look after, and she had the rest of the stable. Communicating was very difficult and Selma was starting to get embarrassed, especially after Heinrich became aware of the problem.

I have never liked tension, and when I saw it was affecting Selma I decided that I had done all I could and things had now reached boiling point. There was no way Unn would leave. All I could do was hand in my notice.

Selma accepted with sadness. I think she was torn between Unn and me, and didn't know how to resolve our conflict. Heinrich was also sad to see me go. I handed back the tickets to the World Championships but he refused to take them, saying I had earned the chance to go, even if it was only as a spectator this time.

I also knew that I didn't have much chance of finding an Olympic-standard horse while I was there. It was time for me to go and chase my Olympic dream. I decided to go to England and check out what was on offer there, with the intention of returning to Germany to watch the World Championships in a few months' time. There was no bad feeling when I left, but definitely a sense of many things left unsaid. When I reached England I wrote to Selma to try to explain my feelings a bit more. I think, and hope with all my heart, that it smoothed the troubled waters a little.

In England I stayed with Baroness Barth von Whrenalp, who was a patron of Mark Todd's. She had recently moved to Wincanton House, a huge mansion. We had become friends after meeting at events in England, and she had been keen for me to work for her. In between working her horses I spent time with Hamish Cameron, a New Zealander who was on a scholarship with Captain Mark Phillips. At this time the captain was still married to Princess Anne and they lived at Gatcombe Park, not far from the baroness's home. Their cook, a red-haired girl, was also a friend of mine and I sometimes went to visit. One day, Princess Anne walked in as I was chilling out in the stables. She sat down and chatted with me for a while, mostly about horses. I was struck by the fact that this royal woman had no airs or graces, just a deep love of horses, and concern for the sport.

'What do you think of them using shredded newspaper for bedding?' she asked me. This was a new thing in England, and we discussed the pros and cons. I got the feeling she might have thought shredding tabloids was the best thing you could do with them, although this was before the newspapers began to really get their claws into the royal family. Hamish was riding for the Queen at one event and we went in Anne's little truck, which had the number-plate ANNE 1. Just like the princess, it was nothing fancy, just a good practical truck that got there and back without any fuss.

While I was at Wincanton House I suddenly heard from my dear stepmother Bud, the gracious, upper-class woman who had married my down-to-earth no-nonsense Kiwi dad Stan.

'My dear, we are in London,' she said. 'My mother is having her 90th birthday and we are here for the party, staying at a little place near Victoria Station. It would be simply wonderful to see you. Can you come?'

It was not long since I had met up with Bud's mother Vera. She had fallen and hurt her hip at the time, and wasn't doing well. The baroness had suggested a different doctor, whose name sounded familiar. I should have guessed really. He was the Queen's personal doctor. He was happy to see Vera, and whatever he prescribed — I think it was a homeopathic treatment — did the trick.

The party was to be held in Kent at the home of Pippa, one of Bud's nieces. I took the train to the apartment in London where Stan and Bud were staying. Excited at the prospect of seeing Stan again, I walked in with a big smile on my face, ready to hug him and tell him how much I loved him. Not a chance. He was watching showjumping on television and didn't even look up. Bud was embarrassed.

'Stan? Peter is here to see you, darling.'

'Shhhh, I'm watching something here,' he replied grumpily.

I hid my disappointment. All my life I had wanted to be closer to my father and to be accepted by him. He hadn't seen me for years, but I was still an annoyance. For a moment I was back in the garage of our house in Whangarei, wondering how I would feign excitement at the chance to oil some sprockets, or whatever they were called.

Kind, gentle-hearted Bud saw my sadness and gave me a warm hug. 'Don't mind him, Peter. He's pleased that you are here, he truly is. He's just preoccupied at the moment, and a bit jetlagged. Don't take it to heart.'

But I did. How could I not take it to heart? Things got even worse at the party, where I heard my father waxing lyrical about the pride and joy of his life. 'He's such a clever boy, he really is. I'm very impressed by how far he has gone.' No, it wasn't me. It was Bud's grandson Matthew that he was talking about. I never got a mention all day and Stan barely acknowledged me as his son.

When he did finally talk to me, I wished he hadn't.

'Peter, you've been a chef. Why don't you go behind the table and serve everyone?' he said.

I was taken aback. Although I knew Vera quite well and was a guest at the party, my own father was treating me like a servant in front of these upper-class people. I couldn't wait for the party to end.

Years later, I would find out that Stan had dreaded going to England and having to mingle with Bud's aristocratic family. A true working-class Kiwi bloke, he believed everyone was equal, and he didn't know how to fit in. But whatever the reasons behind his behaviour towards me it was wrong, and it hurt. I didn't stay over. I headed straight back to Wincanton and back to work.

I must have been having a streak of bad luck, as not long after this I fell off a mare I was working and dislocated my shoulder. The baroness, like the Queen's doctor a great believer in homeopathy, rubbed arnica into the traumatised joint. From then on I would keep arnica and comfrey, both soothing treatments, in my horse gear for use on the horses and me.

Despite the baroness's kindness and the pleasant surroundings I wasn't settled in England. I wasn't earning enough money to compete at the best levels and the horses weren't as good as I had hoped. I didn't even have the money for the fare to Germany for the World Championships, which were a few weeks away in August 1982. I ended up giving the tickets Heinrich had given me to Beth Fife, the friend who had hidden Fez for me, and who was now in England. She was very happy and later wrote to tell me she had met up with Mark and his parents at the event, finding them charming people.

I decided to go to London and earn some decent money so that I could ship myself, my saddle and my gear over to America, then on to Australia. I wasn't sure why I chose Australia as my destination, but it had been a good place for me in the past, and my sisters were both based there.

My first night in London was spent at Bud's family apartment. As I was walking the streets around the area, looking for a job, I passed a place called Café Smiles in Jermyn Street. A card in the window said 'Waiters wanted'. The position was evenings only, but I took it anyway. I had already found a place in a boarding house, and now I needed to get a second job.

I noticed an ad for masseurs in a men-only club in Old Bond Street, underneath a very posh barber's shop. I was told that at 30 I was a little old for massage work but just perfect as a daytime supervisor and receptionist. I started the next morning. It was a very respectable place, with a sauna and massage area in the middle of a gym. Everything was glass, so there was nowhere for anyone to have sex except the sauna. And some of that did go on. One of the masseurs was an absolutely huge boy of 17 who was training to be a weightlifter. He was saving money to go to the British Championships. I worked at the club until 4pm each day, then I started at Café Smiles. Soon I had enough money for my fare to the US. The plan was to fly from London to Miami, where Joan was now based, then later travel on to Australia, having accumulated sufficient funds for ongoing travel. Once I arrived in Miami the desire to contact Karen overwhelmed me. I rang and told her how much I had missed her.

'Can I come and see you, try again?' I asked gently. She had been quite cold throughout our chat, but I had known she would be like that. She was proud and fiercely protective of herself, and already wounded emotionally. I knew it would be a tough job to win her over again.

She paused before answering. 'No, I can't have you back, Peter. You broke my heart.'

'I want to come back to you, Karen. I really want you in my life. We can try again.'

'We can't. Sorry. It can't be.'

She hung up and I sat there in Joan's apartment letting the reality sink in. As heartbreaking as her decision was, I was determined to make something of my time in America en route to Australia. I started to look through the small ads in the newspapers and noticed a position for a secretary and companion to an elderly gentleman in Biscayne Bay, just south of Miami.

Frederick McLean Bugher was a billionaire with a fixation on his late mother. She had owned the Hope Diamond and was a leading socialite. Basically, I got the job because I told him I had a close relationship with my own mother.

'Ah, if you are good to your mother, you must be a good boy,' Frederick said. 'You are hired, starting immediately.'

His house was majestic, full of treasures and portraits. There was just me, Frederick and the security guard (a man in his mid-thirties who had started as a companion to the old man); the cook and the maid came in each day. I knew I needed $400 to get to Australia, and I was determined to stick it out long enough to save the money. But from the first day it was clear that this was one weird job.

'Sit with me in the Japanese room,' Frederick instructed, indicating an atrium with silk tapestries on the walls and permanently drawn blinds. Apart from the guard, whose footsteps I would hear on the gravel outside the window every hour, I only heard and saw the old man. It took him two days to regale me with the story of his life. We broke for dinner, which we ate in a large, long dining room with a black-and-white marbled floor. I learned that the reason he had the guard was because a burglary had netted two million dollars' worth of art and antiques.

Every so often Frederick would pee in his pants and I would have to sit there with a hairdryer, drying them off, as he droned on and on. It didn't take me long to realise that I was basically a prisoner of this mad old gent. I wanted to see the gardens, but he wouldn't let me out of his sight. Being his secretary meant I also had to deal with some paperwork. For instance, one day he received a letter from the US Government offering a billion dollars for some tin mines he owned in Omaha. He refused to accept the Government's offer, even though the letter said that if it came to a time of war they would take the mines anyway because the material was needed, and would pay him a much lower amount. Frederick just snorted and said he was pretty sure that wouldn't happen.

For someone so rich, he was incredibly stingy. He allocated $50 a week to food for himself, me and the security guard. Not 50 each, 50 in total.

'I'm pretty hungry, Frederick,' I admitted once or twice, but he just scolded me for gluttony.

'You need to chew slower and make your food last longer,' he rasped in his croaky voice. He didn't have an ounce of fat on his bones and I wasn't surprised at all.

At night I slept in his mother's room, down the end of a long, narrow corridor. That first evening, after Frederick was in his bed, I tried to sneak down to the kitchen to get some food. His room was next to mine and connected by a small doorway. This was to remain unlocked, so he could call through to me in the night. Between Frederick's room and the kitchen there were seven doors. I quickly discovered that every single one was kept locked at night, and the keys were held by Frederick.

The job got even more bizarre in the morning after I had slept a poor first night, with a rumbling stomach. I had to go through to Frederick's room in my T-shirt and underpants and sit in the bed with him. He didn't touch me or anything like that.

'I just like a nice young man beside me,' he explained, as if it was the most reasonable request in the world. So there I was, half-dressed and sitting in bed with a man old enough to be my great-grandfather, with the looks of a tortoise minus its shell. I had to sit there while the maid, let in through the seven doors by the security guard, brought him a cup of tea in bed. The poor girl looked quite startled when she walked in with her tray and saw the two of us sitting side by side.

'Stop gawping, girl, and put the tray down. Carefully, don't you dare spill a drop,' Frederick snapped. I tried to give the girl an 'it's okay, don't worry, just put up with it' look, but she was obviously pretty unsettled by his rudeness.

I ended up staying in the house for eight days, and Frederick sacked three maids in that time. I couldn't stay any longer with the crazed old control freak. Since I had been kept prisoner in the house I hadn't spent anything, and the amount I was due for my first week was $400, the very sum I needed for my ticket to Australia. During the eight days I had had to listen to his life story four times. The only time I was allowed out was to go to the supermarket with the cook, a lovely black lady, and even then Frederick was petulant about being left for an hour.

'Be careful, honey,' the cook told me. 'He's a crazy old thing. But then, you're a smart young boy, and I don't think you'll be around for too long. Just take care.'

I realised that the way to get out of this unbearable situation was the same way I had got in. I played the 'mother' card.

'Frederick, I'm afraid I have to leave your employ,' I said, praying it would work. 'My dear mother needs me immediately. I have to go to her. I'm sure you understand.'

Frederick's wrinkly old face crumpled with emotion. Of course I could go, he said, as mothers mattered most in the world. A tidal wave of relief flooded me.

I phoned Joan and asked her to come and get me. She was a bit puzzled, as I had only been gone just over a week. 'I can't tell you anything at the moment,' I whispered down the phone. 'Just come and get me. Please.'

Before I left, I made sure Frederick knew that I expected to receive the $400 in wages that I was owed.

'Ah yes, pay, pay, I shall arrange that immediately,' he said. 'I'm afraid I don't keep cash in the house. Burglars, you know. Will a cheque do?'

Having seen some of the paperwork attesting to his wealth, I had no fears that a cheque would bounce. 'A cheque will be fine,' I said.

He pressed the cheque into my hand as I left and I wanted to whoop with joy.

Sadly, I had underestimated the cunning old weasel. As the gates clanged shut behind my mother's car and we drove away from that divine prison, I glanced at the cheque and groaned. It was unsigned. I returned later that day and with a grumpy resignation, he signed the cheque.

Chapter 19

I had no reason to stay in America. I couldn't work legally because I didn't have a green card, and Karen didn't want me. The only chance I had of getting to the Olympics was to make some decent money and get a first-class horse. My sisters were both in Australia — Yvonne in Sydney and Kay on the Gold Coast, near Surfer's Paradise — so I borrowed the fare, packed up my saddle and meagre belongings, and headed to Sydney, in time for Kay's birthday. It was the winter of 1982.

I stayed briefly with Yvonne, who now had two children: a baby called Sarah and a three-year-old, Anna. Then I travelled to Kay's home, which she shared with her husband Ron and their two children, six-year-old Chris and three-year-old Vicky. Within minutes of my arrival Vicky had bowled me off the camper stool where I was sitting, drinking a beer with Ron.

'Hey, Uncle Peter, watch me,' she chirped, and immediately scampered up a nearby tree, where she started to perform amazing trapeze tricks.

'Wow, how does she do all that?' I asked Kay.

Kay smiled. 'She's a live wire. It's constant.'

She clearly took after Kay. I admired my sister and the new life she had made for herself in Australia. She had a business making lingerie items in her home, piece-work. Every day she would run off 200–300 pairs of crotchless knickers edged with fluffy swansdown, and the little feathers seemed to be all over the house. As well as this she had a small leather-gear shop called Leather and Lace, which included bondage clothes. Ron had a busy air-conditioning business. Everything had fallen into place for my special baby sister and I couldn't have been happier for her.

I decided to stay in Surfer's Paradise, where I found work in restaurants, made some good friends, played backgammon for money sometimes, got a great tan, rode some horses, and enjoyed the fun, relaxed lifestyle. At Christmas Joan came over for a family reunion with her mother, Myrtle. Myrtle, you may remember, had had four husbands. She had given up Joan and her sister Betty when they were just babies, something Joan had never forgiven her for. I knew Myrtle had a mean streak but this reunion would open my eyes to just how nasty she really was. It would also give me a heartbreaking insight into why Joan had found it so hard to be a mother herself.

The reunion was to begin with a party at my aunt Betty's house on Christmas Eve. Betty had moved many years before and had done well with motels, wholesale grocery barns and making T-shirts for the tourist trade. The day before the big gathering — which was to include Kay, Yvonne and Betty's family as well as Joan — we all met at the house for afternoon tea. It was nice to see Auntie Betty again. As soon as she saw me she said, 'Goodness me, Peter, you look just like my father. Your eyes, the shape of your face and your chin are exactly like his. You are his image.'

It was a sweet thing to say, or so I thought. As soon as I met Myrtle, however, I found out that this wasn't quite the compliment I thought it was, at least in her eyes. I had only met Myrtle a few times, and the last time was when I was about 12. Throughout her life Joan had a stormy relationship with Myrtle, and was always seeking her love. The problem was that Myrtle didn't seem to have an ounce of love in her for anyone.

I walked in, smiled at Myrtle, and said, 'Hello Gran.' Immediately she stared at me and her face turned a dark purplish colour. 'Oh my God, you look exactly like George Allen. Get away from me. I hated him and I hate you!' She turned away.

I'd never had much time for Myrtle, having seen how she treated my mother, so I tried not to let this get to me. I just shrugged, saying, 'Ah well, I guess that's it for you and me then, Gran.' I went to the other side of the room and started chatting to some cousins. At one point I caught Myrtle checking me out with undisguised disgust and I made a point of making eye contact. She immediately turned away.

I managed to get through the afternoon but there was more to come the following day, Christmas Eve. By now Joan and Betty's half-sister Lexie, from Myrtle's third marriage, had also arrived for the reunion, and the three sisters decided to have some time with Myrtle on their own. It was supposed to be a happy time, during which they would share memories and maybe bury a few hatchets.

Myrtle, however, was determined to make it memorable for all the wrong reasons. I heard about it from my mother later. Apparently she went quite berserk, pointing at Joan with a trembling finger and letting loose all her poison.

'I hate you,' she shrieked. 'I love Betty and Lexie, but I hate you. You were conceived out of hate. From the very start, you were hateful. That George virtually raped me that night and you were the result.' She was so enraged that she began foaming at the mouth. Betty and Lexie tried to calm her but Myrtle was having none of it, screaming over and over, 'I hate you, I hate you.' Joan was devastated and left. Betty and Lexie decided to take tough action with their mother.

'You can't treat Joan like that,' Betty told Myrtle, who had calmed down amazingly quickly once she realised her tantrum had had the desired effect on Joan. 'If you can't keep yourself under control you'll have to leave.'

Then they told Myrtle exactly what they thought of her years of torment of Joan: she had manipulated the family all her life, been selfish, and hated her own daughter for something that wasn't her fault. Myrtle just looked smug and refused to accept that she had done anything wrong.

A decision was made and Myrtle was put on a bus to her sister in Sydney. Christmas Day went ahead without her and we all had a wonderful day. Joan was perfectly gracious at the reunion and hid her pain well. But I knew now just how toxic Myrtle was to my mother, and it was so awful my heart ached for her. I realised that much of what she had done when I was a child was simply because she didn't know any better. She had been mothered with hate, manipulation and guilt, and that was all she knew. But she had managed not to transfer the sheer poison of Myrtle to us and had given us some happy memories too, such as days at the beach or walking in the bush, cooking together or simply helping her get ready for a night out. She was the best mother she could be and she loved us.

With the family gathering over, it was time for me to make a move. The year had passed with astonishing ease, but now it was time for me to concentrate and work on my goals. My Olympic dream remained unfulfilled and I had still to find the perfect horse. I thought about ways in which I could make big money quickly.

Sex, drugs and rock-and-roll seemed to be the best means. I couldn't play guitar, I wasn't in a position to become a big dope dealer, at least at this stage, so that left sex. I would do anything to secure the horse I needed. So I became a sex worker.

I sold most of my horse gear and moved to Sydney, the heart of the gay sex industry in Australia. Working on the street was a definite no-no; I wanted to work out of an establishment. I managed to get an interview for Brett's Boys, a well-known men's brothel in Paddington. I thought this might involve taking my clothes off, but no, I must have looked just fine as I was. Tanned, muscular and looking good, I passed the interview straight away and was offered a job, starting at 10am the next morning.

I was a tiny bit nervous as I pushed open the door to Brett's Boys the next day and went inside.

'Who are you?' said a piercing voice.

I turned around and saw a tall, quite broad transsexual with a big, blonde helmet of hair and lashings of make-up. She looked me up and down, and I remember seeing her nails, huge curved talons that seemed more of a disability than any kind of asset. Remember, this was 1983, and everything had to be big to be fashionable: hair, nails, shoulder pads and egos.

'I'm Peter,' I said.

'Ah yes, the new boy. Hello, I'm Stella. Come on, darling, sit down, sit down.'

It didn't take me long to work out that Stella was one of the madams and therefore somebody to be in favour with. A pre-op transsexual, she had a fine pair of implants that created a cleavage you could get trapped in, but she still had to have the final surgery.

I was to meet many transsexuals during this time. Some were incredibly beautiful, including one who became the face of Max Factor cosmetics. Another was Tiffany, who was stunningly beautiful and had a successful modelling career but became hooked on heroin. I remember her coming in once with her lovely cleavage all speckled with stubble because she was too wasted to shave her chest. The other transsexuals, or 'queens' as they were known, quickly became fed up with her drug addiction. The worst thing a queen can use to another is her male name and Tiffany, originally Terry, was nicknamed Terry-dactyl. It was apt but cruel. If you get on a queen's bad side, you're in big trouble.

I cottoned on within five minutes of arriving at the brothel that Stella was strong-willed, sharp-witted and a real force to be reckoned with. As I sat down the phone rang and she picked it up. I saw her scowl and a string of expletives come out. Slamming the phone down, she turned to me, immediately calm. 'Bloody school holidays and kids with nothing better to do. It's always the same, darling. Little bastards.'

Stella then quizzed me about my assets. Yes, I had an all-over tan, yes, there was some hair on my chest, oh, and yes, I was above average. She wasn't asking about my IQ. Then Stella gave me a tour of the building, a beautiful old brick terraced house in Paddington's Boundary Street. First there was the lounge area, where the clients came in and sat on sofas while the boys came in from the kitchen, said their names, walked around the room and out again. The madam would then go in, ask which boy they wanted, and allocate a room for the boy to take them to.

There were four rooms. The Blue Room was decorated with underwater scenes on the walls and had a high window. The Green Room had fake leopard-skin everywhere and Japanese parasols over the lights, as well as a big tiled mirror behind the bed. The theme in the Yellow Room was antique, and the bed had huge carved ends and side tables featuring those classic art-deco lamps with nudes curling around them. Finally, the Red Room had a harem look about it. It was at the back of the house, and had red velvet curtains, a big mattress on a low base, piles of velvet and satin cushions and a canopy over the top. It was quite a popular room if the client was ugly because it was the darkest.

At noon I got my first client, a truck driver. Stella had briefed me well. I took him to the Blue Room and told him to make himself comfortable.

'Undress if you like. I'll just get some towels and be back in a few moments,' I said, remembering Stella's advice to let the client get a sense of anticipation (which saved on foreplay) and a chance to decide if he wanted to be naked or not. I went downstairs, grabbed two towels and returned, pausing at the door to the Blue Room. This was it. It wasn't bad or good; it was just a job. After it was over I showed the client to the main bathroom so that he could freshen up. This was a hideous room, covered with grey marble tiles, with a big raised bath in bright pink bearing taps in the shape of swans' heads.

After that it was downstairs and payment, which was handed over to the madam. The rates were $30 for half an hour or $40 for an hour. Fifty percent of this went to the brothel. As far as wages for sex work went, men didn't earn much. Transsexuals earned $100 for a half-hour and $160 for an hour. Female prostitutes also made much more money than the men. I worked out pretty quickly that the best way to make decent cash was through tips. My wages for that first day were $30 plus $10 in tips. I knew I had to lift my game and gain Stella's confidence so that I would get more work. During the next few days I learned a bit more about Stella and Donjalle, another transsexual who helped Stella run the brothel. The chat between them was amazingly fast, and quite indistinguishable.

'What language are you talking?' I asked, completely unable to translate it.

'It's called Polari,' Stella explained. 'It came from the British merchant seamen and is still spoken on a lot of the big cruise liners. Think of it as a kind of Cockney rhyming slang with a twist.'

I soon picked up some of the words, which was handy when you needed to speak in front of clients without them knowing what you were saying. 'Riah' was hair, 'jarry' meant food, to 'ogle' something meant to look at it, 'down your screech' meant down the throat, while going for 'a gin' meant a walk. That didn't have anything to do with the drink gin. It was a local addition to the lingo from the word for Aboriginal women, which was 'gin', and it meant going walkabout. We used it when we needed to pop out to the shops across the road or take a breath of fresh air.

It didn't take long for the clients to blur. An Irish guy I was flatting with thought it was interesting to know a sex worker and used to quiz me about my clients. But unless they were particularly good-looking, very odd, had a giant appendage or a great sense of humour, I didn't remember them. I was fortunate to be 30, because this meant I didn't have to go with the much older men. They preferred the teenage 'himbos' who worked in the brothel and were happy to go with anyone.

I was living in a flat in King's Cross at this time; in a weird twist of fate, it was next door to the place I had stayed at when I came to Sydney for the first time, at the age of 16. I worked a lot in hotels, going on out-call, and Stella obviously liked me as she soon started passing me regular clients. In fact we became good friends and soon took on the role of big sister and big brother to the younger workers. Some of these boys had gone through incredible hardship and their stories were heartbreaking. I felt very protective of them. Apart from the sex work, I also had a job at a catering agency where I was rated as the best class of waiter and got lots of high profile jobs. I had switched to the night shift at the brothel and worked during the day for the catering agency. I also had a third job as a riding teacher at Centennial Park, something I fitted in when I could. I didn't mind having so much work — it was all for one reason: to get that Olympic-grade horse.

One of the positions the catering agency got me was as function supervisor for a prestigious wine company. I kept the books correct for them, and was able to take leftover food away at the end of functions. I would drop this at Brett's Boys for the workers, as some of the young ones didn't eat properly. As soon as they got any cash in hand they spent it on drugs. There would sometimes be two or three bottles of wine left over after functions, as clients might order and pay for a package of wine but not use it all. I would take this back too, and store it up so the boys could have a decent Christmas. Many of them had low self-esteem and no ambition, and Stella and I worked together to improve their situation. We helped them dress better, improve their speech and told them that they could make something of their lives.

Transsexuals always like to give people nicknames, and Stella called me Vera, because I was always dabbing aloe vera on myself or the boys for anything from grazes to spots. It's amazing stuff. One day Stella was talking about my love of aloe vera when I walked in. 'Ooh, 'allo Vera,' she quipped, and the name stayed. She never called me Peter again.

I ended up working at the brothel for nearly five months, and during that time I realised that the job was 25 percent sex and 75 percent counselling. Most of my clients were between 24 and 45, and wanted someone to take to dinner, talk to, and who would be good company. The sex only took up ten minutes of the whole time we spent together on each call. Kissing was always out. They tipped me if they wanted extra, and the more extreme the extra, the bigger the tip. But I didn't do anything too extreme very often, so the money had to be very good indeed. There were a few bizarre clients, such as the young man who just wanted me to bear-hug him naked then throw him against the wall. A rather well-known football player came in because he and his wife were going swapping and he wanted to know what to do with men. He was gorgeous and I didn't mind playing teacher. I also remember having one rather boring client, and tracing out dressage moves on his back while he did his business. Afterwards he gave me an extra tip for 'that nice thing you were doing on my back'.

I developed quite good relationships with some of the clients and spent about three nights a week at the Menzies, Regent and Wentworth Hotels, seeing about five clients each night. Ironically, the Menzies was the hotel I was supposed to get married in not long after this episode in my life.

During this time I was still looking for the horse of my dreams. I knew exactly what I wanted, so when I saw him I just knew he was the right one. His name was Dunedin and he was a soft sandy colour with a black mane and tail. The colour is called dun, and that's where his name came from. He was quite a mixed breed, but very talented and immediately I knew I had to have him. There was only one problem — his owner, Greg.

I met Greg the first time I went to the stables in Centennial Park where Dunedin was kept, and knew straight away that he was a gay man. He was dark, gorgeous and very attractive. We flirted, and I tried to find a way to get him to sell Dunedin. In the end he agreed to lease him to me. As Dunedin was only three years old I knew I had some time in which to work out a way to get him off Greg. By leasing him, I could start training him for bigger things while keeping in with Greg. I began seeing Greg and we ended up moving in together.

Greg was very handsome but terribly lazy. He knew I was a sex worker, and although I tried to have a break from it for a while, I ended up going back because Greg wasn't bringing in much money from his job in the railways. Sometimes I would act as the madam or sleep overnight at Brett's Boys, which brought in extra cash. One night Damien, who owned the catering agency, came in with

Graham, the man who owned the brothel, and there was an awkward moment as we chatted. Neither man knew I worked for the other.

'So, are you a client?' Damien finally asked.

'Actually, I work here,' I admitted. 'I guess I'm going to get fired by both of you.'

Graham and Damien looked at each other, had a brief discussion, and decided it was fine for me to do both jobs. I breathed a huge sigh of relief.

After we had been living together for about three months, Greg decided I could buy Dunedin. The price was $3000. I had that much money saved up, and I wanted to finish as a sex worker. I also wanted to split with Greg as it really wasn't working. I had been hanging in there only to keep him sweet so that I could eventually buy Dunedin. Soon after I paid him for the horse I moved out. I knew it would take four years to get Dunedin ready for the 1992 Olympics and I was keen to get started.

On my last night at the brothel I had one of those clients sex workers dread. I had gone pretty sour on the whole job, and when this man asked me to turn him on I told him to do it himself because I was only getting paid $15. Suddenly I felt him clasp me around the throat with both hands. My immediate reaction was to slap him.

'Don't do that,' I told him.

The man was quite upset, and said he wanted to go to the spa, which was downstairs next to the kitchen where the boys waited. Around the spa were plastic flamingos and artificial plants. That night the water in the pool seemed to have more chlorine in it than usual. It was not a pleasant place to be and I was keen to get it over with. Then the man tried to kiss me. It's the golden rule of sex work that you don't kiss clients, especially ones you're not that keen on. He was unhappy when I refused and in the end I told him to get out.

The next job was a young man who looked very handsome. 'I don't want to take my jeans off,' he said.

I told him it was okay for him to be naked and that I was fine with it. I wondered to myself why this attractive man wasn't out partying with his friends and having fun. But I soon found out. When the jeans did come off, I realised that he had a colostomy bag. As a professional, and a former hospital worker, I wasn't fazed at all. But when the third call of the night turned out to be another bloke with a colostomy bag I wondered if it was fate telling me to get out of that line of work. This man was very sweet, in his fifties and quite self-conscious about the bag, but I put him at his ease and it went well.

I don't remember the fourth client I had that night, but I do remember the fifth. He came in at 2am, just before I was about to finish. I kept hoping he wouldn't pick me, so that I could go home, but luck was against me. We went to the Red Room, and although it seemed a straightforward job to start with he began asking for all kinds of strange things. That was it. As soon as I was finished with that client I went to Stella and told her I wasn't going to do it anymore. She was disappointed to see me go, not least because we had become great friends, but I knew the burn-out rate was high and I never wanted to get close to that. In September 1983 I walked out of the sex industry and into the next big adventure of my life, one that would take me to the brink of marriage.

Chapter 20

While I was working as an instructor at the Centennial Park stables I had noticed a dark-haired girl who hung around with the other rich girls. These pampered young women had nothing better to do than shop and wait for the perfect husband to come along and take responsibility for keeping them in the style to which they were accustomed. Some of them took up riding to fill in the wait for marriage, and Varda was one of these.

A sleek, dark-haired Jewish princess of 20, she singled me out for attention, even though she knew I was bisexual and working in the sex industry. She was impossible to ignore. Her figure was perfect, like a thoroughbred horse, and she had short hair, cut in a fashionable style. Her huge brown eyes — her best feature — were fringed with long lashes. Like the other girls at the park, she only wore designer clothes and had the very best in horse gear for riding her collection of pretty pony hacks.

I wasn't looking for another relationship, with either man or woman, as my entire concentration was taken up with improving Dunedin. I adored this horse. He was so young but eager to learn. His colouring reminded me of a koala, with his soft fawn muzzle, black mane and tail, and creamy dun body.

Varda would ask me questions about the horse and occasionally about my job at the brothel, smiling coquettishly as I answered. She liked to flirt with me, and I knew not to take her too seriously. I wasn't particularly attracted to her, although I did appreciate her good looks. We became quite good friends.

When I quit as a sex worker, I decided I wanted to find a horse-related job so I could work on Dunedin at the same time. I've always been fortunate that, whenever I have needed employment, something has come out of the blue at just the right time. And this time was no exception. A racehorse trainer called Deirdre offered me a position at Bathurst, where her husband played polo and ran a stud. The horses they bred were first checked out for their racing abilities and if they were too slow — what is known as a 'sacked' racehorse — then they would be tried as polo ponies.

When Varda found out I was leaving for Bathurst, she was upset. 'Don't worry, I'll still be around,' I said, to cheer her up.

'Why don't I come too?' she suddenly suggested. 'I'm not doing anything much here. I'd love to learn more and improve my horsemanship.'

Even though it meant no money for her, she didn't care. Her father gave her plenty. Before I knew it, Varda was coming along and the two of us were stuck together in a tiny caravan in Bathurst. It was the autumn of 1984 and the weather was chilly. Of course, it wasn't long before we ended up in bed together to stay warm. The next step was predictable. We began having a relationship.

Varda was an easy girl to get along with. She knew I was bisexual and accepted it, and I was happy to be in a monogamous relationship. Things seemed to fall into place for us. We got on well and felt comfortable together. The next step was for me to meet her family.

Her father owned a huge kosher catering company that provided food for Sydney Airport, as well as its own restaurant and Jewish centres in the city. Varda's mother had died of cancer two years earlier, and just before she passed away Varda's oldest brother Peter was killed in a motorcycle accident. Her other brother, Stephen, had made a good match with a beautiful young Jewish woman who was about to have their first baby.

When I met Varda's father I was immediately fascinated by this tall, grey-haired man who lavished so much on his daughter and surviving son. 'What do you do?' he asked me. I told him about my qualifications and experience in the restaurant industry, as well as my equestrian achievements. He nodded gravely and I could tell he was reassured.

'So, you work in food. Good, that's good,' he murmured. 'I am in food also, as I'm sure Varda has told you. She loves horses too. I like her to have her horses. They keep her happy.'

I nodded, relieved that I seemed to have his approval.

Shortly after this, Varda's father offered me a job in his restaurant in Sydney. But there was more. He wanted to give us a house, one that he had found in Glenorie, a lifestyle suburb on the outskirts of the city. It had five acres and stables. I was blown away by his kindness. In the past I had always turned down gifts like this, but I was in a committed relationship with Varda and felt this was a good step for our future together. What's more, he was offering me a team of horses. How could I refuse?

In November 1984, Varda and I moved onto the property, bringing Dunedin and Varda's horses. I started working at the restaurant as kitchen supervisor, and eventually moved to front of house. At 4pm each day a junior rabbi would come and bless the kitchens. Everything seemed to be going so well. I became close to Varda's father and looked up to him as a father figure. He seemed to understand me and I thought I was getting to know him. We would talk for hours and were relaxed in each other's company. He called me Schneider, which is German for 'cloth-cutter' and the closest the language had to the word 'tailor', my surname. He didn't mind that I wasn't Jewish and that I wasn't going to convert.

I almost blew it one afternoon in the restaurant, however, when an elderly rabbi came in. A lovely man, he would usually choose something light and traditional from the menu, but that day he was having trouble deciding. I pointed out a few things that he might like to try, but nothing seemed to take his fancy.

'I know,' I said. 'What about a ham, cheese and tomato toasted sandwich?'

There was a silence as everyone in the restaurant stared. I had asked a rabbi if he wanted ham. Was I mad? Just as I realised my mistake the old rabbi started to laugh, waving away my apologies. He chuckled for a long time, and from that point on everyone knew I was not Jewish. But it didn't matter. I worked hard and kept the kitchens running well. It was an easy job for me. I don't like to twiddle my thumbs, so I started doing the market run every morning at 5am, collecting the fresh produce and delivering it to the restaurant. I would then work on the farm during the day, including training with Dunedin, fencing, remodelling the farm, and so on.

Early in 1985 Varda and I got engaged and began planning our wedding. Initially I was sure this was what I wanted. Everything seemed to be going well. However, I couldn't shake a creeping feeling of unease as we started making decisions about our big day. The wedding would be for 50 people, just a small affair. Varda's mother had always wanted her to get married in the Sydney Opera House, and we looked at a function suite there but decided against it, instead choosing the Menzies Hotel. This was one of the places where I had worked as an escort, and it seemed more than a little ironic that I would be getting married here almost two years later. The date was set for April 1985, a couple of months away. I noticed that Varda was starting to get increasingly insecure and didn't like me working at the restaurant. 'Don't leave me here,' she would say, pouting. But what could I do? It was my job.

I noticed that when she was at the restaurant she would walk past the till when her father was there and just stand, waiting, with her hand out. He would open the till and put some notes into her hand. If she felt it wasn't enough, he would pull out more money and give it to her. When she had enough, her perfectly manicured fingers would close over it and she would give him a huge, heart-melting smile and kiss him tenderly on his stubbled cheek.

Her father was kind enough to buy me a ute, which was an incredibly generous gift. I really appreciated his kindness, and I thanked him from my heart. We needed a ute for the smallholding, but this one was brand new. He also decided to buy Varda a new car. She chose the make, something sporty and compact, and ordered it in red. One morning the telephone rang and it was a man from the car company. They didn't have the car in red, only in blue. Was that okay, the man asked? I was just so grateful to have any vehicle, whatever the colour, that I said it was fine, and hung up without a second thought.

When Varda came in from checking her horses I mentioned the phone call.

'Blue?' she gasped. 'But I want red!'

'I know, but he can't get a red one so I said the blue one was fine.' I was puzzled by her expression. What happened next shocked me. Varda began to stamp her feet like a toddler. The stamping increased until she was virtually jumping.

'I want red! I want red! I don't want blue. Red!' she shrieked.

I realised that this was a full-scale tantrum on a scale I had never seen before, let alone from a grown woman. It sowed a seed of doubt in my mind. How well did I know this person that I was about to vow to spend the rest of my life with?

I bottled up my concerns and carried on as if everything was normal. But Varda became more and more erratic. I would find her crouched in a stable, crying and rocking like a distressed baby.

Comforting her was difficult, and at times she was inconsolable. I wondered what was changing this young woman into such an emotional wreck. Everywhere I went on the property, she followed me. If I was out building fences, there she was, watching my every move. Varda became a desperate shadow that haunted me. Occasionally she would break down and insist I was going to leave her. I would reassure her but that dark look never left her huge eyes. One night she refused to let me go to work. When I took off my farm clothes, she tried to put them back on me. Then she grabbed my restaurant clothes and ran off with them to stop me getting dressed.

'Don't leave me here,' she repeated over and over. 'I don't want to be alone. Don't go, I hate it when you go.'

'Varda, darling, I have to go to work,' I said, trying to grab my pants from her. I was used to dealing with Joan's mood swings and that helped me deal with Varda's behaviour. However, I was starting to work out that something much deeper was going on with her, and I wondered if this was the first time in her life that this needy, dark, troubled personality had surfaced.

For three days she did the 'taking my clothes' trick to keep me from going to work. By that stage she had begun screaming at me. Finally I had had enough of it, and I said loudly and firmly, 'That's enough!'

Varda was horrified, then furious. She picked up a cup and hurled it at me. Luckily it missed and smashed against the wall. I grabbed my clothes and went to work. Later I went to see her father.

'Peter, is everything all right?' he said with concern. I shook my head.

'I'm worried about Varda,' I told him, describing her behaviour over the past few weeks. He looked at me, his expression increasingly stony.

'Has she ever done anything like this before?' I asked. I felt so relieved to have told him, and I waited for him to advise me, like he usually did. Instead, he leaned towards me, his eyes suddenly cold and dead.

'You either marry her or you fuck off,' he said menacingly. I stared. This was totally out of the blue.

'What? I thought you and I got on well. What do you mean? I don't understand,' I said.

'No, you do understand. This was a deal. It was all arranged.'
That's when everything fell into place. The house, the horses, the job; it was all part of the deal for taking his daughter off his hands. Varda was disturbed and desperately needy, but with me as her husband the burden would be mine and not his. I understood immediately and it felt sickening. I had genuinely cared for Varda and wanted to be married to her but I couldn't go through with it now. It was all a sham, a business deal with her father. I was being bought.

When I got home that night Varda had gone to one of her friends' houses so she wasn't on her own while I was at work. I packed a trunk, put it in the van that I used to get the vegetables from the market, and then tried to get some sleep. The next morning I took the van to work and left a note at the kitchen to say the key could be found under the spare wheel. The note also said thank you and informed the restaurant that I was going back to New Zealand. I arranged for a friend with horse connections to pick up Dunedin. I knew it was likely that I was going to have to sell him and put my dreams on the back burner once again. But the Olympics were something I had to do on my own terms or not at all.

Then I rang Varda at her friend's house.

'I'm not coming back to you, Peter,' she sobbed.

'It's okay. I've got to go anyway. It's not working for either of us,' I replied. She didn't want to come back to the property and it ended up being taken over by her brother Stephen.

I had no idea what I was going to do or where I would go. New Zealand had been my first thought. I rang a few friends to let them know my circumstances had changed. Through another friend I heard of a job going at a bloodstock agency not far from Sydney. The agency was run by three guys who showjumped as well as bred horses, so it was a chance to go on the showjumping circuit and learn how it worked. I threw myself into the work, partly because I loved it and partly because I wanted to forget about the Varda disaster. At the end of the showjumping season, in May 1985, the agency went bankrupt and I couldn't even be paid. It was a sad finale as I had enjoyed my time there.

Once again I was wondering what to do with my life when fate stepped in. I mentioned to Philip, the friend who had taken Dunedin for me, that I was looking for a job. Philip is an internationally renowned poodle breeder and knows many people in the dog world. Apparently a man who bred Afghan hounds at his house in the Blue Mountains was looking for a housekeeper. Did I fancy the job? I jumped at the idea. The Blue Mountains is a beautiful area of Australia and I liked the idea of living there for a bit while I worked out what to do about my Olympic goal.

The Afghan breeder, Desmond, lived in a huge colonial house in beautifully tended grounds. Unfortunately I soon came to dislike him. He was pompous, arrogant and very racist. Jowly and unpleasant, he would make the most awful comments and not think twice about it. It was strange that this overweight, inconsiderate man was also a well-known bonsai specialist. These tiny stunted trees were displayed outside his house and took my breath away. How could someone so utterly repugnant produce such beautiful creations? It was as if anything pleasant in him had gone into the bonsai.

Seven of Desmond's Afghan hounds lived in a bedroom of the house. They were house-trained, but part of my job was to pick up their droppings in the garden. Desmond also had a Kerry blue terrier, a breed that is notorious for its unpredictable nature, as I was to find out. My employer went away quite often — he was a good friend of Imelda Marcos and travelled to the Philippines twice a year as her guest — and while he was on a trip the Kerry blue attacked an elderly poodle that Desmond adored. After my experience in America, when almost the entire kennel of English bulldogs had died of heatstroke, I had a horrible sense of déjà vu. I knew Desmond would be livid if his dog died. Luckily, the poor beast made it, after receiving 70 stitches to patch up the wounds. One thing was clear though; Desmond needed a kennel maid rather than a housekeeper. I found a young man who was willing to do the job and felt relieved to have that part of Desmond's lifestyle taken out of my hands.

Meanwhile, my sister Yvonne had been in contact with me. She had started a networking business that had really taken off and she needed someone to prepare food for meetings. I had been working for Desmond for two months and was keen to escape this vile man. I quit, loaded up my little Ford car with my belongings and went to see Yvonne. On the way I passed through a little village called Mid Dural, and decided to stop at a real-estate agent's office. I explained that I was looking for somewhere with a nice, big, well-equipped kitchen to rent.

Not long before this I had found out that Dunedin, the horse I had worked so hard to buy, had finally been sold for $4500. I had a plan up my sleeve to get an equally good, if not better, horse for my Olympic dream. The real-estate agent, a pleasant woman called Vicky, looked vaguely familiar and she was giving me that 'I know you' look too. We both laughed as we worked out that we had met before through a mutual friend, Marissa. Vicky told me Marissa had another friend with a large rural property she couldn't manage. It was in a remote, beautiful area called Cattai, and best of all, the house had a lovely big kitchen. Did I want to rent it?

Of course I did. A new adventure was about to begin.

Chapter 21

I called my catering business Madigan's Kitchen, and ran it from my new home in Cattai. It was my friend Stella who came up with the name. Sometimes, instead of Vera, she called me Elvira, as we were both huge fans of the film Elvira Madigan. So Madigan's Kitchen it was.

I produced a whole range of food, from gourmet meals and buffet food to delicatessen products such as mustards and flavoured vinegars. Work came in from Yvonne's company, and word got around. I was soon extremely busy in the big kitchen of that country house.

My friend Marissa moved in for a while but she was so untidy that it was impossible and she eventually got her own home. I kept chooks in the garden, including one black hen and several white ones, who were called Gladys Knight and the Chicks. They roamed the big gardens, finding tasty titbits, and their eggs were delicious. It was an idyllic setting. There were only two or three houses around me, and they weren't that close. At the bottom of the property there was a gorgeous lagoon populated by pelicans. The owner of the house and land, Marlene, was busy looking after her young daughter after the loss of her husband, so I ended up taking care of her fields and some retired horses of hers as well.

I would feed, worm and water the 20 or so horses, making sure their last days were relaxed and easy. I gave them hay when the grass was low and occasionally, when it became clear that one was on its last legs, I would ring Marlene, break the news to her and arrange for it to be put down. In some ways I didn't feel too sad when they went, because I knew they had enjoyed a good few last years in retirement. But I dreaded those goodbyes as my mind would go back to my beloved Fez.

The house was quite secluded and, liking the occasional joint, I decided to plant a few cannabis seeds. It was too difficult to get to the city to buy any, so growing my own seemed a good idea. I had 40 seeds that I had bought, and I planted them outside, behind the house. I was pleased when they all sprouted, and I made beds for them using some 200-year-old red-gum-wood posts and spreading the plants out to grow. I fertilised the bed with some good-quality manure that I got from a horse friend who stabled his horses on peat, watering it down so it could be easily absorbed. They grew and grew. Soon they were huge, and I needed to screen them off by growing climbing plants such as sweet peas around them. My garden looked innocent and blooming from the outside, which was just how I wanted it.

It was at this time, in July 1985, that I found out I was HIV-positive. After leaving Varda I had decided that I was no longer going to get involved with women sexually and would be solely gay. I had to be true to myself and, at heart, I wanted to be with men. It was quite a profound decision to make but I felt relieved as soon as it was reached.

While working in the sex industry I had always used condoms, and I had been monogamous with Varda. As a responsible gay male I had regular sexual health tests and these had all been clear. HIV was something that was just beginning to be talked about. I had heard about it in 1983 and knew of a couple of men who had contracted it and died, but they had been regular drug users and in poor health. I was fit and healthy so I didn't think it was really a risk for me. When I went to Sydney on business or to meet friends I would go to a sexual health centre in Taylor Square for a check-up. One day, after I had been in for my usual check-up and blood test, someone from the clinic rang and asked me to come back in. I didn't feel too concerned at having to go back, assuming it was just something routine.

As I sat in the chair in the doctor's office, I heard him say, 'I'm sorry, Pete, you are HIV-positive.'

HIV-positive? I just looked at him. It didn't really sink in for a second. I thought about it. What did that actually mean? I wasn't sick; I was fit and didn't feel any different. It wasn't affecting my life.

As the doctor explained that it could become AIDS and eventually kill me, I had a moment of feeling, 'Should I be sad? Should I be angry? Should I think why me?' That lasted just a few minutes and then I thought, 'What the hell, why not me? I'm an active gay man.'

I worked out that I must have contracted it after leaving Varda and I accepted it as part of my life. I was HIV-positive but I wasn't dead, and there was no way I was going to lay down and let this thing consume me. I'd never done that with any of the other challenges in my life and there was no way I'd do it with HIV. I was too busy to let it drag me down. I learned all about having safe sex and what warning signs to look out for, and left the clinic determined to carry on with my dream.

At the house my cannabis plants were growing tall and strong. I would work during the day on the catering business, and spend a wee while each evening in my garden, tending the plants and tipping the heads to encourage growth.

I soon made friends with Sharon, a girl who lived nearby and had horses. She was a voluptuous, dark-haired lesbian with a great sense of humour and we got on really well. We would sometimes smoke dope together. One morning I heard a knock at the door and found Sharon standing there, dressed totally in men's clothes. Her face was pale and she was looking very upset.

'Sharon, what's wrong?' I asked, bringing her inside the house.

'My house has burned down,' she said. 'I've lost everything. One of my dogs saved me by pulling me out of the house.'

I used to slash Sharon's yard for her and I knew her two Rottweilers, Miss Fritz and Atom, who was a top stud dog. They were devoted to her and I could imagine they had acted quickly to save her. But why the men's clothes?

'I ran out naked and grabbed them off the next-door neighbour's washing line,' she explained. 'It was all I could find. Thank God I got out. It burned to the ground in 10 minutes, Pete. Everything's gone.'

And that's how Sharon came to move in with me at the end of December 1985. She was great fun to live with. Her Rottweilers also made sure nobody dared to check out my dope beds at the back of the house.

Sharon had horses and, by now, so did I. Madigan's Kitchen was doing so well that I had been able to buy two good horses, Look Sharp and Larwood. Then, in April 1986, I brought in my first crop of dope and sold it through a contact in Sydney. I was surprised and pleased by the amount it earned, and there seemed no point in slaving away at the catering business any more when I could make that kind of money growing cannabis. So Madigan's Kitchen ended and I became Pete, the dope grower and handyman, helping out on properties around the area.

I was so set on my dream of going to the Olympics that I was quite prepared to take the risks involved in this occupation. I needed the money for my equestrian campaign, and I was growing the cannabis for that reason alone. Nothing else. It wasn't greed; it was necessity.

Being a grower also freed me up to work on my horses. Look Sharp was a four-year-old chestnut thoroughbred with a racing background. He had been sold off as part of his owner's divorce settlement. I liked the fact that, although he was a gelding, he was bursting with hormones and constantly showing off. It was early days with him and I knew he would need about four years' work to bring him up to standard for the 1992 Olympics, but he had the potential, without a doubt.

Larwood was 12 years old, and brown. I had tried to bid on him at a sale as I needed an experienced horse for competitions until Look Sharp was ready. I didn't win him at the auction but the boy who bought him returned him when he turned out to be lame. I couldn't believe the state he came back in. He was miserably thin, and it was obvious he hadn't been fed. I can imagine the previous buyer thought there was no point in feeding a horse he couldn't use. I got him for the bid I had made and took him to my vet. An X-ray showed arthritis creeping in and he needed prompt treatment, which I got for him. In the end he became a great three-day event horse and I will always remember him for that.

In June 1986 I went to the World Championships, but once again I wasn't competing as I didn't have any horses ready. The championships were being held in Australia for the first time and I was very excited about attending. It was wonderful to see international talent at its best, and I even got to meet royalty. Prince Philip was there and almost busted me smoking dope. He appeared from behind a tent and said sharply, 'What are you doing?' Luckily I managed to bluff my way out of it, saying something about a quick cigarette. It was a funny moment.

At this time I also ended up with two dogs of my own. I had looked after an Old English sheepdog called Bumble, who was depressed, and the owner was so grateful to me for cheering her dog up that she bought me another Old English sheepdog. I named him Sebastian and kept him clipped short. I also had a cute little Jack Russell called Ozzi. I had acquired Ozzi one night when I was at a friend's house for dinner and the little six-week-old pup had walked in and eyed me up cheekily. The last of his litter, he was still needing a home, so I ended up forking out money for this little character.

In addition to growing dope I was caretaker of a nearby property and worked as a builder's labourer. One job involved working at the house of a friend, building fences and suchlike, and during one of these times, in August 1986, I noticed a young man while I was painting the house. He was blond, handsome and well-built. Of course, I admired him, but thought nothing more of it. Then, during morning tea, we started talking and got on well.

'Do you like Bette Midler?' he asked me at one point. I thought it was a weird question but still didn't pick up on what he was trying to say. His name was Ross, he was a carpenter, and he was looking for somewhere to build furniture. There was a shed on Marlene's property that wasn't used, and I told him it might be available. We arranged for him to come and look at it. As we were walking around, little Ozzi decided he didn't quite like the friendliness between us, and out of jealousy he gave Ross a bite. He had never bitten anyone before and I was very embarrassed.

'Sorry about that,' I said. 'I have no idea why he did that. Naughty Ozzi.'

Ross smiled.

'It's okay. Don't worry about it,' he replied. I was starting to wonder if he was interested in me but couldn't be sure. Then, as we had a cup of tea at the house before he left, he looked at me shyly and said, 'Would you like to know me better?'

I did, in a safe way, of course, and after that day we were smitten with each other.

Ross, who was 11 years younger than me, came from the same small town as Mel Gibson. Being gay just wasn't an option there, and for a long time he had tried to hide it. When we started seeing each other he decided it was time to be upfront with his very Catholic family. The news didn't go down well, especially when he said he wanted to go to the Sleaze Ball in Sydney, which raises funds for Mardi Gras. They told him to move out and I asked him to move in.

Ross and I lived together until 1988. We were very happy, sharing the house with the lovely Sharon and her dogs. She moved out eventually and a stuntwoman called Avril moved in. She could fall from a three-storey building and do other amazing things as part of her job. Avril was one of the top stuntwomen in the world, and no wonder. Ross and I helped raise money so she could go on an expedition to climb the world's second highest mountain. She was an amazing woman and we both liked her very much.

In February 1988 Ross decided he wanted to go on his OE. I had already travelled extensively and didn't want to go as I was concentrating on bringing Look Sharp and Larwood on. I told him he had to go, and that he had my blessing. It broke my heart as I watched him pack up and leave, but there was no point in continuing our relationship. It wouldn't have been fair to either of us.

With Ross gone, I continued to grow dope, work odd jobs and bring on my horses. During 1988 I competed in all five three-day events in Australia and both horses did well. That was also the year I went onto the anti-AIDS drug AZT after my T-cells, depleted by HIV, dropped to a low level. The doctor I had been seeing, who was based at St Vincent's Hospital in Sydney, called me to say he had some important news for me. At this stage I had been having blood tests every six months to check my T-cell level.

'I'm pretty busy. I have a paddock to slash,' I said, being a practical country bloke. But the doctor insisted, so I drove the one and a half hours to Sydney.

When I walked into the waiting room I saw several young men sitting there, all in various stages of the illness. Most were very sick indeed, and some had family members there for support.

'They look so thin, sick and cold,' I thought as I sat down to wait my turn. 'Is this what I have to look forward to?' Healthy and fit, I couldn't imagine being so ill.

'Your T-cells are now below 100 and that's low, Peter,' the doctor explained when I went into his consulting room. 'It leaves you open to opportunistic infections. I want to put you on a new drug called AZT.'

The drug trial was taking place at Westmead Hospital in Parramatta, which was closer to where I lived. It was to run for eight weeks and I had a weekly appointment with the team there. Whenever I went in I was heartened by the cheerful nurses, the great doctor and the counsellors. I took the drug every six hours, made sure I kept fit, ate healthy food and slept well. Even more importantly, I maintained a positive attitude. Every time I took the pills I imagined they were little Pacmen, from the well-known video game, chasing the virus and eating it. After three weeks of making myself visualise this, it became an automatic response. I thought of the drugs as making me well, rather than stopping me being sick. The power of being positive played a huge role in keeping me going and not letting HIV take over my health and my life. I also knew all about the importance of safe sex, and when I broke the news of my HIV to Ross, he accepted it.

I moved out of the Cattai property in April 1989. An international-standard golf course had been built nearby and there were up to 10 helicopters going over each day: not exactly ideal conditions for growing cannabis. What I had produced had helped take me around Australia on the three-day event circuit, but I was ready for a change. At the end of the event season I had retired Larwood. His arthritis was catching up with him and it was time for him to take it easy. He went to keep another retired horse company, leaving me with Look Sharp.

Through Vicky, the real-estate agent who had put me onto the Cattai house, I found out about a family who were looking for a trainer. Their 15-year-old son Shane was a promising rider but had behaviour problems as well as dyslexia. I moved onto their property, where there was a little cottage for me to live in, and where I discovered the barns were overrun by rats. My Jack Russell Ozzi and my black-and-white cat Patches spent eight days killing the lot. By the end they were skinny and exhausted but happy. Avril, the stuntwoman, came with me to this new job, which was in an area called Duffy's Forest.

I began working with Shane, and before long word got around about how well he was doing, not just as a rider, but with his behaviour too. I ended up with about ten pupils who either stabled their horses at the property or lived nearby on smallholdings and were able to keep their ponies there. Many of the kids had behaviour problems. Annie, a tall, gangly 13-year-old, was autistic. She hadn't said a word for years. After a good riding lesson I told her she could ride Look Sharp. Riding the instructor's top-ranked horse was the biggest treat the kids could have; a special reward for hard work. I helped Annie get on and she sat there, waiting.

'Honey, if you want him to move, you have to say "Walk on",' I said.

Annie stared at me with huge eyes and I prayed that she would do it. A minute passed and then she whispered, 'Walk on.'

Of course, the horse didn't respond.

'You'll have to speak a bit louder so he can hear you,' I said gently.

'Walk on,' she said. Look Sharp pricked his ears and took a few steps. Her face was a picture of delight. She had spoken and she had made him walk. I was as thrilled as she was. Over the next few lessons I let her ride Look Sharp and soon she was talking more. Her parents rang me to say that she had started talking at home and thanked me for getting her to speak. I will never forget that.

While I was living in Duffy's Forest I would take Look Sharp along the bush trails, seeing lyre birds, snakes, black kangaroos and lizards. It was a magical place. We would go to the beach at Long Reef and I would swim him there before the ranger came on duty, as it wasn't technically allowed. Sometimes, when it was hot, the children would come too on their ponies.

But through it all, I was still missing Ross. To take my mind off him, I decided to go on holiday to Europe in October 1989. I travelled for two months, catching up with a former lover, Claudio, visiting Greece, Nice, Barcelona, Lisbon and Paris, then returning to Sydney in December. Between then and March 1990, I continued eventing. The last three-day event was at a new course in Lochinvar. Look Sharp and I were the first to go over it and we came in third. This event was also significant for one other reason. It was my last one before retirement.

Something had changed for me. I had wanted to go to the Olympics so much, and I was encouraged to carry on by the Australian selectors who thought I was virtually a sure thing for the national team. Having an Australian mother meant I would have been eligible to compete in the 1992 Olympics in Barcelona for Australia. But I was tired. I felt that I had lost my edge. I couldn't go into such a big event without feeling totally committed to it and determined to succeed. The heart had gone out of it for me and I no longer wanted to continue on the event circuit. I wanted horses to be part of my life but I didn't want to be in competition any more. With my Olympic dream so close to my grasp, I let it go. I also had no more money to fund myself for the two years until the games. I couldn't give Look Sharp what he deserved as a top horse. It was a big decision for me and I felt heavy of heart when I told the selectors to cross me off their list of potential riders. I began losing my big muscles in my legs and did not want to let down a team for not delivering my best.

I was certain that my Olympic dream was over. Little did I know what was around the corner: an opportunity that would take me to Barcelona after all.

Chapter 22

Nobody in Australia would buy Look Sharp. The horse people there couldn't understand why a decent, first-class horse was being sold off. There had to be a catch, didn't there? No, I told them, he was sound, fit and well. There was no catch. But nobody wanted to take the chance. It was hard for people to understand why I no longer wanted to continue on the gruelling path to the Olympics. To them it seemed as if I was so close, but for me the two years leading up to the Olympics would be heartbreakingly difficult, with no money to fund the campaign and no steam left in me.

In November 1990, with a heavy heart, I packed up my belongings, my dogs and my horse and headed back to New Zealand. The three trunks didn't seem a lot to show for my life — one filled with saddlery, another with cooking equipment, and the third with my clothes, bedding and a few personal items. When I arrived in New Zealand I sent Look Sharp to stay with Beth Fife's daughter, Nicoli, in Putaruru. Nicoli was a good rider and trainer, and I knew she would look after my boy well. I got a job at Harbourside Restaurant in Auckland, through my old Le Brie partners Tony and Larry. It was just what I needed to put the heartache of ross and relinquishing my Olympic dream behind me.

Look Sharp did well on the dressage circuit with Nicoli and was spotted by Susan Humphries, an equestrian agent, after two impressive wins. Susan's business partner was a top Canadian rider, Nick Holmes-Smith, and together they bought Look Sharp. Soon after they had bought the horse they arranged for Blyth Tait to ride him at an event in Pukekohe. He did well and got only one rail down, finishing second. I was pleased to see Look Sharp do well, as he deserved the recognition, but as I was leaving the showground I noticed him tied up at the back of a trailer with no rug on, no water and nobody to look after him. I was furious, and when I saw Nick I told him exactly what I thought.

'Your management of the horse stinks,' I said. 'After all he has done for you today, after all he has achieved, how can you leave him like that, just tied to a truck with no care?'

Nick went quiet and I walked off. It was hard to leave Look Sharp but I had to remember that he wasn't my horse any more, and I had made my concerns clear. I couldn't do any more than that. A couple of days later I was surprised when Nick and Susan came into Harbourside, where I was working. I was even more surprised when Susan said, 'You were right, Peter. The management of the horses does need looking at. Would you like a job as Nick's manager?'

I thought about the offer. It would mean moving to Canada, where Nick was based.

'Of course, Nick will have to interview you formally to see if you are suitable,' she continued.

'No, I will interview him and see if he is suitable for me,' I said firmly. 'After all, it's me who will be travelling across the world, and there's no point in doing that if we aren't going to work well together.'

Susan agreed. Then she said something I hadn't expected to hear. 'It means getting Nick ready to go to the Olympics in Barcelona in 1992. You'd be going too. Is that okay?'

More than 13 years after I had first made it my goal to go to the biggest games in the world, and now that I had finally made a conscious decision not to go, the opportunity had arisen once again. It was as if I was fated to go. I almost laughed. Something wanted me to go to Barcelona, that was for sure. How could I refuse?

In January 1991 I flew with Look Sharp and two other New Zealand horses to Cave's Creek in Phoenix, Arizona. All three were to be sold on the American market. Before I left I had to go to the dentist. HIV had affected my jawbone and I had already had major surgery on my gums after developing gingivitis. The gum was cut right back in July 1987, but it wasn't enough. It was now clear that drastic action was needed to improve my mouth. I had 17 teeth removed and was left with only the front top six. It was good to get rid of the ugly teeth the gingivitis had left me with, and I was happy with the dentures I was fitted with.

Basically, Nick and Susan took orders from riders and found horses overseas to match their needs. There were already buyers lined up for the three horses they had bought in New Zealand, but they had to be put through their paces on the American circuit to

show their abilities, and that was part of my job. While Nick rode his two Olympic horses in the top classes of the big competitions, I rode the 'dealer horses', as we called the ones that were being sold on, in
the lower classes.

Nick and I had agreed to work together for one month and see how it went. If either of us felt the arrangement wasn't working I would be flown back to New Zealand. Nick's Olympic horses were Ruderpest, who was known as Rudi, and Sir Lancelot, or Lance as we called him, a Kiwi-bred buckskin-coloured horse. Rudi was an elegant silver-grey horse who excelled in all three disciplines of three-day eventing, while Lance was tough, cheeky and determined to have a go at anything we threw at him.

Once we had arrived in Arizona we put all five horses into Nick's old truck and set out to drive through the States to Canada. It was an incredible road trip. On the way we stopped to see Karen, my former girlfriend, who had a pair of handmade riding boots for me. Despite the fact that I had broken her heart we were still in contact and remained good friends. She had had the boots I had ordered and made for me.

'But you have to pick them up,' she had told me. 'I won't be posting them.'

I was so happy to see this beautiful, vibrant woman again. She admitted she hadn't stopped loving me, and a part of my heart felt the same. By the time I left I felt that bridges had been mended, and that our friendship could continue.

The following day we crossed into Canada, and four hours later we arrived at Checkmate Farm, which was Nick's base in Ontario. I had seen photographs of this place, but nothing prepared me for the real thing. Snow was piled up around the yard and doorways, and all I could see initially were white drifts with trees sticking out of them. Finally I made out the log cabin, the walls and the traditional barn, half-buried in the ground to keep it warm in winter and cool in summer. Built over a hundred years ago, it was a craggy monument to past farming methods. But I couldn't shake off a feeling of shock at the sheer rawness of the place. It was cold and basic. 'What've I got myself into now?' I wondered.

There were two old caravans in which Nick and I would live. The wind was blowing at 60 kph and the temperature was below freezing. So you can imagine how I felt when I realised the door to my caravan wouldn't shut. I had to stretch a bungy cord across to hold it closed, but even then the icy wind whistled through. It was also a filthy hovel, as it hadn't been cleaned properly. I had never been so cold in my life, and wore all my clothes in layers so thick that I could barely walk.

The three New Zealand horses looked very grumpy. They had come from a Southern Hemisphere summer to a freezing winter. I had to smash the ice in their trough and teach them to drink immediately, before it froze over again.

A young rider called Darci Ecker, who was training with Nick, arrived from Alberta with her horses and we immediately became good friends. Lynn, an English girl, also joined us as a groom, and for the next few weeks we muddled through. We had to, because Checkmate Farm was to host the Canadian International Three-Day Event in May, just three months ahead, and I had grave fears about whether we would be ready. Fortunately Nick and I both agreed after the one-month trial period that things were going well, and that I would stay on.

Just before the big event, spring suddenly happened. This might sound strange, but I have never seen such a rapid change in the seasons. In one week the new buds and leaves were through, followed by thick meadow grass. The farm was transformed, and just in time. The 200 hectares around the farm, which contained 40 cross-country fences, were now ready for the event. Both Nick's horses went well, and Nick qualified as the top Canadian rider. Nick and I were a good team. The horses bloomed under the two of us, and I was pleased with all their progress.

Look Sharp had been sold to an American who wanted an Olympic-grade horse. He was renamed Sandscript, because the millionaire who bought him for his son wrote the amount he was willing to pay in the sand at Cave's Creek. I had sold Look Sharp to Nick and Susan for NZ$20,000, and it had cost them another $10,000 to send him to the US. When I found out the American had agreed to pay US$50,000 for him I gave them a nudge to say I thought it was a bit mingy, making such a vast profit, and they gave me another thousand to keep me smiling. Look Sharp then went onto the American circuit, but I was to meet up with him again, in very traumatic circumstances.

At this time, however, I was focusing on Nick's horses and getting ready for the Olympics. I worked hard through the season and we were feeling confident and happy at the end of it. By then I was ready for a break. I had earlier fallen ill with a bacterial infection related to my HIV, one of the few times the virus had caused me any problems. I was at an event in California at the time and took a three-day course of antibiotics, which sorted the problem out. But after a gruelling, though also fulfilling, spring season, I felt I needed a holiday to recharge my batteries.

In June 1991 I headed off to Spain, where I met up with Claudio again and had a wonderful time in this fragrant, colourful country. Claudio looked after me well and filled my holiday with surprise trips to amazing beauty spots, delicious cuisine, fine wines and incredibly interesting people. It was just as well that I felt revived when I arrived back in Canada two months later. Nick met me at the airport sporting a huge black eye and a badly bruised nose. He had fallen from Lance and they had both suffered a knock to their confidence. I had some work to do to rebuild their trust and get them back on track for the games.

In August 1991 we all moved closer to Toronto, as the official Canadian team training camp was to be held at a farm just outside the city. The riders were all hopeful of a spot in the final four for the games. We still had the three-day event autumn season in Canada, Holland and America to get through, and the Canadian Equestrian Federation decided that the team would go to the final qualifier in Holland. It was the first time we had travelled as part of a team, and it wasn't without drama. On the way over, our flight had to be diverted when an oil seal on the plane needed to be replaced. Once at the Dutch venue, I set up our stable unit within a huge tent that held a hundred horses. Officials tested the air quality each day and opened the flaps if the methane got too high, from all that horsey wind.

Nick and Lance did well in the dressage, but after the cross-country stage they had 13 time faults. I was not happy with Nick. 'Did you use your watch?' I asked him.

'I misread it at the halfway point,' he said.

I wasn't accepting that excuse. 'Bloody long way to come to misread your watch,' I said, taking Lance back to the box.

I wouldn't tolerate such a silly mistake. Yes, I was tough, but that's what I had to do to get results, both as team stable manager and Nick's groom/personal manager. The team finished ninth overall, putting them within the top 10 and thus qualifying them for the Olympics.

Once again, getting back to Canada was no easy trip. There was a storm over the sea so we ended up being diverted to the North Pole, of all places, which added three hours to the trip. One of the riders, Rachel, had left her passport in a trunk that had already been loaded onto the plane, putting my management and negotiation skills to the test. The car we had hired in Holland got smashed by a truck, which meant more problems to sort out with the hire company. I also had to battle with the airline officials to be allowed to stand with the horses at take-off. As we had paid Can$100,000 for our tickets, it was the least they could do, I told them. I got to stand with the horses.

During the flight, Paige (another rider) and I had to sit on the little jump seats at the back of the plane because it was overbooked by the airline. The rest of the group had nice comfortable seats in first class and we weren't even offered food. When I complained, the stewardess told us we just had to hope someone would fall asleep so there would be a meal available. In the end, we had a small piece of fruit each. Paige and I were too far away to hear the words of the film, Robin Hood, so we made up our own, giggling to ourselves at lines like, 'So, Little John, you like the cut of my green pantyhose, do you?' Or, 'Maid Marian, I'd kiss you but your moustache is too bristly.' The only high point of the flight was when a friendly steward gave us each a Baileys on ice to cheer us up. We were very glad to get off that plane.

Not that there was much of a break after the flight. I had two days to unpack and repack before the team left to go to Dalton, Georgia, for the Pan American Games. This was to be Rudi's last event before the Olympics. Lance had already finished his season after the event in Holland and was put out in the big paddock for a well-earned rest. It was the end of October 1991, and he had been working hard since February.

Dalton was icy cold and Lorrayne La Framboise, the team manager, who had been an Olympian herself, gave us little pocket warmers to keep our hands from seizing up while we were plaiting manes and tails. There were ninety horses from six countries at the Pan American Games. Mark Phillips had designed the course and it was awe-inspiring. I was very happy to see Look Sharp or Sandscript as he was now, and he whickered when he saw me. The team did well, With Nick and Rudy claiming the gold medal. The pressure had been on and it was very cold, and there was great jubilation at such a successful result. Back at the farm, I put Rudi into the paddock with Lance and watched them greet each other, snuffling and whickering. They were both wonderful horses and I was proud of them, I thought, as I pulled my scarf over my nose to try and stay warm in the minus-five-degree temperature. I'd had enough of the chills. I was heading home to New Zealand for the summer, to coach, and then it would be back to Canada for the final countdown to the Olympics.

Chapter 23

As the plane circled Barcelona airport I managed to persuade the pilot to let me stand in the cockpit so I could see the incredible view of this golden, sun-baked land. I wanted to whoop with joy as we approached the landing strip. After thirteen hard years, I was finally at the Olympics.

My role was as stable manager and assistant to Lorrayne La Framboise, the manager of the Canadian Olympic equestrian team. The riders were Nick, Rachel Smith, Rob Stevenson and Stuart Young-Black. The trainer was a taciturn man called Jack, who had the red face of a hardened drinker.

Before heading for Barcelona we had been in Surrey, England, for our final training camp, some events and to put the horses through quarantine. While there, the grooms for the Olympic-bound teams had stayed at the house of the famous children's writer Monica Edwards. She had a little new house that had been built in the grounds of her former family home, a beautiful 14th-century farmhouse where she had lived until the death of her husband in a tractor accident. The property was edged with woodland that was home to a thousand-year-old badger set. Monica, who had written two books about the badgers, had tracked and followed five generations. Now in her seventies, she was almost blind, but still loved her contact with these fascinating creatures. They would come up to her house from the set and she would feed them with nuts and sultanas. She was full of stories, and I spent hours talking and listening to her. I even fed the big male badger after he appeared at the ranchslider door, standing up and banging on the glass.

Even in England, I was finding Jack quite difficult to deal with. One morning as we were preparing for an event he told me to pull the hair from the top of Rudi's tail. This was a way of shaping the tail, an alternative to plaiting, that had recently become the fashion. Although Rudi was usually placid he hated having his tail pulled so I would trim it with scissors just before a competition.

'It's not a good idea, Jack,' I cautioned, when Jack insisted on pulling Rudi's tail. 'He doesn't like it if you're rough.'

Jack ignored me, and began pulling the horse's tail, which upset Rudi. I wasn't going to allow the horse to become disturbed before an event and asked Jack to leave the box. 'What did you say?' he growled, furious that I had the nerve to speak out. I repeated my request. He then took me behind the stables and lectured me for 45 minutes, dramatising his fury by throwing his half-finished cigarettes in the air and slicing them with a lash of his dressage whip. I was used to dealing with alcohol-inflicted ravings so after a few minutes I just switched off. Jack even threatened not to take me to Barcelona, but he didn't go through with this because I was popular with the riders and worked very hard.

So I arrived in Barcelona, as part of an Olympic team. The first thing I noticed was the heat. It was intense and dry, but the organisers had provided plenty of water in fridges everywhere. Security was very tight, even though the Basque separatists had agreed to stop any action during the two weeks of the games. We had to pass through metal detectors and two checkpoints to get into the stable complex.

Denis Frappier, our vet, kept the horses well-hydrated. Five and a half tons of ice would be used on cross-country day. Mark Todd, who was there as the president of the Event Riders Association, assured everyone that there would be more ice and plenty of cooling stations.

The three-day event was being held at El Montayna, a resort in the hills, about 60 kilometres from Barcelona. It was very glamorous and filled to the brim with staff from the various teams, who made the most of its huge swimming-pool and bars. The riders were based in the Olympic village 60 km's further down the hills.

Having been in the sport for a while I knew some of the people at the resort already. But it was also a chance to meet new people and swap lapel pins. The evening after the dressage I teamed up with the Irish stable manager, who wanted to swap his groom, Maggie, for Rob Stevenson's lovely groom, also called Maggie.

'Ah, come on, Peter. Your Maggie might be a sweet little thing but my Maggie is six foot two and can lift a tack truck all on her own. You'd be mad to say no to a deal like that,' he joked. Of course, there was no way our Maggie was going to swap sides. She was my back-up and I couldn't do without her.

At the stable block we were based next to the Russian team. The situation had been the same in Holland, where I had helped them with a mare that had damaged a tendon. Denis had helped them out for nothing, as they had no vet help, and I had given them bandages and poultices. I admired their ability to keep going when they didn't have the expensive equipment and back-up of the other teams. They had driven for five days just to get to the event in Holland.

Apart from the heat, one of the other really noticeable things was the number of sandflies around the place. I had already been bitten a few times on my legs, but although the bites were itchy I didn't think too much about them. At the time they were simply an annoyance — only later would I find out about the terrible legacy they had left me with.

The Russians didn't have any rugs to protect their horses from the sandflies so I gave them a leftover set of old red flysheets, since I had been given several sets of new white and red rugs with white maple leaves on them. Hey, red was the Russians' colour after all. They were amazed and touched. I also had boxes of apple juice, which was added to the water to encourage the horses to drink. I had trained our horses to accept water with molasses so we didn't really need the apple juice. I took some to the Russians, who looked a bit wary.

'It's okay. It's safe,' I said, realising they thought it might be poisoned to jeopardise their chances at the games. 'No, no, see, it's good. Here, I'll drink some.'

I opened one of the tins and had a glass of the juice. Reassured, they all had some too. I didn't expect anything in return so I was touched when they invited us to their rooms — and after being plied with golden vodka and stuffed herrings, Denis and I could barely walk. The Canadian team's apartment was quite crowded and I had been put in with the Bulgarians. As I tottered into the apartment I was met by a row of huge men all crowded around the telly watching MTV, something they had never seen at home. They smiled at me and said, 'Ah, Canada,' which I think was the only English word they knew. Immediately, I was poured a glass of Bulgarian plum brandy. It was the last thing I felt like, and I knew

I had to escape. After one or two brandies MTV got their attention again and I beat a retreat.

In the bar I found my Irish friend drinking poteen, a spirit brewed from potatoes. I couldn't say no this time, and had a taste. It reminded me of the moonshine I had tried in Arkansas. As I eventually wobbled back through the resort to my bed I wondered how I would get up at 4.30am with a clear head, ready for the cross-country competition.

I had spent months getting Nick ready for this part of the event and knew he was ready. Lorrayne and Jack inspected the course with Nick, and when they returned Lorrayne looked disturbed.

'I think Jack's knocked Nick's confidence about fence 13, a complex one,' she confided to me. 'He doesn't think Nick will get the horse over it. I hope Nick hasn't taken it too much to heart.' I was concerned too, as I knew Nick respected Jack's opinion. It all hung in the balance.

The weather was beautiful and the temperature nudged 30 degrees. Rachel and her horse, Plantagenet, went first and did well over the testing course, with one stop at a fence. Rob and Stuart both went clear but got a few time faults. Nick, as the main rider, went last on Lance. The round went well until they came to fence 13. Lance stopped. Then, Lance didn't take one of the last fences properly and Nick fell off. He wasn't injured, but I was worried because this wasn't like Lance or Nick. I was there to take Lance when they came in and I noticed the dirt and grass streaks on Nick's shirt. Nick was disappointed and we both knew Jack and the pressure had undermined his confidence, making it difficult for him to ride at his best.

But where was Jack? He was missing for part of the day and turned up at 2pm, by which time Lorrayne and Jill, a general team manager for the Canadians, had worked out the rides between them. It sent him a clear message. But it wasn't the Jack situation or the fall that stood out as the worst part of the day. While waiting for Nick, I had witnessed something that made my blood boil. I was thrilled to see Sandscript on the American team, being ridden by a young man called Todd. I watched them go through the start of the course and winced when Todd made a bad mistake at the sixth fence, although the horse, being clever and intuitive, managed to get over.

I was there at the finish line when Sandscript and Todd appeared, trotting in after what seemed to be a very gruelling round in the full heat of the day. I immediately realised that Sandscript was in severe distress. As soon as they crossed the line Todd got off and six people had to hold the horse up to stop him collapsing. It was heartbreaking. He had been cooked by being whipped over the last two fences while not being hydrated properly. Todd was eliminated for abuse.

The support team immediately began covering the sick horse with ice to cool him rapidly. With four people on each side, they helped him stagger up and down. If he stopped, he would fall over and never get up. The American vet worked hard to get fluid back into Sandscript, and once he was stabilised the horse ambulance took him back to the stable block. The scene brought tears to my eyes. How could this man do such a terrible thing to a willing and courageous horse? Todd's ambition had led to cruelty and his victim was the horse I had invested so much in. Later, Todd jogged past me as I was walking back to the stables.

'Your horse went well today, Peter,' he said blithely. I couldn't believe his callousness and was barely able to look him in the eye as I let loose with my views on his treatment of Sandscript.

'You broke that honest horse's heart today,' I spat. 'Don't talk to me. You're despicable.' I turned in disgust and walked off.

At the stables, I saw Sandscript being led up and down by his distressed groom. The horse had tubes sticking out of his neck to enable more fluids to go in. I could see he was exhausted and barely able to walk.

'I think you should take him back to his box,' I told the groom.

'I can't,' she said, looking at me with tear-reddened eyes. 'Todd told me to keep walking him so he doesn't stiffen up.'

'Todd is no longer responsible for any decisions regarding horses. He's forfeited that right,' I said firmly. 'Take the horse back to the box and let him rest. I hope he makes it.' She looked relieved as she slowly led Sandscript to his box.

Todd was given a one-year ban that night. He was made to leave the games site and return to America. I briefly saw his mother at the stables as they were leaving. 'We will take good care of your horse,' she said. They still referred to him as 'my horse'. On his arrival in the US Todd was met by animal rights activists protesting about his treatment of Sandscript.

But my job wasn't over and I had to refocus on the games after the Sandscript incident. I had an early night in preparation for the show jumping the following day. This part of the event was taking place in Barcelona, at the Real Polo Club. Seventy-eight horses left in convoy from the stable block for the one-hour drive to the city. Nine trucks made up the convoy, which had a police escort.

The arena was very impressive. Nick had one rail down, and at the end of all three parts of the event the Canadian team ended up in 14th place overall. The New Zealand team took the silver and the Australians gold, so I was pleased for both countries. After a long day, we headed back again in convoy to El Montanya. We should have been back by 6pm but the police got the entire convoy lost and we didn't get in until 11pm. Even then, the truck carrying the French and Russian horses was still missing. They didn't get back until 1am, by which time the French stables manager was absolutely furious.

A high point of the next day was the chance to ride over the cross-country course bareback on Lance. I was accompanied by top rider Ian Stark's groom on his famous grey, Glenburnie. He also led Ian's other grey, Murphy Himself, as we toured the course, which was now empty of people and cameras. The following day I had some free time so I went down to watch some of the other Olympic events. I had a pass that allowed me free access virtually everywhere. At the main arena I sat in the competitors' area and watched the final of the men's 100-metre sprint. A woman sitting one seat away from me had long painted fingernails studded with gems and cheered loudly as the athletes raced. I realised later that she was the famous American runner Florence Griffith Joyner — Flo-Jo.

It was a wonderful end to my time in Barcelona. From here I returned to Britain for more events with Nick, then I had a two-week holiday sailing around the Eolian Islands with Claudio in Italy, and finally headed back to Auckland to coach during the summer of 1992.

I didn't yet know it, but I was carrying something else in addition to memories. The sand fly bites on my legs had almost faded, but inside my body something sinister was happening, something that would change my life for ever.

Chapter 24

It was good to be back in Auckland after my Olympic experience, and I enjoyed the summer there. In May 1993 I was asked to take on the role of executive director of the Pukekohe three-day event, which was due to take place at the beginning of December. The event had been held at Pukekohe before, but now, for the first time, it was part of the world leader board riders' rankings, and on the Oceania circuit for World Championship qualification in Holland in 1994. There was no way the organising committee could afford to put on a second-rate event: everything must go smoothly.
It was a huge job, involving months of preparation, 250 volunteers and a committee of 25. My job description was simple: bring the event up to international standard and make a profit. For the past eight years, since it had started, it had always made a loss. I was delighted to be given the job, and felt ready for the challenge.
The next six months flew by, filled with meetings, chasing sponsorship and organizing staff and competitors, as well as preparing the venue. In November, a month before the competition, I went to Australia to manage a friend who was competing there, and was able to secure a good Australian rider to come to our three-day event. She was the girlfriend of Shane, the young man I had trained at Duffy's Forest, and he came with her to act as her groom and coach. Shane was now a rising young star of the equestrian circuit himself and I was proud of his achievements.
Having worked in the hospitality industry as well as in equestrianism, I was able to think outside the square and organize some great entertainment for the event. There were trade stands and a Mouse circus. Before the show jumping on day three, my father dressed up as Father Christmas and came in on a horse and wagon, accompanied by a troupe of little ballet girls in fairy costumes who handed out sweets to the VIP's and sponsors. In the arena we had dressed a horse as a Push Me Pull You, the two-headed creature from Dr Doolittle, and had tumbling clowns as well as a stilt-walker. Mark Todd's horse Charisma was celebrating his 21st birthday and the pair made a guest appearance,

much to everyone's delight. Charisma's breeders gave him a neck wreath of carrots and a carrot cake to celebrate.

The whole event went extremely well and I was thrilled when I added up the takings and found that we had actually made a profit. It was a great moment.

As I was finishing off the Pukekohe work I was contacted by Sue Ockenden, the chairwoman of the Canadian eventing committee. She had come over for the event with an American client, heir to a large global drink company, who wanted to buy some New Zealand horses. Would I help him find the best horses, she wondered. I was happy to help. I drove them around the North Island and eventually we bought three stunning, unbelievably well-trained horses. It was arranged that I would take the horses to the US, where they would be quarantined in Los Angeles, then take them across America on a five-day trip to North Carolina. I would then stay on for six weeks and help the man, a lovely, gentle bloke of 47, get to know the three new horses and learn how to ride them. I had taken many flights as a groom and we arrived, safe and sound, at the quarantine station at midnight. All went well, but I was glad to get to bed at the end of the 40-hour journey via Sydney and Tahiti. But at 4am, as I was sleeping at the house of a horse importer, I was suddenly woken by a shaking sensation. It was an earthquake. There was a glass skylight directly above me, and I breathed a sigh of relief that it hadn't shattered. I had encountered earthquakes before during my travels and felt reassured that this one wasn't too bad, although I knew there could be more aftershocks during the night. However, nothing prepared me for the carnage that I saw the next morning. Los Angeles was devastated by the notorious quakes of January 1994. Freeways and skyscrapers collapsed. Sixty people died and there was US$30 billion worth of damage to the city.

I was shaken by the sheer, deadly scale of the destruction. Buildings had crumpled like paper and roads had folded like soft toffee. Luckily the horses were safe, and as soon as they were released from their two-day quarantine I set out on the drive to North Carolina. I was glad to get out of Los Angeles. The damage to the roads meant there were several diversions, adding many hours to the journey. The truck was a big 15-horse one that came with two drivers, and they took turns at the wheel. We also had to pick up several other horses on the way. In Kentucky we hit a snowstorm that caused the temperature to plummet. It was so cold the horses' manure froze to the ground. It was very hard on the New Zealand horses, fresh from the warm summer weather. When we finally got to Southern Pines in North Carolina there was relief all round, for horses and humans.

Just before leaving on this trip I had met my new partner, Geoff, in Auckland. A former lieutenant commander in the navy, now working in human resources, he was tall, with dark hair, green eyes and bundles of intelligence. I couldn't wait to get back to Auckland to see him again. Not long after I arrived back I caught up with Andy, a friend of mine who worked in real estate. We had talked about running a small bar in Auckland and he had just bought a building that was suitable for what I had in mind. Setting up a bar isn't a quick process. Getting a license is a mission in itself, but I got the process underway and began making plans for my dream bar.

While this was happening I had a joint birthday party with Geoff, who was a week younger than me. During the celebrations my good friend Doug George, who designed women's shoes and was a wonderful drag queen, told me he wasn't in the best of health. I had known Doug in Sydney, and in Auckland he and I were known as the 'ambassadors of fabulosity' on the social scene. I was devastated when he told me about his lymphatic cancer, the same illness that Jackie Onassis was suffering from (she died three weeks before he did). Doug lasted for two months after Geoff's and my birthday party. I still miss him, all these years later. Sadly, I wasn't able to attend his memorial party: I had accepted a job as assistant coach and stables manager for the Canadian team's trip to the World Championships. The licence for my bar hadn't yet come through. I had to go to Canada to start work.

At the training camp in Canada I was given the task of bringing a depressed horse out of its shell. I made enough of a difference in just two weeks of camp for him and his rider to be able to join the squad for selection for the World Championships in Holland.

I wasn't prepared for yet more devastating news. One day my sister Yvonne rang to say my father Stan was sick. It was prostate cancer. In the last few years Stan and I had forged a new friendship. He had finally asked me about my sexuality in 1988, and said he wanted to be my friend. We shook hands on it, and since then it had been a lovely relationship. Bridges had been rebuilt and I had said everything I needed to say to him. Although I was heartbroken at the news of his illness, I knew that if he died before I was able to get home, our peace had been made.

I went to the World Championships in Holland with the Canadian team, fulfilling another dream to be there in a competitive capacity. Everything went smoothly as we were such a good, well-organised team. We set up the cooling tent that we had had at the Olympics for the cross-country, which meant getting in seven tons of ice. The horses went into this deliciously chilled area to cool down after their round. Although we didn't win, Morayne and I were recognised for the cooling system and thanked for helping out a Hungarian rider whose horse was very heat-distressed.

After the World Championships I made an important decision. Lorrayne Laframboise sensed it was coming.

'This is my last event,' I told her. 'I'm retiring.'

It was hard to say those words but the time was right. Lorrayne and I had been a good team, had made our mark on the equestrian world, and I was leaving on a high. Vaughan Jeffries, a New Zealander from Cambridge in the Waikato, had won the title of world champion.

The rest of the Canadian team returned home, leaving me in Holland with the final few horses and one groom, Sarah, a tiny, feisty English girl with a shock of red hair.

'I'm going out for a ride,' she said one day, indicating the horse she looked after.

'That's not a good idea,' I replied. 'He's recovered from the competition and he's really fit.' Unfortunately she decided to go out on the horse anyway, and within seconds I heard a thump as she fell, followed by a plaintive cry for help. I ran out and found Sarah lying on the ground, badly injured.

'He bucked me off,' she groaned. At the hospital a scan showed her back was broken and she was immediately put in traction. Luckily the break hadn't severed her spinal cord, but the fracture took months to heal. In a twist of fate, the accident was to lead to a new career for this headstrong young woman. She later studied the back and became a leading osteopath, working with both horses and people. Once I knew she was fine, I left for New Zealand. The news had come through that my bar licence had been approved, and everything was in place for the next big adventure in my life. As I sat on the plane, I thought about my plans for the bar. I already had a name. I'd seen it on a T-shirt that I had bought in Canada. It was a line from The Wizard of Oz and said simply, 'Surrender Dorothy.'

Chapter 25

It was the size of a shoebox but overflowing with fabulosity. Surrender Dorothy, my special little bar, opened in Auckland's Ponsonby Road on November 1, 1994, and it was an instant hit. For three months I had been supervising the fitting out and decor of the bar, which measured just three and a half metres wide and 12 metres long, including the toilets and storage. Everything had to be just right for the grand opening.

The decor was eclectic, to say the least. Some people thought it was kitsch, others described it as camp. One thing was certain. Nobody had ever seen anything quite like Surrender Dorothy before.

The concept was unusual. I wanted people to feel they were coming to my lounge for a drink with me. On the walls were photographs of my horses, Olympic memorabilia and other snapshots of my life. Then there was the unique trademark of the shoes left to me by my dear friend Doug George. His design brand was Georgia D, and when I first got the shoes I wondered what I could do with them. I wanted to commemorate my friend in a very special way.

I put in a memorial to him above the fuse box. It had his photograph and the shocking pink plastic carnations from his shoe shop in Auckland's Lorne Street. He would have loved it, which is why I wanted to do his shoes justice. And what better way than stuck to the wall and up onto the ceiling of Surrender Dorothy? The shoes were soon joined by others given to me by patrons, usually women. I would decide if the shoes were fabulous enough or had a great story attached to them, and if so, they were added to the ceiling. Within a year the bar had shoes going completely across the ceiling and right back towards the rear: strappy silver lamé shoes, leopard-skin shoes, stilettos, often by top international designers. People fell in love with Dorothy and wanted to contribute. Soon I had pieces for the walls, such as bright-coloured plates, fantastic pieces of pottery, Wizard of Oz souvenirs and, of course, a range of gorgeous little ruby slippers.

Within the first three months my tiny bar had been written up in seven magazines, including the prestigious House and Garden. The reputation I had for my banter and the wonderful staff were attractions in themselves. It was a safe place for women to have a drink with girlfriends, straight or gay. The music wasn't so loud that you couldn't speak, and we kept a close eye on straight men to make sure they didn't hassle the women. It was not an overt pick-up joint and we had no trouble. I had originally covered the barstools in leopard print but the wear was far greater than I expected, and soon they were recovered with more hardwearing sheepskin. Patrons who turned up in drag were given free drinks. Our motto was 'Don't Postpone Joy' and we certainly didn't. Geoff and I lived above the bar. I worked seven days a week and Geoff was my support person on Friday and Saturday nights, co-hosting the bar and collecting glasses. We were a good team. The place was licensed for 27 people, but on the second night there were 50 and it just got busier. On special occasions I would get in Bertha, a fabulous, full-figured Samoan drag queen who had performed with two others as the Funky Divas. She was very well-known, and at our first New Year's Eve party she performed 'Over the Rainbow' by Patti Labelle. About 150 people crammed into the bar and spilled out into the street. Bertha's performance literally stopped traffic on Ponsonby Road. People at the restaurant across the street came out to watch, the crowd screamed and Bertha basked in the glory.

The drag queens who performed never charged me. They supported my concept and I supported the community. Living above the bar as I did, I was able to immerse myself in the scene. I joined the local business association and contributed to as many projects as I could afford. I loved the theatre of being behind the bar, knowing it was my place and I could do as I wished. My banter had been learned from the drag queens I had known. A good queen has to be witty, intelligent but never hurtful. Bitchiness only lasts two minutes before it becomes boring. I remembered the names of 200 patrons and what they liked to drink. I wanted every patron to leave feeling better than they had when they arrived. I greeted each person who came in as if they were the only person in there. They loved the recognition and attention.

'Love, sit down, take the weight off your slingbacks and I'll get you a drink,' I would say. Or, 'That shirt looks hideous on you. It would look fabulous on me. Get it off.' It was fun, never pretentious and always discreet. I never divulged who I had seen or who they were with. The staff took their cues from me and we were the hit of the city.

I also got to decide who was allowed to stay for a drink, just as I would if it was my own living room. If a person didn't seem appropriate, usually a straight rugby drunk, I would put on a pair of dangly earrings and some sparkly red lipstick and say in a very masculine tone, 'Come on, this isn't the bar for you.' They always left.

Within ten months I had paid back every cent I had borrowed to set up Surrender Dorothy. Having cash again meant I was able to rebuild my assets, have a proper holiday and go to Sydney three times a year for dance parties. At the first anniversary party I dressed in drag as Bet Lynch, who was retiring from Coronation Street. I loved drag. My sisters thought I looked like my mother, Joan, when I was dressed in it.

I lost my father in July 1995, and although it was devastating I felt we had become friends and shared much love since putting our differences aside. The prostate cancer took him and though it was a release from suffering when he eventually let go, I will always miss having him in my life.

Geoff was actually a father himself, and had a beautiful eight-year-old daughter named Alexandra. A super-bright blonde child, she came to stay with us each Friday after school until Monday morning when her mum Bridget would collect her and take her to school. Bridget and Geoff were still good friends, and Alexandra was a charming, smart, well-loved girl. She and I got on fantastically, and still do.

As I became more successful with Dorothy, I became ready for another challenge. In October 1995 I took over the space next door to the bar and opened a gift shop selling cards, T-shirts and books for the gay market. It was called Friends of Dorothy. Even so, retail didn't push my buttons in the way hospitality did.

The Hero Parade was now an item on the gay calendar. In 1996 it had moved from Queen Street to Ponsonby Road and was bigger than ever. I entered two floats, one from the bar and one from the shop. Dorothy's float featured a yellow brick road, with Dorothy played by Ronny Buck, a little drag queen, in her blue gingham dress and ruby slippers. The lion and the straw man were two bodybuilder friends, and the tin man was another gorgeous man wearing very few clothes. Good witch Glinda was superbly played by an old girlfriend of mine who now worked in the gift shop; she had a collection of vintage clothes so had no trouble looking the part. The Wicked Witch of the West was a female actor who had been my stilt clown at the Pukekohe three-day event. I was the driver, and had decorated the cab with over a thousand tulle flowers and a rainbow made of coloured sequin material. My friend Steven (a university art teacher) and I made a pair of polystyrene stilettos covered in red glitter, standing over two metres high, and these sat on the cab.

The other float, for the shop, was covered with three layers of tulle, more than 250 metres, to make a skirt. An actor friend in a very high wig sat on the cab looking like a doll. Behind the cab was a huge purple-papered gift box with a yellow bow and sash. An incredible amount of work went into both floats. When I drove out from the assembly point and onto Ponsonby Road in the first lorry, a roar went up. I saw 200,thousand of delighted, cheering faces. 'Wow!' I gasped. 'This is bigger than Ben Hur!'

Surrender Dorothy sold out that night. After that we closed the bar and went to the Hero Party.

In the first week of March 1996, Geoff and I went to Mardi Gras in Sydney, then had a holiday in New South Wales. I could feel Iris the virus, as I called my HIV, attacking me. I had no energy and a few health problems that were the result of lowered immunity. I only really hit the wall about once a year, and it was usually caused by doing too much.

I had sold the gift shop so I could ease my workload. It had also been a strain on the bar, and my bank account was now in the black again. April 2 1996 was Good Friday, one of the few days of the year when the bar was closed. At 2.30pm I felt strangely cold. I spent the day at Okura, just north of Auckland, with my family, including my stepmother Bud, my sister Yvonne, her husband and the kids. I remember we were watching Ben Hur on television. By 5pm I was starting to shake. I excused myself, and went home with Geoff.

When we reached home I got the key out of my pocket and tried to unlock the door to the flat. My hands wouldn't stop shaking, and I needed both of them to open the door. I went straight to bed, and by 6pm I was blacking out. My temperature soared and sweat soaked the sheets. Four times this happened. Geoff changed the sheets twice, then put down towels twice after that. When he went to work at 8am the next day I lay there, drained and weak. I thought it was a bout of Iris the virus. Two more sweats hit me during the day, and I knew it was time to take my HIV seriously. My staff at Dorothy took over for me. Del, the bar girl, became manager and Harris, a gorgeous Dutch guy, took over some of the other shifts. We later took on Tom, a dark haired South African pal of Harris's, to fill the other shifts.

After a month of illness I was very weak. I often had sounds rushing through my head and had zig-zags in my vision, like a migraine. Geoff took me to Fiji for nine days to help me get warm again but the weather was dreadful, although the resort was nice. I noticed that my muscles were starting to wither. By the end of the trip almost all my muscle had gone: no chest, just ribs, no butt, no biceps. I still had quite muscular legs though, from over 20-odd years of riding.

On my return I went to my doctor, but he was on a research sabbatical, so I saw a specialist in infectious disease, Sally Roberts. She thought I had a muscle-wasting condition and noticed my spleen was beginning to enlarge. Blood tests showed changes in the shape of my red blood cells. The symptoms were strange and not altogether typical of HIV-related illness. Something sinister was going on.

In May 1996 Michael, a friend of ours, had gone to Sydney to consult a doctor called Cassy Workman. Michael also had HIV, and after seeing this doctor he had been started on a treatment involving a new kind of anti-HIV drug called a protease inhibitor. Protease inhibitor drugs prevent T-cells that have been infected with HIV from producing new copies of the virus. T-cells are a type of white blood cell that are crucial to the immune system, and are the ones attacked by HIV. I had already had my T-cell count drop below 100 before and had gone on the experimental drug AZT. Michael's experience with protease inhibitors had been exceptional, even better than AZT.

By the time I arrived in Sydney in July 1996, my T-cell count was down to only 27. Cassy did all the tests and started me on a cocktail of drugs that included protease inhibitors. She also found out that bactrin, a drug used to control one of the many opportunistic infections that I faced, was no longer working for me. Cassy also noticed my enlarged spleen and suggested I have some tests done when I got back to Auckland.

Every three months, either Michael or I would need to go to Sydney to get the drugs, which were not available in New Zealand at this time, for both of us. Michael had improved and my T-cells increased to 200 within six weeks. Checks for the amount of virus in my body revealed it was below detection. This meant there was very little left, and the remaining infected cells were probably hiding in the lymph glands. My doctor in Auckland decided there was no point in testing the spleen because it looked like a clearcut case of rapid HIV progression.

But by October 1996 my spleen, usually a compact, fist-sized organ sitting just under the ribs, was so big and painful that the main spleen had almost ceased to function and four tiny baby spleens were growing off it. My doctor, Sally, had a certain look on her face when she delivered the news. It was that 'I don't know how to tell you this' expression and I knew, when she told me to sit down, that it was going to be bad news.

'Peter, I'm afraid you only have eight weeks to live, at best,' she said gently. The words sank in and I took a deep breath. This was it. I'd battled for years and now I was tired. I left the office, thinking about the practical issues of dying; what to do about my assets and preparations for my funeral.

Spleen pain is an extraordinary form of agony. My internal organs were pushed to one side to accommodate the swollen spleen, which was now the size of a football. The spasms would flash through me and I would involuntarily cry out in pain. It constantly felt as if my lungs were being pushed through my ribs and back. Breathing was hard because my lungs had so little room to expand. I was on slow-release morphine to give me a break from the pain. This put me into a deep sleep for three hours and I would wake feeling disorientated, as if my hands and feet didn't belong to me. By the time I arrived home — having purchased the house in Arch Hill for Geoff and me in September — I had decided to sell

Dorothy, deregister from GST, and various other practicalities. I still had the emotional impact to face up to, and the sad task of telling my friends and family. This was more difficult than I had imagined, not for me, but for them. They knew me as vibrant and positive, full of life. The idea of my death was just too removed to seem real. I explained that I was living in terrible pain and that meant I was living a compromise. I was ready to go. It was hard to see that look of sadness on their faces and the hopelessness in their eyes at not being able to do anything to alleviate my suffering. As the reality sank in, it was me with my arms around them, comforting them and telling them that it would all be fine in the end.

As the time approached, I rented a bach at Piha on the wild west coast beyond Auckland, close enough to the sea to hear the waves crashing. And I waited for death to take me.

Chapter 26

The bach was above the beach, opposite a hillside covered with manuka scrub where tuis liked to perch and sing. Their calls reminded me of being a small child on a Northland farm again. It was a comforting sound.

I was on my own, taking time out to reflect and sort through my photographs. I read a journal of my holiday in the Mediterranean in 1989 and planned my funeral. I didn't want it to be sombre and depressing. I wanted people to dress up in colours, the drag queens in their finest clothes, and to celebrate my life, rather than mourn my passing. As a farewell song I wanted The Communards' 'Don't Leave Me This Way', a song I had danced to many times in the past.

It was good to be alone, and not to have to provide support for someone else's vulnerability. Geoff came over once a week. My sister Yvonne would bring him out, so she could see me and drop off some KFC. I was so weak I could barely open a bottle of ginger beer. I would get my visitors to break the seals on the bottles so I could open them when they weren't there. I ate very little, perhaps half of a small mince pie, a slice of bread and butter with Colby cheese, or something from a tin. I noticed in the mirror that I actually looked quite green, and I was so thin that I couldn't shave under my cheekbones because my face was so sunken. As I stared at myself, I saw hollows had appeared in my temples. That was an undeniable sign of approaching death.

I drove myself back to the city just before Christmas and went to the house in Auckland's Arch Hill that Geoff and I had moved to. I managed to say goodbye to the last two friends. I was desperately weak and softly spoken as I lay on the couch talking to them. One was Steven Lovett, who had the drag name Pepper Burns. We had done some wonderful satirical drag together. It's crucial to have wit when you're in character, and we used to bounce cheeky comments off each other. I gave Steven all my drag stuff because he was the same shoe size as me, and he had applied my make-up the last few times we had dressed up. Being an artist and an accomplished drag queen, he always made me look fantastic. He knew how important my gift was, as a way of saying thank you for the wonderful times we had shared.

On December 19, eight weeks and three days after I was told about my impending death, I lay on my bed, looking out the bedroom door, through the open front door, and beyond to the garden. I knew it was my time, and I felt myself slipping towards a coma. It wasn't painful or frightening. A sense of peace began to wash over me and I felt my body becoming numb. I was alone, but in my heart I had everyone I needed with me and I wasn't afraid. It was a chance to lose the pain and finally sleep. My eyes fluttered closed and I slipped deeper and deeper into the coma. It could not have taken long, but as I was going Yvonne came in. She sat beside me, held my hand and began to pray. I knew she was there even though I couldn't speak to her.

Deeper, deeper, my mind began to slow and my body started to shut down. And then, I was no longer sinking, I was suddenly going back, away from the quiet, pain-free place. I started climbing out of the coma, my body waking up again as everything restarted, kicked back into life. It was the strangest thing, as if something had decided that my time wasn't up and there was still more for me to do. I came to, looked into my sister's face, and smiled. Ten minutes later I was sitting up in bed, propped on pillows, having a cup of tea with Yvonne.

'What now?' she said, overwhelmingly relieved to have me back. I thought about it and grinned. I knew what I wanted to do.

'Let's go shopping,' I said.

And we did.

The following day the sale of Surrender Dorothy went through and I had put another stage of my extraordinary life behind me. On December 23 I went to a dinner party and my appetite returned. I ate chicken and really enjoyed it, as if my body was saying, 'Hey, time to refuel.'

The following day, Christmas Eve, I felt quite ill again and vomited eight times during the day. It was quite difficult to finish off my Christmas shopping when I kept having to stop and throw up, but nothing would get in the way of buying the food for the Christmas Day feast I was hosting. It was for my gay family, people I had said goodbye to, not even expecting to be there at Christmas, let alone cooking for it.

Geoff and I went on a round of Christmas Day lunches with both our families and friends, then in the evening the special meal was held at our home. Sharing that day with my families and friends was unbelievably precious to me. Everyone I had said goodbye to and comforted as they mourned me had had a chance to share another extraordinary moment in my life. I wasn't going anywhere. I had too much to do.

Two days after Christmas, Geoff and I went to Rarotonga for a holiday. I had sold Surrender Dorothy for a decent nest egg and this was a treat from that money. I went to Barkers to buy some clothes for the trip and could barely find anything to fit me because I was so skinny. Thankfully, baggy clothes were in fashion. A blood transfusion boosted my energy for the trip. For 10 days we were warm and relaxed, hand-feeding fish, snorkelling and eating fresh tuna. Then we returned to Auckland and Geoff went back to his job in human resources at Auckland Hospital.

By February 1997, two months later, I was wondering why the effects of the blood transfusion hadn't worn off. I wasn't feeling exactly well, but I was definitely feeling much better. I went back to Sydney and saw my doctor, Cassy, again.

'Are you absolutely sure this is HIV?' I asked her. 'My spleen is huge and that's not part of the virus.'

Cassy agreed and pulled a book down off a shelf. It was all about the causes of enlarged spleens.

'Basically, there are three possible causes and you've already been tested and cleared of two of them, Peter,' she said, frowning as she read through the little book. Then she pulled down another book, a medical dictionary.

'Have you ever been to Spain?' she asked me. I was puzzled but said yes, for the Olympics and a holiday.

'Did you get bitten by sandflies on those trips?' she asked.

I replied that I had, but only in Barcelona during the 1992 Olympics, when the sandflies were everywhere.

Cassy looked at me and closed the book.

'Well, Peter, I think you've got Visceral Leishmaniasis donovani,' she said, then she explained what it was.

Leishmaniasis is a disease caused by a microscopic parasite that lives on dogs and rodents. It is transmitted to humans by sandflies that have previously bitten an infected animal. I remembered seeing wild dogs in Barcelona, and the sandfly bites on my legs. The pieces of the puzzle began to fit together as Cassy explained the disease. Also called kala-azar, it attacks the internal organs and causes fever, anaemia, weight loss and an enlarged spleen. The parasites live in the spleen and liver and attack the bone marrow. The puzzle was solved. When I had gone to bed to die two months earlier, it hadn't been from HIV. It was down to this mysterious disease that I had never heard of before.

The bone-marrow tests were done at the Prince of Wales Hospital in Sydney under anaesthetic, two days after the gay and lesbian Mardi Gras, which I had gone to. Two hours after I had woken up from the operation, the results were in. My bone marrow was riddled with the leishmania parasite.

'Okay, well, that's that sorted out,' I thought. But there was more to come.

Nobody with HIV had lived longer than between three and 20 months once they had become ill with Leishmaniasis donovani. I had been sick for 11 months. I had, at most, nine months to live. Once again I was told to prepare for death.

There is a major leishmaniasis centre in London and tests there with a cytotoxic drug named Stiboglutonate had shown some success in controlling the parasite. Cytotoxic means poisonous to cells, and the drugs are used as chemotherapy for the disease. But nobody had been cured of Leishmaniasis donovani. The idea was to keep the disease from progressing and killing me. I had a line put into my arm and a tube into my heart, and was started on the drug two days later. After four days I went back to Auckland to continue treatment, and it was arranged that the drug would be sent over. Unfortunately the drug was held up at Customs and I was given another until it arrived. The substitute drug was terrible, but cheap, and I got one dose every day for eight weeks. It affected my heart, made me stagger and caused vomiting. The drug also damaged my hearing quite badly.

Finally the Stiboglutonate arrived and my treatment was started. I received the drug through a catheter that went straight into my heart. It was so corrosive that it couldn't be put into a vein because it would make a hole in it on contact. The side effects were dreadful and included aching joints, thirst, exhaustion and vomiting. This happened with every single dose, and the line between drug and illness became blurred. After a treatment I would go home and sleep for two hours, feeling as if I had done 10 rounds with a revolving door, two rounds with Muhammad Ali or had a very rough ride on a bad horse, with every muscle hurting from trying not to be bucked off.

By October 1997 I had lived past the nine months, once again beating a time limit I had been given. The doctor who had been administering the treatment, Mark Thomas, told me it was good that I had beaten the deadline, but there was a serious downside. The health system couldn't afford to pay for the expensive chemotherapy drugs I needed to survive. I had to find a country to treat me or I would die. It was as shockingly simple as that. I could hardly believe it. But I wasn't going to just give up and wait for death. No way. I contacted the Sydney-based team that had brought over the Stiboglutonate for me and they agreed to treat me. It was an opportunity for the medics too. I was the only person with leishmaniasis in Australasia, so they would benefit from studying the illness and I would benefit from the treatment. I sold my house, I sold my car, and I sold my share in a new bar on K Road that I had gone into with my old friend Larry.

I'm not one for just going somewhere and putting my feet up. Even though I was heading to Sydney for gruelling and still experimental chemotherapy, I wanted to find a job. I applied for a fantastic one at Centennial Park, the place where I had met my former fiancée Varda all those years before. The position was manager of the riding facility there. They picked me over five other candidates. Once again, I packed up everything and crossed the Tasman for a new start and a chance to stay alive.

I started work and chemotherapy in January 1998. The treatment was three afternoons a week, one of them a Saturday, and I would go to the Prince of Wales Hospital for the intravenous chemotherapy. I had moved to Sydney ahead of Geoff and found a good two-bedroom, two-bathroom apartment with a lock-up garage and a swimming pool in Surry Hills. Geoff had got a job as a senior manager for a health organisation and the apartment was close to his job, as he didn't drive.

I would drive to the hospital and back, stopping to vomit on the side of the road. I also had a bucket in the garage at home to be sick into when I arrived, as I often could not make it to the bathroom. I made throwing up into an artform.

The job took some adjusting to. I hadn't worked for a public service before, and the Centennial Park and Moore Park Trust had many businesses centred on the park. The stables was just one of them, and the plan was to turn it into a world-class facility. But there was a lot to do and a lot of money needed to make it as good as the trust hoped.

At full capacity the Equestrian Centre, as the stables were called, could accommodate 220 horses, 350 clients and parking for 200 vehicles each day. On a good weekend there could be 450 people riding and watching. My office oversaw other businesses as well, including a vet practice, fodder store and five riding schools. My position as manager of the Equestrian Centre meant I supervised and controlled the two-hectare centre in the park itself, and a horse track that went around the park. The park was used by six million people each year, which meant endless traffic. The stables were situated on an arterial road that had to be crossed to access the park, so safety issues were a constant concern.

I worked hard to get the place into shape in those first few months, and had to spend Aus$180,000 of trust money to sort out problems that had been caused by previous managers, as well as resurface the three riding arenas. A few weeks after I started there, other cytotoxic drugs were added to my treatment, along with painkillers and anti-inflammatory drugs to stop my body rejecting the poison that was being pumped into it. My hair began to break off and thin. I looked as if moths had been nibbling me so I got it clipped to a number one and wore a hat.

After four months at the centre I hit a bureaucratic brick wall when I tried to find out why so many mistakes had been made in the past. Although my contract was for three years, I threatened to leave unless things improved and I was in a position where I was proud to put my name to the project. I was then offered a deputy director, Judith Peters, to help me. Judith, a kind and helpful woman in her forties, had useful experience in the public sector and taught me a lot about areas I had never dealt with because I had usually been self-employed. The management became more supportive, realising I was going to make the facility a world-class, efficient, horse-friendly place, using my horsemanship and my business experience, two fields I was passionate about.

Each month of my treatment started and finished with a bone-marrow biopsy to check the activity of the parasite. In April 1998, there was some incredible news. The parasite was inanimate under the microscope and my bone marrow was clean. It was a momentous result. Had we killed it? Was I the first person to be cured of this illness?

Three months later I was tested again and the parasite was back. It was a huge blow to the whole team and a major disappointment to me. I carried on with my three days a week of drug therapy and looked very washed out when I got back to work after each treatment. I worked a full schedule to make up for the time I took off on Tuesdays and Thursdays for my hospital visits. I had told the staff that I was at the hospital during those afternoons, but not the management team. But the drugs took their toll and I looked ragged and thin. I finally told my bosses, and they were fine about it. I worked hard, I did my job well and I got results, so there was no problem as long as I could cope. I more than coped. I was now responsible for putting part two of the multi-million dollar stables complex in place to bring it up to full capacity. I started a jumping club and dressage group every fortnight, to give riders a chance to take part in a simulated competition. Finally, by the end of that first year, I felt the centre was on track and where it should be.

For the next year, I worked hard and continued with the treatment. I had a few more health worries. I collapsed in pain and 22 gallstones were found. They were eventually removed after two more attacks. Three times I had horrific headaches, vision problems and vomiting that turned out to be a reaction to the drugs, which caused my brain to swell and jam against my skull. In December 1999 I saw a specialist about this problem and he looked through my eyes to my brain. There were tiny cataracts in my eyes but nothing more.

At the start of 2000, the new millennium, Geoff and I finally split up. I had caught up with my old friends and he had made new friends through his work. We didn't socialise together any more, apart from the occasional dance party. Geoff was determined to immerse himself in the gay culture but I had other concerns. The cracks had started to appear in our relationship six months after we arrived in Sydney, but I had always hoped they would mend. Eventually the situation became intolerable and I asked Geoff to move out. After six years together, including two years in Sydney, I was single and celibate.

I felt relieved. The break-up came at a time when things were going well at the centre. My position was established at the stables, I had achieved my targets and was surrounded by a network of good friends. Although I had some major problems from the drugs, they didn't stop me riding, not even when I got bucked off a young horse and burst my nose. I was a bit concussed, but that's the way riding goes sometimes.

By April 2000 I had been on chemotherapy for three years. I had been treated with Stiboglutonate on and off during this time but it was tough on me, causing hearing loss and possible heart damage, meaning I had to have an ECG every week. But I was about to find out the true legacy of these drugs, which would cause the biggest crisis of my life.

I had recently noticed that I needed stronger glasses. It was just a slight change to my vision, and I had some new lenses put in. Then, I was returning from the hospital one afternoon when a car suddenly appeared in front of me, virtually instantaneously. I braked and narrowly missed hitting it.

'Phew,' I thought. 'That was close. Why did I not see it?'

I drove the rest of the way home with extra care. The next morning I went to the bathroom and, as I was washing my face, I glanced in the mirror. I couldn't see my face. It was just a blur. I looked around the bathroom and couldn't read the labels on any of the bottles. Everything was blurry.

'Okay, well, this will pass,' I said to myself.

I walked to work, thinking the visual problem would improve as the day went on. I opened up the office, turned on the computer and waited for it to boot. I glanced at the phone on my desk and realised I couldn't see the numbers. Then I looked at the computer screen. I knew it was on but I couldn't see anything. Gillian, a friend who also worked with me at the stables, came in, chattering cheerfully. As soon as she saw my expression, she stopped.

'What is it, Peter?' she asked, worry flooding her voice.

'I think you'd better call the hospital,' I said calmly. 'I think there's something very wrong with my sight.'

Chapter 27

I could hear the click of heels on the hospital room floor and immediately turned towards the sound. I was expecting a visit from my sister Yvonne, and I waited for her to speak. She often came to see me in Sydney, whenever she was passing through back to NZ. This time I had been admitted because I had such an upset stomach that my weight had gone down to 58 kg and I was not getting vital nutrients.

'Hi Pete,' she said.

'Is that you, Yvonne?' I asked.

'Yes.' I could tell from her tone that she was puzzled.

'I'm partially blind. I can't see you from there,' I explained. There was silence. She hadn't known about my eyesight and it was a huge shock to her, just as it had been to me.

Her visit came several weeks after my sight had gone in April 2000. It had taken a month to work out what had happened.

A neurologist checked me out first and found nothing. Then, a toxicologist found out that the heavy-metal poisons used in my chemotherapy had strangled my optic nerves. The cataracts that had been found previously were removed but the limits to my vision remained. An eye specialist confirmed my worst fear: the damage
was irreversible. I was basically blind.

The only vision I had was around the edges and even that was blurry, like a fly screen smeared with Vaseline. All definition was gone, although colour remained. I had so much to learn in my new, visually limited world. Even basic things had to be taught to me, like putting a finger at the top of a glass when filling it with water so I didn't overfill it, or applying toothpaste to my mouth rather than my brush. I could still cook because, as a chef, I could literally do it with my eyes shut. But I had to rely on my memory much more when doing ordinary tasks.

Yvonne and I shared some tears that day in the hospital. For the first time in my life, I was frightened. I had very few of my savings left, having supported Geoff for two years, and I had 10 months of my contract to work. Used to my independence and freedom, I suddenly felt trapped. How would I live, or shop, or even take care of my home? I could no longer drive. I couldn't use the phone, read print or use the computer. And I couldn't ride horses any more. I couldn't even coach. And there were the hearing problems, which made it even scarier. My world was closing down and I had no idea what to do.

Thankfully, I had support from friends and family to get me through. Gillian collected me in the morning for work, as I was too sick to walk, and took me home at 2pm for my rest. Another good friend, Yuri, took me shopping each Saturday morning. Slowly, things began to fall into place.

There was another reason I got through this toughest of times. When I first lost my vision, I prayed for it to return. I asked God for a miracle to heal my eyes and return my life to the way it had been. I thought it would be easy for God to do this, but nothing happened. Both Yvonne and Joan are born-again Christians, so I asked Yvonne about this.

'Why isn't it working? Why isn't God listening to me?' I asked her.

'Under what authority do you pray?' she replied.

I had no idea I needed authority to seek help from God. I thought it was just a question of praying and being answered.

'You have to have a personal relationship with Jesus, give your heart to Him,' Yvonne explained. I thought about her words.

Two months later she came to see me at Centennial Park and we had lunch at the Fox Studios next door. I was so sight-impaired that I spent ages chasing a baby beetroot around my plate with a fork.

'Yvonne, I need to be saved. If I'm going to do this properly, then I'll give my heart to the Lord so my prayers have a hundred percent chance of working,' I said.

Yvonne was thrilled, as was Joan, who had prayed for my salvation.

I officially became a born-again Christian on 17 July 2000. I felt as if a huge burden had been taken off my shoulders and euphoria flooded through my body. I was so excited. This was another adventure. I had joined the top club in the world. I approached each church meeting as a lecture in understanding a very complicated book, the Bible. I wasn't miraculously healed but I realised that I would receive progressive healing. God works in His own timeframe, I knew, not mine.

I found new energy and purpose in my life. Gillian became my eyes at work and I completed my contract, saving several thousand dollars for my future. The stables were fully leased out for the next six months, and in my honour the Trust dedicated a Port Jackson fig tree to me and made me an honorary Friend of Centennial Park. This was a wonderful accolade in recognition of my effort and achievements at the Equestrian Centre. I finished at the stables in January 2001 with a send-off party that was truly awesome.

I had made it happen. I hadn't given in. I had learned from a young age to believe in myself and never lose hope, and this had allowed me to accomplish some incredible feats as an adult. I knew my father Stan would have been proud of me. He always used to say, 'Peter, I don't know how you do it, but you can fall in a bucket of shit and come out smelling like a rose.' And I'd done it again. But I have to admit that, as a rose, I was feeling pretty wilted. Once again, fate stepped in.

The doctors had now decided to change my treatment. When I was diagnosed with leishmaniasis I had not been expected to live longer than nine months. I was now four years on from that. The doctors wanted to try giving me treatment every day, Monday to Friday, two weeks on, two weeks off. I knew it would be tough but I decided to give it a go, not just for myself but for the other leishmaniasis sufferers around the world. I was now the longest-living person with the illness in the world. Others were still dying three to 20 months after contracting it. I started the new treatment in February 2001.

It was an extreme regime. The idea was that the chemotherapy drugs would attack the parasites full-on and kill them, once and for all. Seven months of this left me incredibly weak, a vomit machine. I was still living in an apartment across the road from the clinic, and it was all I could do to stagger across to the clinic then stagger back to my bed, full of the poisons they had pumped into me. I ate little and would smoke half a joint of marijuana to ease the agony and feelings of sickness. Marijuana was recognised by the doctors as the most effective treatment for pain management during chemotherapy. The relief came within ten minutes of smoking it and lasted for about three hours. My quality of life was so poor that I cried out to God, 'Kill me or cure me, because I can't live like this any more.'

I was to get an answer in November 2001. It was while I was visiting Joan, who was now living in Surfer's Paradise. I was feeling so desperate that I went down to the beach and cried, 'Help me, God, because I just don't know what to do anymore!'

And I actually heard someone answer me. Just two words, but so loud that I turned to see who was speaking to me on the beach — and no one was there. The words were: 'Leave it.'

'But you don't know how tough it is,' I replied, throwing my arms in the air.

Then I heard the voice say: 'Peter, let go of the past. If you do this, I'll protect you.'

I looked towards the water, wondering what to do next. Then, I know this might sound weird, but I saw an image of Jesus in front of me. I couldn't see his face as I had no central vision, but I felt him raise his arms and pour something over me. I think it was blood. It ran down my face and body, and all I could think was, 'Wow, this is spooky!'

Symbolically, I think the blood meant I was protected and nothing could go wrong. It gave me an incredible sense of hope and new confidence to carry on.

I went to see Joan five times that year, travelling to Surfer's Paradise between treatments. Although we never addressed past problems, I remained confident and went to church with my mother. I was able to see my aunt Betty and my cousins, as well as going to Noosa to visit my sister Kay and her daughter Vicky, who had recently became a mum herself.

I also caught up with Donjalle, one of the transsexual madams at the male brothel where I had worked years earlier. She had a terminal lung disease, the result of inhaling spores from an infected person. Donjalle had decided to educate herself and returned to studying, graduating with a degree in social work. I adored her sharp wit and black humour, and the two of us spent time hanging out together. We were both very underweight, so we would go to a local café chosen for its comfortable chairs, as anything aluminium was like sitting on a cheese slicer. I called her Wonder Woman. She died in April 2003.

Eight months into the new treatment regime I could not take it any more. I had developed an infection in the catheter that carried the drugs to my heart. The doctors later told me that they had given me four days to live. Just four days. But once again, I fought back. I had platelet transfusions and was operated on to remove the catheter. After so many infusions of antibiotics, my arms were black and blue. Feeling better after the catheter removal, I told the team I was going home. They were disappointed, as they had hoped I would be staying in the clinic for another two months for daily treatment.

'Two months is a long time,' I said. 'I can't take any more of it. I've had enough.'

I left the clinic, saying I would visit them after the weekend. But as I walked out of the clinic I knew I would stick with my decision to give up. I wanted to see how long I could go without the chemotherapy keeping the parasites at bay.

Two days into my eighth week without treatment my body went into revolt. The pain and nausea were extraordinary and I had a headache that would knock a cow over. Never in my dreams had I thought I would ask for the poison to be put back into my system, but there I was at the clinic the next day, pleading to have chemotherapy. I was two or three days away from death. I now knew what to expect. At least my death would be quick, and with pain control I knew it would be simple.

Now, to this day, I live on an eight-week cycle. Seven doses of chemotherapy then seven weeks off. I have recently found out there is further deterioration as a result of the parasite causing protein to leak from my kidneys and intestine. I have a top-up of albumen protein halfway through each cycle.

In January 2002 I returned to Auckland. It was time to go home. I had phoned Auckland Hospital to ask if there was any possibility that I could receive my chemotherapy there, and to my delight they said yes. The treatment programme was now established and no costly new drugs were expected to be introduced. It was wonderful news.

In July that year I went for a trip to Bali with two good friends, and while there I decided to study massage therapy. I had to earn money and I had massaged in the past. Being so visually impaired made it difficult to find work, and massage therapy seemed ideal. I decided to specialise in massage for sporting injuries, and trained for six months. It was challenging, because of my sight problems, but my sense of touch worked very well, and I got good results.

I also found another field of expertise. Several times Yvonne had asked me to speak at business meetings and the response I had received was amazing, so I decided to pursue this option too. I had been motivating people for years, I realised, so why not take my unique story out there. More than anything, I had motivated myself many times when everything seemed bleak and hopeless. If I could do that, I could also help others. I found out about Celebrity Speakers, and the organisation was happy to take me on. My first speaking engagements took place in 2003 during a tour of several cities. I was quite nervous and wondered if my story would touch people. I was delighted when I got standing ovations and heart-warming feedback from the audiences. It sure beats the hell out of crocheting doilies or packing pens.

I now live in a cute little city apartment with my dog Barney, a cross between a dachshund and a very determined Labrador. He is my link to the rural life that I love so much. We go for walks whenever I am up to it, and apparently we have become part of the city's landscape, the almost-blind man and his short-legged dog. My life is full, with speaking engagements around the country, seeing massage clients, and spending time with friends and family. I have no intention of giving up or copping out. While there is breath in my body, and value and good friends in my life, I will always have a reason to carry on fighting.

I don't have time to wallow or worry. I never have. I grew up, got over it and got on with it. I relish my life and live for the moment. And I have never postponed joy. Nobody should.

Chapter 28

When I left home at 15, my father Stan shook my hand, wished me luck and said, 'To thine own self be true.' This principle has stayed with me throughout my life. It reminds me to critique my motives and has guided me in making decisions.

Most of my life has been spent working in hospitality and with horses. Both have taught me lessons. From my equestrian career, I learned to look at myself when faced with a tricky situation. Even if the problem seemed to be the horse, I had to look at myself and how I had handled it. Had I made a clear and fair request of staff or the horse? Had I tried to be consistent, respectful, kind and sympathetic? Or had I been demanding something with frustration and lack of understanding? Was I being affected by my emotions and had I considered the horse's emotions? Maybe he was having a bad day or he was the kind that needed clearer communication? To truly understand a horse, you have to understand yourself first. As I grew personally through my progress as a rider and coach, I gained more respect, love and empathy with the horses. I also learned to understand that we all have different personalities and motivations, and that this is the key to being a winning combination.

As I mastered this technique, I applied it to people. When negotiating or in a leadership role, I realised that people respond to the same values. This establishes loyalty, reward and recognition. Attitudes remain positive. People become willing to go the extra mile.

When I was with the Canadian team preparing for the World Championships in June 1994, a horse and rider hoping for a place on the team arrived at the two-week training camp. The horse was deeply depressed and stood at the back of the stable with his head down. He turned away from anyone who approached and also had a low-grade virus, which showed in his runny nose. His groom was inexperienced and the rider had some alcohol issues. I had known the horse since 1991 when he had arrived from England. He had a lot of potential then but I had seen him become unruly under another unsympathetic, ego-driven rider. Now he had been given to this rider, and although he was doing better on the circuit, he had become submissive and miserable. In my position as stables and operations manager, and assistant coach, I took over his care, grooming and management.

I had worked a lot with problem horses during my career, using my own life experiences as a starting point. To gain this horse's confidence, I gave him respect, time, gentleness, constant reassurance with a quiet voice, and lots of praise. I called a vet to treat his virus, and rejigged his feed and exercise programme. I knew it would take a week, at the very least, for the horse and rider to trust me, and there were only two weeks before the flight to Europe for the World Championships. I would help the rider to mount then work quietly with them both, reassuring the rider and making sure he used the same techniques of empathy with the horse.

Every day, they improved. By the end of the first week the horse would face the door when a staff member entered the stable complex. He no longer pulled his legs away when his feet were being worked on. Whether or not he would go to the competition hung in the balance. In the end he was taken to Europe but wasn't a sure starter. That gave me another week with him there, and when the competition started he was selected to compete. He was a different horse. He would now put his head out of the box for a scratch and call to me, and he was first to the front at feeding time. He had become a sheer delight to work with.

This gentle technique, applied to horses or people, has been the mainstay of my life philosophy.

When I look back at my life, I'm glad I was born a baby boomer. My generation had new freedom. But freedom brought perils. During the 1990s I attended many funerals of friends who had died of HIV and AIDS.

I don't regret the choices I have made. They gave me freedom, and I used this to overcome fears, follow my dreams and work in the fields I wanted to. I did some crazy things to fulfil these dreams. Some may feel I was irresponsible, but I took full responsibility for every choice I made. I wanted to be sure that my life was not dictated by tradition but by personal decisions. As a result, I laughed, partied, loved and worked extremely hard. With anything

I have taken on, I have made it happen. I have given things a go and have shared my life with the most amazing, inspirational people. Even the ones who were heartbreaking to encounter brought new meaning and experience to my life. The fact that I have survived them and learned from them is testimony to that. The only regret I have is not being there when my horse Fez was put down. But that is all.

Some people might wonder if it has all been worth it, given the suffering of my illness. I think it has.

To date, I have had 529 doses of chemotherapy, 22 bone marrow biopsies, three CAT scans, three MRI scans, cataracts removed from both eyes, a lumbar puncture, brain swelling, infections, ultrasounds and numerous surgeries, including the recent removal of skin cancers. My eyesight continues to be exceedingly poor and, until I received new hearing aids recently, I could barely hear a thing. My hearing continues to deteriorate. I suffer from swollen legs, painful spasms from my spleen and constant fatigue. Pain is part of my life now. If vomiting was an Olympic sport, I would be a definite gold medal-winner. Blood transfusions are regular events. But I won't give up. Three times I have been told I would die, and I'm still here, remaining vigilant, cheerful, positive and cooperative.

I choose to make all the things that I do in my life positive things. I don't allow myself to think of negatives, and if they sneak in I quickly banish them. I can't afford to sink into depression because I don't know if I would climb back out. I believe in keeping a positive attitude at all times. My will to survive is strong and I have always taken responsibility for all my decisions and actions. Next time you have a bad day, or even a bad week, think of ny years staring death in the face, of 13 years working for an Olympic dream to happen, and decades of coping with the legacy of a difficult upbringing.

As a result of losing my sight, I have discovered that beauty has a different meaning. I see beyond a person's appearance to their generosity, warmth and spirit. Memory and intuition serve me well. I don't need to see things in detail. I know that when I leave home for another treatment, my dog Barney's eyes will be filled with sadness. I know what the veins on a leaf look like, and continue to look like, even though I can't see them. And I have wonderful memories of a life well lived.

I continue to take every opportunity that presents itself and embrace each new day as a fresh challenge. I am continuing to further my training in massage therapy and have a regular list of clients who are very pleased with their progress. I have touched and inspired people with my public speaking. I remain cheerful and at peace with myself. I have strong bonds with my family. My mother Joan and I haven't spoken about the past but I wish her well. I am thrilled by the arrival of baby Taylor, who is a symbol of so much hope for the future. He's a very special little boy.

I always felt I had purpose in my life, something to aim for. Driven by passion, I made things happen for me. My life has been about joy, the warm feeling that I get in my heart when I look back and think, 'I did it.' It's a deep-seated satisfaction.

I don't know how much longer I will be here or what will happen next in this amazing, unpredictable life of mine. Even as I finish this book, there have been new developments in my health. My bone marrow is now so full of parasites that it can't make new white or red blood cells. I appear to have built up resistance to the four chemotherapy drugs that I am given, and emails have been sent to the UK centre for leishmaniasis. There are now two new drugs available and the doctors are hoping to try them on me. It's an exciting prospect and I am happy to give them a go.

I continue to keep death at bay. I have defied it three times, and my doctors know there is no point in making any predictions about how long I will last. I'll only see it as another challenge and beat it again.

It's not over until God calls me home.

Epilogue

June 2012, 7 years later.

'No I have not fallen over the rainbow,' as some readers may have thought. This book was published in 2005 and sold out. Last year 2011, I regained the ownership of this manuscript and have edited this copy ready for new global distribution.

I am writing the sequel of this autobiography ,'Don't Steal My Joy' as a request by many readers who wish to know what has happened in the past seven years. It is my hope to have 'Steal' on the Amazon Kindle list by the end of this year.

After a set of studying short university writing courses in 2005, I wrote my first novel which placed in the Canadian Aid Literary awards, 'Best Foreign Entries List', in 2007. This project is now being rewritten for the Amazon Kindle market and will be released by the end of this year

My blog, 'How's your day,' is a collection of how I think and deal with my daily life as inspired by my sister Yvonne. Like many of her friends, she wants to know how I do the continued treatment and deal with the new uncertainties that my life, health and all round positive well being brings. It is often funny, inspiring, and deep and a social comment on different issues. With readers around the globe, this series 1 to 75 will be available on Amazon Kindle by the end of June.

As an ambassador of 'the Pin Drop Foundation', an organization providing cochlear implants to severely deaf NZ'ers, myself and other consumers seek parity and extra funding from the NZ Government and offer information via talks to Rotary Clubs and other sources. I am now a bi-lateral cochlear user, the most significant change in my life in the past two years. More about my profound deafness in the sequel.

Again, prompting by my sister Yvonne, I began speaking again last year after stopping in late 2006. At the end of April, I gave two inspirational presentations in Sydney to the corporate sector. With great success, my future as an International Speaker is assured with several bookings for this year. On May 29th I won both the Bright Star and the Inspirational Speaker of the Year at the National Speakers Assn, Auckland Chapter. I am available for speaking engagements worldwide.

You can view my work on my U Tube channel or my website; www.peterataylor.biz

For any wish to contact me, you may do so via my website.

I hope you have enjoyed my book and will appreciate you recommending 'Don't Postpone Joy', to your friends. Please write your comment on the Amazon recommendation page and give it as many stars as you feel.

With thanks, Pete Taylor, Auckland New Zealand.

Printed in Great Britain
by Amazon

17398422R00129